Praise for *Architecting Data and Machine Learning Platforms*

T0093373

Becoming a data-driven company requires solid data capabilities that can fit the company strategy. This book offers a 360-degree view of strategies for data transformation with real-life evolutionary architecture scenarios. A must-read for architects and everyone driving a data transformation program.

—Mattia Cinquilli, Data and Analytics Director
for Telco and Media at Sky

Cloudy with a chance of data insights! This book is the Mary Poppins of the data world, making the complex journey of building modern cloud data platforms practically perfect in every way. The authors, a band of seasoned engineers, are like data whisperers, guiding you through the labyrinth of machine learning and analytics. They help turn the abandoned carts of your organization into free-shipping success stories. If you're looking for a book that simplifies data and ML platforms while making you chuckle, this is your golden ticket!

—Priscilla Moraes, PhD in AI and NLP,
Director of Applied Sciences at Microsoft

The authors' experience dealing with evolving data and AI/ML practices show throughout the book. It's a comprehensive collection of wisdom dealing with data at scale using cloud and on-prem technologies.

—Bala Natarajan, Former VP, Enterprise Data Platform, PayPal

Architecting Data and Machine Learning Platforms

Enable Analytics and AI-Driven Innovation in the Cloud

Marco Tranquillin, Valliappa Lakshmanan, and Firat Tekiner

Beijing · Boston · Farnham · Sebastopol · Tokyo

Architecting Data and Machine Learning Platforms

by Marco Tranquillin, Valliappa Lakshmanan, and Firat Tekiner

Published by O'Reilly Media, Inc., 1005 Gravenstein Highway North, Sebastopol, CA 95472.

O'Reilly books may be purchased for educational, business, or sales promotional use. Online editions are also available for most titles (*http://oreilly.com*). For more information, contact our corporate/institutional sales department: 800-998-9938 or *corporate@oreilly.com*.

Acquisitions Editor: Megan Laddusaw	**Indexer:** Potomac Indexing, LLC
Development Editor: Virginia Wilson	**Interior Designer:** David Futato
Production Editor: Gregory Hyman	**Cover Designer:** Karen Montgomery
Copyeditor: nSight, Inc.	**Illustrator:** Kate Dullea
Proofreader: Shannon Turlington	

October 2023:   First Edition

Revision History for the First Edition

2023-10-12:   First Release

See *http://oreilly.com/catalog/errata.csp?isbn=9781098151614* for release details.

978-1-098-15161-4

[LSI]

Table of Contents

Preface

What is a data platform? Why do you need it? What does building a data and machine learning (ML) platform involve? Why should you build your data platform on the cloud? This book starts by answering these common questions that arise when dealing with data and ML projects. We then lay out the strategic journey that we recommend you take to build data and ML capabilities in your business, show you how to execute on each step of that strategy, and wrap up all the concepts in a model data modernization case.

Why Do You Need a Cloud Data Platform?

Imagine that the chief technology officer (CTO) of your company wants to build a new mobile-friendly ecommerce website. "We are losing business," he claims, "because our website is not optimized for mobile phones, especially in Asian languages."

The chief executive officer (CEO) trusts the CTO when he says that the current website's mobile user experience isn't great, but she wonders whether customers who access the platform through mobile phones form a profitable segment of the population. She calls the head of operations in Asia and asks, "What is the revenue and profit margin on customers who reach our ecommerce site on mobile phones? How will our overall revenue change over the next year if we increase the number of people making purchases on mobile?"

How would the regional leader in Asia go about answering this question? It requires the ability to relate customer visits (to determine the origin of HTTP requests), customer purchases (to know what they purchased), and procurement information (to determine the cost of those items). It also requires being able to predict the growth in different segments of the market. Would the regional leader have to reach out to the information technology (IT) department and ask them to pull together the necessary information from all these different sources and write a program to compute these statistics? Does the IT department have the bandwidth to answer this question and the skills to do predictive analysis?

How much better would it be if the organization has a *data platform*? In this case, all the data will have already been collected and cleaned up and be available for analysis and synthesis across the organization. A data analyst team could simply run an interactive, ad hoc query. They could also easily create or retrieve forecasts of revenue and traffic patterns by taking advantage of built-in artificial intelligence (AI) capabilities and allow a data-driven decision to be made on the CTO's request to invest in a new mobile-friendly website.

One possible way to answer the CEO's question is to procure and deploy a real user monitoring (RUM) tool. There are lots of specific tools available, one for every one-off decision like this. Having a data platform allows the organization to answer many such one-off questions without having to procure and install a bunch of these specific solutions.

Modern organizations increasingly want to make decisions based on data. Our example focused on a one-time decision. However, in many cases, organizations want to make decisions repeatedly, in an automated manner for every transaction. For example, the organization might want to determine whether a shopping cart is in danger of being abandoned and immediately show the customer options of low-cost items that can be added to the shopping cart to meet the minimum for free shipping. These items should appeal to the individual shopper and therefore require a solid analytics and ML capability.

To make decisions based on data, organizations need a data and ML platform that simplifies:

- Getting access to data
- Running an interactive, ad hoc query
- Creating a report
- Making automated decisions based on data
- Personalization of the business' services

As you will see in this book, cloud-based data platforms reduce the technical barrier for all these capabilities: it is possible to access data from anywhere, carry out fast, large-scale queries even on edge devices, and take advantage of services that provide many analytics and AI capabilities. However, being able to put in place all the building blocks needed to achieve that can sometimes be a complex journey. The goal of this book is to help readers have a better understanding of the main concepts, architectural patterns, and tools available to build modern cloud data platforms so that they can gain better visibility and control of their corporate data to make more meaningful and automated business decisions.

We, the authors of this book, are engineers who have years of experience helping enterprises in a wide variety of industries and geographies build data and ML platforms. These enterprises want to derive insights from their data but often face many challenges with getting all the data they need in a form where it can be quickly analyzed. Therefore, they find themselves having to build a modern data and ML platform.

Who Is This Book For?

This book is for architects who wish to support data-driven decision making in their business by creating a data and ML platform using public cloud technologies. Data engineers, data analysts, data scientists, and ML engineers will find the book useful to gain a conceptual design view of the systems that they might be implementing on top of.

Digitally native companies have been doing this already for several years.

As early as 2016, Twitter explained (*https://oreil.ly/OwTy4*) that their data platform team maintains "systems to support and manage the production and consumption of data for a variety of business purposes, including publicly reported metrics, recommendations, A/B testing, ads targeting, etc." In 2016, this involved maintaining one of the largest Hadoop clusters in the world. By 2019, this was changing to include supporting the use of a cloud-native data warehousing solution (*https://oreil.ly/xeud3*).

Etsy, to take another example, says (*https://oreil.ly/4vckj*) that their ML platform "supports ML experiments by developing and maintaining the technical infrastructure that Etsy's ML practitioners rely on to prototype, train, and deploy ML models at scale."

Both Twitter and Etsy have built modern data and ML platforms. The platforms at the two companies are different, to support the different types of data, personnel, and business use cases that the platforms need to support, but the underlying approach is pretty similar. In this book, we will show you how to architect a modern data and ML platform that enables engineers in your business to:

- Collect data from a variety of sources such as operational databases, customer clickstream, Internet of Things (IoT) devices, software as a service (SaaS) applications, etc.
- Break down silos between different parts of the organization

- Process data while ingesting it or after loading it while guaranteeing proper processes for data quality and governance
- Analyze the data routinely or ad hoc
- Enrich the data with prebuilt AI models
- Build ML models to carry out predictive analytics
- Act on the data routinely or in response to triggering events or thresholds
- Disseminate insights and embed analytics

This book is a good introduction to architectural considerations if you work with data and ML models in enterprises, because you will be required to do your work on the platform built by your data or ML platform team. Thus, if you are a data engineer, data analyst, data scientist, or ML engineer, you will find this book helpful for gaining a high-level systems design view.

Even though our primary experience is with Google Cloud, we endeavor to maintain a cloud-agnostic vision of the services that underlie the architectures by bringing in examples from, but not limited to, all three major cloud providers (i.e., Amazon Web Services [AWS], Microsoft Azure, and Google Cloud).

Organization of This Book

The book has been organized in 12 chapters that map to the *strategic steps to innovate with the data* that will be explained in detail in Chapter 2. The book concludes with a model use case scenario to showcase how an organization might approach its modernization journey.

The visual representation of the book flow is reported in Figure P-1.

Chapter 1 discusses why organizations should build a data platform. It also covers approaches, technology trends, and core principles in data platforms.

In Chapters 2 and 3, we dive more into how to plan the journey, identifying the strategic steps to innovate and how to effect change. Here we will discuss concepts like reduction of the total cost of ownership (TCO), the removal of data silos, and how to leverage AI to unlock innovation. We also analyze the building blocks of a data lifecycle, discuss how to design your data team, and recommend an adoption plan. In Chapter 4, we consolidate these into a migration framework.

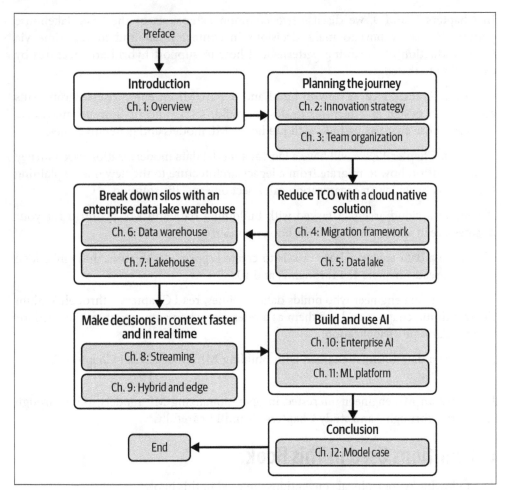

Figure P-1. Book flow diagram

In Chapters 5, 6, and 7, we discuss three of the most common architectures for data platforms—data lakes (Chapter 5), data warehouses (Chapter 6), and lakehouses (Chapter 7). We demonstrate that lakehouses can be built in one of two ways, evolving to this architecture starting from either a data lake or a data warehouse, and discuss how to choose between the two paths.

In Chapters 8 and 9, we discuss two common extensions of the basic lakehouse pattern. We show how to make decisions in context faster and in real time via the introduction of streaming patterns and how to support hybrid architectures by expanding to the edge.

Chapters 10 and 11 cover how to build and use AI/ML in enterprise environments and how to design architectures to design, build, serve, and orchestrate innovative models. Those chapters include both predictive ML models and generative ones.

Finally, in Chapter 12, we will have a look at a model data modernization case journey with a focus on how to migrate from a legacy architecture to the new one, explaining the process by which an organization can select one specific solution.

If you are a cloud architect tasked with building a data and ML platform for your business, read all the chapters of the book in order.

If you are a data analyst whose task is to create reports, dashboards, and embedded analytics, read Chapters 1, 4 through 7, and 10.

If you are a data engineer who builds data pipelines, read Chapters 5 through 9. Skim the remaining chapters and use them as a reference when you encounter the need for a particular type of application.

If you are a data scientist charged with building ML models, read Chapters 7, 8, 10, and 11.

If you are an ML engineer interested in operationalizing ML models, skim through Chapters 1 through 9 and study Chapters 10 and 11 carefully.

Conventions Used in This Book

The following typographical conventions are used in this book:

Italic
> Indicates new terms, URLs, email addresses, filenames, and file extensions.

`Constant width`
> Used for program listings, as well as within paragraphs to refer to program elements such as variable or function names, databases, data types, environment variables, statements, and keywords.

This element signifies a general note or tip.

O'Reilly Online Learning

For more than 40 years, *O'Reilly Media* has provided technology and business training, knowledge, and insight to help companies succeed.

Our unique network of experts and innovators share their knowledge and expertise through books, articles, and our online learning platform. O'Reilly's online learning platform gives you on-demand access to live training courses, in-depth learning paths, interactive coding environments, and a vast collection of text and video from O'Reilly and 200+ other publishers. For more information, visit *https://oreilly.com*.

How to Contact Us

Please address comments and questions concerning this book to the publisher:

O'Reilly Media, Inc.
1005 Gravenstein Highway North
Sebastopol, CA 95472
800-889-8969 (in the United States or Canada)
707-829-7019 (international or local)
707-829-0104 (fax)
support@oreilly.com
https://www.oreilly.com/about/contact.html

We have a web page for this book, where we list errata, examples, and any additional information. You can access this page at *https://oreil.ly/architecting-data-ml-platforms*.

For news and information about our books and courses, visit *https://oreilly.com*.

Find us on LinkedIn: *https://linkedin.com/company/oreilly-media*

Follow us on Twitter: *https://twitter.com/oreillymedia*

Watch us on YouTube: *https://youtube.com/oreillymedia*

Acknowledgments

Writing a book like this one is rewarding because you are sharing not only your knowledge but also the fruits of experience, and that experience was obtained in the trenches with so many people. Writing the book reminded us of all these people who we have had the fortune to work alongside, learn from, and celebrate with. It would be impossible to mention everyone without violating confidentiality, so we'd like to just give a big thank you to the extended data analytics, data engineering, and data science communities.

We are deeply grateful to our amazing tech reviewers—Sami Akbay, Mike Dahlin, Kevin George, Jonathan Gerhard, Noah Gift, Sanjay Ramchandani, Joseph Reis, and Vicki Reyzelman—for reviewing the draft manuscript and providing us with invaluable feedback and suggestions.

O'Reilly is the publisher of choice for technical books, and the professionalism of our team is a testament to this. Megan Laddusaw guided us through the process of creating a compelling outline. Virginia Wilson and Melissa Potter diligently managed the entire content development. Gregory Hyman supported us in shaping a fantastic final production of the manuscript, even helping us with the design of all the schemas. Thank you for all your help!

Marco: I would like to express my gratitude to my wonderful wife, Lara Maria Gessica, who is my guiding light and has been incredibly supportive throughout the entire journey, as well as my adorable sons, Walter and Nicholas, who make my life amazing and incredible every single day.

Lak: Many thanks to Abirami for 25 years of love and companionship. The protests are getting a little thin at this point, but I'll try not to let the empty nest result in too many more of these writing commitments!

Firat: I dedicate this to the three ladies who continue to shape my life and who made it all possible. To my daughter, Evre, for curiosity and joy. To my wife, Yontem, for perseverance. And to my mother, Emine Ayla, for never-ending belief and confidence in me.

The three of us are donating 100% of the royalties from this book to Girls Who Code (*https://girlswhocode.com*), an organization whose mission is to *build a large pipeline of future female engineers*. The more central data becomes to many aspects of business, the more important it is that the workforce building it is diverse and inclusive.

Modernizing Your Data Platform: An Introductory Overview

Data is a valuable asset that can help your company make better decisions, identify new opportunities, and improve operations. Google in 2013 undertook a strategic project to increase employee retention by improving manager quality. Even something as loosey-goosey as manager skill could be studied in a data-driven manner. Google was able to improve management favorability (*https://oreil.ly/MN6eZ*) from 83% to 88% by analyzing 10K performance reviews, identifying common behaviors of high-performing managers, and creating training programs. Another example of a strategic data project was carried out at Amazon. The ecommerce giant implemented a recommendation system based on customer behaviors (*https://oreil.ly/URxN_*) that drove 35% of purchases in 2017. The Warriors, a San Francisco basketball team, is yet another example; they enacted an analytics program (*https://oreil.ly/dFZRW*) that helped catapult them to the top of their league. All these—employee retention, product recommendations, improving win rates—are examples of business goals that were achieved by modern data analytics.

To become a data-driven company, you need to build an ecosystem for data analytics, processing, and insights. This is because there are many different types of applications (websites, dashboards, mobile apps, ML models, distributed devices, etc.) that create and consume data. There are also many different departments within your company (finance, sales, marketing, operations, logistics, etc.) that need data-driven insights. Because the entire company is your customer base, building a data platform is more than just an IT project.

This chapter introduces data platforms, their requirements, and why traditional data architectures prove insufficient. It also discusses technology trends in data analytics and AI, and how to build data platforms for the future using the public cloud. This chapter is a general overview of the core topics covered in more detail in the rest of the book.

The Data Lifecycle

The purpose of a data platform is to support the steps that organizations need to carry out to move from raw data to insightful information. It is helpful to understand the steps of the data lifecycle (collect, store, process, visualize, activate) because they can be mapped almost as-is to a data architecture to create a unified analytics platform.

The Journey to Wisdom

Data helps companies to develop smarter products, reach more customers, and increase their return on investment (ROI). Data can also be leveraged to measure customer satisfaction, profitability, and cost. But the data by itself is not enough. Data is raw material that needs to pass through a series of stages before it can be used to generate insights and knowledge. This sequence of stages is what we call a *data lifecycle*. There are many definitions available in the literature, but from a general point of view, we can identify five main stages in modern data platform architecture:

1. *Collect*
   Data has to be acquired and injected into the target systems (e.g., manual data entry, batch loading, streaming ingestion, etc.).

2. *Store*
   Data needs to be persisted in a durable fashion with the ability to easily access it in the future (e.g., file storage system, database).

3. *Process/transform*
   Data has to be manipulated to make it useful for subsequent steps (e.g., cleansing, wrangling, transforming).

4. *Analyze/visualize*
   Data needs to be studied to derive business insights via manual elaboration (e.g., queries, slice and dice) or automatic processing (e.g., enrichment using ML application programming interfaces—APIs).

5. *Activate*
   Surfacing the data insights in a form and place where decisions can be made (e.g., notifications that act as a trigger for specific manual actions, automatic job executions when specific conditions are met, ML models that send feedback to devices).

Each of these stages feeds into the next, similar to the flow of water through a set of pipes.

Water Pipes Analogy

To understand the data lifecycle better, think of it as a simplified water pipe system. The water starts at an aqueduct and is then transferred and transformed through a series of pipes until it reaches a group of houses. The data lifecycle is similar, with data being collected, stored, processed/transformed, and analyzed before it is used to make decisions (see Figure 1-1).

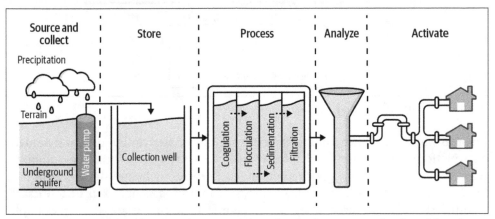

Figure 1-1. Water lifecycle, providing an analogy for the five steps in the data lifecycle

You can see some similarities between the plumbing world and the data world. Plumbing engineers are like data engineers, who design and build the systems that make data usable. People who analyze water samples are like data analysts and data scientists, who analyze data to find insights. Of course, this is just a simplification. There are many other roles in a company that use data, like executives, developers, business users, and security administrators. But this analogy can help you remember the main concepts.

In the canonical data lifecycle, shown in Figure 1-2, data engineers collect and store data in an analytics store. The stored data is then processed using a variety of tools. If the tools involve programming, the processing is typically done by data engineers. If the tools are declarative, the processing is typically done by data analysts. The processed data is then analyzed by business users and data scientists. Business users use the insights to make decisions, such as launching marketing campaigns or issuing refunds. Data scientists use the data to train ML models, which can be used to automate tasks or make predictions.

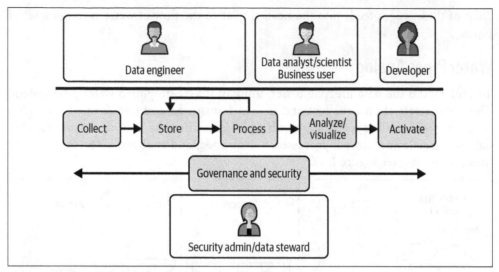

Figure 1-2. Simplified data lifecycle

The real world may differ from the preceding idealized description of how a modern data platform architecture and roles should work. The stages may be combined (e.g., storage and processing) or reordered (e.g., processing before storage, as in ETL [extract-transform-load], rather than storage before processing, as in ELT [extract-load-transform]). However, there are trade-offs to such variations. For example, combining storage and processing into a single stage leads to coupling that results in wasted resources (if data sizes grow, you'll need to scale both storage and compute) and scalability issues (if your infrastructure can't handle the extra load, you'll be stuck).

Now that we have defined the data lifecycle and summarized the various stages of the data journey from raw data collection to activation, let us go through each of the five stages of the data lifecycle in turn.

Collect

The first step in the design process is ingestion. *Ingestion* is the process of transferring data from a source, which could be anywhere (on premises, on devices, in another cloud, etc.), to a target system where it can be stored for further analysis. This is the first opportunity to consider the 3Vs of big data:

Volume

What is the size of the data? Usually when dealing with big data this means terabyte (TB) or petabyte (PB) of data.

Velocity

What is the speed of the data coming in? Generally this is megabyte/second (MB/s) or TB/day. This is often termed the *throughput*.

Variety

What is the format of the data? Tables, flat files, images, sound, text, etc.

Identify the data type (structured, semistructured, unstructured), format, and generation frequency (continuously or at specific intervals) of the data to be collected. Based on the velocity of the data and the capability of the data platform to handle the resulting volume and variety, choose between batch ingestion, streaming ingestion, or a hybrid of the two.

As different parts of the organization may be interested in different data sources, design this stage to be as flexible as possible. There are several commercial and open source solutions that can be used, each specialized for a specific data type/approach mentioned earlier. Your data platform will need to be comprehensive and support the full range of volume, velocity, and variety required for all the data that needs to be ingested into the platform. You could have simple tools that transfer files between File Transfer Protocol (FTP) servers on regular intervals, or you could have complex systems, even geographically distributed, that collect data from IoT devices in real time.

Store

In this step, store the raw data you collected in the previous step. You don't change the data at all, you just store it. This is important because you might want to reprocess the data in a different way later, and you need to have the original data to do that.

Data comes in many different forms and sizes. The way you store it will depend on your technical and commercial needs. Some common options include object storage systems, relational database management systems (RDBMSs), data warehouses (DWHs), and data lakes. Your choice will be driven to some extent by whether the underlying hardware, software, and artifacts are able to cope with the scalability, cost, availability, durability, and openness requirements imposed by your desired use cases.

Scalability

Scalability is the ability to grow and manage increased demands in a capable manner. There are two main ways to achieve scalability:

Vertical scalability
> This involves adding extra expansion units to the same node to increase the storage system's capacity.

Horizontal scalability
> This involves adding one or more additional nodes instead of adding new expansion units to a single node. This type of distributed storage is more complex to manage, but it can achieve improved performance and efficiency.

It is extremely important that the underlying system is able to cope with the volume and velocity required by modern solutions that have to work in an environment where the data is exploding and its nature is transitioning from batch to real time: we are living in a world where the majority of the people are continuously generating and requiring access to the information leveraging their smart devices; organizations need to be able to provide their users (both internal and external) with solutions that are able to provide real-time responses to the various requests.

Performance versus cost

Identify the different types of data you need to manage, and create a hierarchy based on the business importance of the data, how often it will be accessed, and what kind of latency the users of the data will expect.

Store the most important and most frequently accessed data (hot data) in a high-performance storage system such as a data warehouse's native storage. Store less important data (cold data) in a less expensive storage system such as cloud storage (which itself has several tiers). If you need even higher performance, such as for interactive use cases, you can use caching techniques to load a meaningful portion of your hot data into a volatile storage tier.

High availability

High availability means having the ability to be operational and deliver access to the data when requested. This is usually achieved via hardware redundancy to cope with possible physical failures/outages. This is achieved in the cloud by storing the data in at least three *availability zones*. Zones may not be physically separated (i.e., they may be on the same "campus") but will tend to have different power sources, etc. Hardware redundancy is usually referred to as system *uptime*, and modern systems usually come with four 9s or more.

Durability

Durability is the ability to store data for a long-term period without suffering data degradation, corruption, or outright loss. This is usually achieved through storing multiple copies of the data in physically separate locations. Such data redundancy is implemented in the cloud by storing the data in at least two *regions* (e.g., in both London and Frankfurt). This is extremely important when dealing with data restore operations in the face of natural disasters: if the underlying storage system has a high durability (modern systems usually come with 11 9s), then all of the data can be restored with no issues unless a cataclysmic event takes down even the physically separated data centers.

Openness

As far as possible, use formats that are not proprietary and that do not generate lock-in. Ideally, it should be possible to query data with a choice of processing engines without generating copies of the data or having to move it from one system to another. That said, it is acceptable to use systems that use a proprietary or native storage format as long as they provide an easy export capability.

As with most technology decisions, openness is a trade-off, and the ROI of a proprietary technology may be high enough that you are willing to pay the price of lock-in. After all, one of the reasons to go to the cloud is to reduce operational costs—these cost advantages tend to be higher in fully managed/serverless systems than on managed open source systems. For example, if your data use case requires transactions, Databricks (which uses a quasi-open storage format based on Parquet called Delta Lake) might involve lower operating costs than Amazon EMR or Google Dataproc (which will store data in standard Parquet on S3 or Google Cloud Storage [GCS] respectively)—the ACID (Atomicity, Consistency, Isolation, Durability) transactions that Databricks provides in Delta Lake will be expensive to implement and maintain on EMR or Dataproc. If you ever need to migrate away from Databricks, export the data into standard Parquet. Openness, per se, is not a reason to reject technology that is a better fit.

Process/Transform

Here's where the magic happens: raw data is transformed into useful information for further analysis. This is the stage where data engineers build data pipelines to make data accessible to a wider audience of nontechnical users in a meaningful way. This stage consists of activities that prepare data for analysis and use. Data integration involves combining data from multiple sources into a single view. Data cleansing may be needed to remove duplicates and errors from data. More generally, data wrangling, munging, and transformation are carried out to organize the data into a standard format.

There are several frameworks that can be used, each with its own capabilities that depend on the storage method you selected in the previous step. In general, engines that allow you to query and transform your data using pure SQL commands (e.g., AWS Athena, Google BigQuery, Azure DWH, and Snowflake) are the most efficient, cost effective,[1] and easy to use. However, the capabilities they offer are limited in comparison to engines based on modern programming languages, usually Java, Scala, or Python (e.g., Apache Spark, Apache Flink, or Apache Beam running on Amazon EMR, Google Cloud Dataproc/Dataflow, Azure HDInsight, and Databricks). Code-based data processing engines allow you not only to implement more complex transformations and ML in batch and in real time but also to leverage other important features such as proper unit and integration tests.

Another consideration in choosing an appropriate engine is that SQL skills are typically much more prevalent in an organization than programming skills. The more of a data culture you want to build within your organization, the more you should lean toward SQL for data processing. This is particularly important if the processing steps (such as data cleansing or transformation) require domain knowledge.

This stage may also employ *data virtualization* solutions that abstract multiple data sources, and related logic to manage them, to make information directly available to the final users for analysis. We will not discuss virtualization further in this book, as it tends to be a stopgap solution en route to building a fully flexible platform. For more information about data virtualization, we suggest Chapter 10 of the book *The Self-Service Data Roadmap* by Sandeep Uttamchandani (O'Reilly).

Analyze/Visualize

Once you arrive at this stage, the data starts finally to have value in and of itself—you can consider it *information*. Users can leverage a multitude of tools to dive into the content of the data to extract useful insights, identify current trends, and predict new outcomes. At this stage, visualization tools and techniques that allow users to represent information and data in a graphical way (e.g., charts, graphs, maps, heat maps, etc.) play an important role because they provide an easy way to discover and evaluate trends, outliers, patterns, and behavior.

Visualization and analysis of data can be performed by several types of users. On one hand are people who are interested in understanding business data and want to leverage graphical tools to perform common analysis like slice and dice roll-ups and what-if analysis. On the other hand, there could be more advanced users ("power users") who want to leverage the power of a query language like SQL to execute more fine-grained and tailored analysis. In addition, there might be data scientists who can

---

1 Not just the cost of the technology or license fees—the cost here includes people costs, and SQL skills tend to cost less to an organization than Java or Python skills.

leverage ML techniques to implement new ways to extract meaningful insights from the data, discover patterns and correlations, improve customer understanding and targeting, and ultimately increase a business's revenue, growth, and market position.

Activate

This is the step where end users are able to make decisions based on data analysis and ML predictions, thus enabling a data decision-making process. From the insights extracted or predicted from the available information set, it is the time to take some actions.

The actions that can be carried out fall into three categories:

Automatic actions
> Automated systems can use the results of a recommendation system to provide customized recommendations to customers. This can help the business's top line by increasing sales.

SaaS integrations
> Actions can be performed by integrating with third-party services. For instance, a company might implement a marketing campaign to try to reduce customer churn. They could analyze data and implement a propensity model to identify customers who are likely to respond positively to a new commercial offer. The list of customer email addresses can then be sent automatically to a marketing tool to activate the campaign.

Alerting
> You can create applications that monitor data in real time and send out personalized messages when certain conditions are met. For instance, the pricing team may receive proactive notifications when the traffic to an item listing page exceeds a certain threshold, allowing them to check whether the item is priced correctly.

The technology stack for these three scenarios is different. For automatic actions, the "training" of the ML model is carried out periodically, usually by scheduling an end-to-end ML pipeline (this will be covered in Chapter 11). The predictions themselves are achieved by invoking the ML model deployed as a web service using tools like AWS SageMaker, Google Cloud Vertex AI, or Azure Machine Learning. SaaS integrations are often carried out in the context of function-specific workflow tools that allow a human to control what information is retrieved, how it is transformed, and the way it is activated. In addition, using large language models (LLMs) and their generative capabilities (we will dig more into those concepts in Chapter 10) can help automate repetitive tasks by closely integrating with core systems. Alerts are implemented through orchestration tools such as Apache Airflow, event systems such as Google Eventarc, or serverless functions such as AWS Lambda.

In this section, we have seen the activities that a modern data platform needs to support. Next, let's examine traditional approaches in implementing analytics and AI platforms to have a better understanding of how technology evolved and why the cloud approach can make a big difference.

Limitations of Traditional Approaches

Traditionally, organizations' data ecosystems consist of independent solutions that are used to provide different data services. Unfortunately, such task-specific data stores, which may sometimes grow to an important size, can lead to the creation of silos within an organization. The resulting siloed systems operate as independent solutions that are not working together in an efficient manner. *Siloed data is silenced data*—it's data from which insights are difficult to derive. To broaden and unify enterprise intelligence, securely sharing data across business units is critical.

If the majority of solutions are custom built, it becomes difficult to handle scalability, business continuity, and disaster recovery (DR). If each part of the organization chooses a different environment to build their solution in, the complexity becomes overwhelming. In such a scenario, it is difficult to ensure privacy or to audit changes to data.

One solution is to develop a unified data platform and, more precisely, a *cloud* data platform (please note that unified does not necessarily imply centralized, as will be discussed shortly). The purpose of the data platform is to allow *analytics and ML to be carried out over all of an organization's data in a consistent, scalable, and reliable way*. When doing that, you should leverage, to the maximum extent possible, managed services so that the organization can focus on business needs instead of operating infrastructure. Infrastructure operations and maintenance should be delegated totally to the underlying cloud platform. In this book, we will cover the core decisions that you need to make when developing a unified platform to consolidate data across business units in a scalable and reliable environment.

Antipattern: Breaking Down Silos Through ETL

It is challenging for organizations to have a unified view of their data because they tend to have a multitude of solutions for managing it. Organizations typically solve this problem by using data movement tools. ETL applications allow data to be transformed and transferred between different systems to create a single source of truth. However, relying on ETL is problematic, and there are better solutions available in modern platforms.

Often, an ETL tool is created to extract the most recent transactions from a transactional database on a regular basis and store them in an analytics store for access by dashboards. This is then standardized. ETL tools are created for every database table that is required for analytics so that analytics can be performed without having to go to the source system each time (see Figure 1-3).

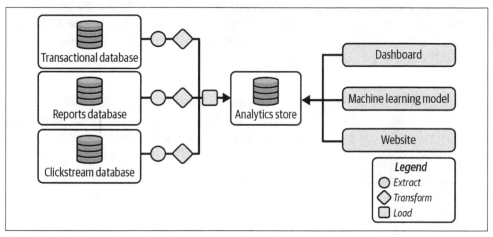

Figure 1-3. ETL tools can help break down data silos

The central analytics store that captures all the data across the organization is referred to as either a *DWH* or a *data lake* depending on the technology being used. A high-level distinction between the two approaches is based on the way the data is stored within the system: if the analytics store supports SQL and contains governed, quality-controlled data, it is referred to as a *DWH*. If instead it supports tools from the Apache ecosystem (such as Apache Spark) and contains raw data, it is referred to as a *data lake*. Terminology for referring to in-between analytics stores (such as governed raw data or ungoverned quality-controlled data) varies from organization to organization—some organizations call them data lakes and others call them DWH. As you will see later in the book, this confusing vocabulary is not a problem because data lake (Chapter 5) and DWH (Chapter 6) approaches are converging into what is known as data lakehouse (Chapter 7).

There are a few drawbacks to relying on data movement tools to try building a consistent view of the data:

Data quality
> ETL tools are often written by consumers of the data who tend to not understand it as well as the owners of the data. This means that, very often, the data that is extracted is not the right data.

Latency
> ETL tools introduce latency. For example, if the ETL tool to extract recent transactions runs once an hour and takes 15 minutes to run, the data in the analytics store could be stale by up to 75 minutes. This problem can be addressed by streaming ETL where events are processed as they happen.

Bottleneck

ETL tools typically involve programming skills. Therefore, organizations set up bespoke data engineering teams to write the code for ETL. As the diversity of data within an organization increases, an ever-increasing number of ETL tools need to be written. The data engineering team becomes a bottleneck on the ability of the organization to take advantage of data.

Maintenance

ETL tools need to be routinely run and troubleshot by system administrators. The underlying infrastructure system needs to be continually updated to cope with increased compute and storage capacity and to guarantee reliability.

Change management

Changes in the schema of the input table require the extract code of the ETL tool to be changed. This either makes changes hard to do or results in the ETL tool being broken by upstream changes.

Data gaps

It is very likely that many errors have to be escalated to the owners of the data, the creators of the ETL tool, or the users of the data. This adds to maintenance overhead, and very often to tool downtime. There are quite frequently large gaps in the data record because of this.

Governance

As ETL processes proliferate, it becomes increasingly likely that the same processing is carried out by different processes, leading to multiple sources of the same information. It's common for the processes to diverge over time to meet different needs, leading to inconsistent data being used for different decisions.

Efficiency and environmental impact

The underlying infrastructure that supports these types of transformations is a concern, as it typically operates 24/7, incurring significant costs and increasing carbon footprint impact.

The first point in the preceding list (data quality) is often overlooked, but it tends to be the most important over time. Often you need to preprocess the data before it can be "trusted" to be made available in production. Data coming from upstream systems is generally considered to be raw, and it may contain noise or even bad information if it is not properly cleaned and transformed. For example, ecommerce web logs may need to be transformed before use, such as by extracting product codes from URLs or filtering out false transactions made by bots. Data processing tools must be built specifically for the task at hand. There is no global data quality solution or common framework for dealing with quality issues.

While this situation is reasonable when considering one data source at a time, the total collection (see Figure 1-4) leads to chaos.

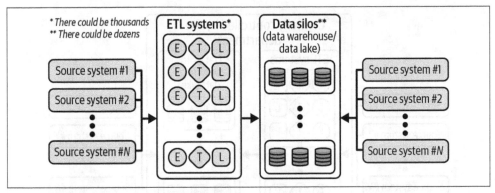

Figure 1-4. Data ecosystem and challenges

The proliferations of storage systems, together with tailor-made data management solutions developed to satisfy the desires of different downstream applications, bring about a situation where analytics leaders and chief information officers (CIOs) face the following challenges:

- Their DWH/data lake is unable to keep up with the ever-growing business needs.
- Increasingly, digital initiatives (and competition with digital natives) have transformed the business to be one where massive data volumes are flooding the system.
- The need to create separate data lakes, DWHs, and special storage for different data science tasks ends up creating multiple data silos.
- Data access needs to be limited or restricted due to performance, security, and governance challenges.
- Renewing licenses and paying for expensive support resources become challenging.

It is evident that this approach cannot be scaled to meet the new business requirements, not only because of the technological complexity but also because of the security and governance requirements that this model entails.

Antipattern: Centralization of Control

To try to address the problem of having siloed, spread, and distributed data managed via task-specific data processing solutions, some organizations have tried to centralize everything in a single, monolithic platform under the control of the IT department. As shown in Figure 1-5, the underlying technology solution doesn't change—instead, the problems are made more tractable by assigning them to a single organization to solve.

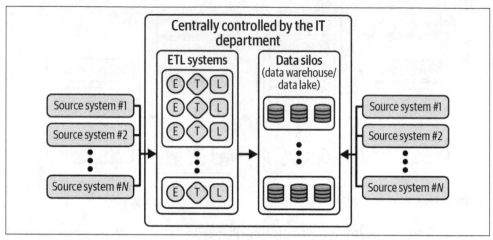

Figure 1-5. Data ecosystem and challenges with IT centrally controlling data systems

Such centralized control by a unique department comes with its own challenges and trade-offs. All business units (BUs)—IT itself, data analytics, and business users—struggle when IT controls all data systems:

IT

The challenge that IT departments face is the diverse set of technologies involved in these data silos. IT departments rarely have all the skills necessary to manage all of these systems. The data sits across multiple storage systems on premises and across clouds, making it costly to manage DWHs, data lakes, and data marts. It is also not always clear how to define security, governance, auditing, etc., across different sources. Moreover, it introduces a scalability problem in getting access to the data: the amount of work that IT needs to carry out linearly increases with the number of source systems and target systems that will be part of the picture because this will surely increase the number of data access requests by all the related stakeholders/business users.

Analytics

One of the main problems hindering effective analytics processes is not having access to the right data. When multiple systems exist, moving data to/from one monolithic data system becomes costly, resulting in unnecessary ETL tasks, etc. In addition, the preprepared and readily available data might not have the most recent sources, or there might be other versions of the data that provide more depth and broader information, such as having more columns or having more granular records. It is impossible to give your analytics team free rein whereby everyone can access all data due to data governance and operational issues. Organizations often end up limiting data access at the expense of analytic agility.

Business

Getting access to data and analytics that your business can trust is difficult. There are issues around limiting the data you give the business so you can ensure the highest quality. The alternative approach is to open up access to all the data the business users need, even if that means sacrificing quality. The challenge then becomes a balancing act on the quality of the data and amount of trusted data given. It is often the case that IT does not have enough qualified business representatives to drive priorities and requirements. This can quickly become a bottleneck slowing down the innovation process within the organization.

Despite so many challenges, several organizations adopted this approach throughout the years, creating, in some cases, frustrations and tensions for business users who were delayed in getting access to the data they needed to fulfill their tasks. Frustrated business units often cope through another antipattern—that is, *shadow IT*—where entire departments develop and deploy useful solutions to work around such limitations but end up making the problem of siloed data worse.

A technical approach called *data fabric* is sometimes employed. This still relies on centralization, but instead of physically moving data, the data fabric is a virtual layer to provide unified data access. The problem is that such standardization can be a heavy burden and introduce delays for organization-wide access to data. The data fabric is, however, a viable approach for SaaS products trying to access customers' proprietary data—integration specialists provide the necessary translation from customers' schema to the schema expected by the SaaS tool.

Antipattern: Data Marts and Hadoop

The challenges around a siloed centrally managed system created huge tension and overhead for IT. To resolve this, some businesses adopted two other antipatterns: data marts and ungoverned data lakes.

In the first approach, data was extracted to on-premises relational and analytical databases. However, despite being called data warehouses, these products were, in practice, *data marts* (a subset of enterprise data suited to specific workloads) due to scalability constraints. Data marts allow business users to design and deploy their own business data into structured data models (e.g., in retail, healthcare, banking, insurance, etc.). This enables them to easily get information about the current and the historical business (e.g., the amount of revenue of the last quarter, the number of users who played your last published game in the last week, the correlation between the time spent on the help center of your website and the number of tickets received in the last six months, etc.). For many decades, organizations have been developing data mart solutions using a variety of technologies (e.g., Oracle, Teradata, Vertica) and implementing multiple applications on top of them. However, these on-premises technologies are severely limited in terms of capacity. IT teams and data stakeholders face the challenges of scaling infrastructure (vertically), finding critical talent, reducing costs, and ultimately meeting the growing expectation of delivering valuable insights. Moreover, these solutions tended to be costly because as data sizes grew, you needed to get a system with more compute to process it.

Due to scalability and cost issues, big data solutions based on the Apache Hadoop ecosystem were created. Hadoop introduced distributed data processing (horizontal scaling) using low-cost commodity servers, enabling use cases that were previously only possible with high-end (and very costly) specialized hardware. Every application running on top of Hadoop was designed to tolerate node failures, making it a cost-effective alternative to some traditional DWH workloads. This led to the development of a new concept called *data lake*, which quickly became a core pillar of data management alongside the DWH.

The idea was that while core operational technology divisions carried on with their routine tasks, all data was exported for analytics into a centralized data lake. The intent was for the data lake to serve as the central repository for analytics workloads and for business users. Data lakes have evolved from being mere storage facilities for raw data to platforms that enable advanced analytics and data science on large volumes of data. This enabled self-service analytics across the organization, but it required an extensive working knowledge of advanced Hadoop and engineering processes to access the data. The Hadoop Open Source Software (Hadoop OSS) ecosystem grew in terms of data systems and processing frameworks (HBase, Hive, Spark, Pig, Presto, SparkML, and more) in parallel to the exponential growth in organizations' data, but this led to additional complexity and cost of maintenance. Moreover, data lakes became an ungoverned mess of data that few potential users of the data could understand. The combination of a skills gap and data quality issues meant that enterprises struggled to get good ROI out of data lakes on premises.

Now that you have seen several antipatterns, let's focus on how you could design a data platform that provides a unified view of the data across its entire lifecycle.

Creating a Unified Analytics Platform

Data mart and data lake technologies enabled IT to build the first iteration of a data platform to break down data silos and to enable the organization to derive insights from all their data assets. The data platform enabled data analysts, data engineers, data scientists, business users, architects, and security engineers to derive better real-time insights and predict how their business will evolve over time.

Cloud Instead of On-Premises

DWH and data lakes are at the core of modern data platforms. DWHs support structured data and SQL, whereas data lakes support raw data and programming frameworks in the Apache ecosystem.

However, running DWH and data lakes in an on-premises environment has some inherent challenges, such as scaling and operational costs. This has led organizations to reconsider their approach and to start considering the cloud (especially the public version of it) as the preferred environment for such a platform. Why? Because it allowed them to:

- Reduce cost by taking advantage of new pricing models (*pay-per-use model*)
- Speed up innovation by taking advantage of best-of-breed technologies
- Scale on-premises resources using a "bursting" approach
- Plan for business continuity and disaster recovery by storing data in multiple zones and regions
- Manage disaster recovery automatically using fully managed services

When users are no longer constrained by the capacity of their infrastructure, organizations are able to democratize data across their organization and unlock insights. The cloud supports organizations in their modernization efforts, as it minimizes the toil and friction by offloading the administrative, low-value tasks. A cloud data platform promises an environment where you no longer have to compromise and can build a comprehensive data ecosystem that covers the end-to-end data management and data processing stages from data collection to serving. And you can use your cloud data platform to store vast amounts of data in varying formats without compromising on latency.

Cloud data platforms promise:

- Centralized governance and access management
- Increased productivity and reduced operational costs
- Greater data sharing across the organization
- Extended access by different personas
- Reduced latency of accessing data

In the public cloud environment, the lines between DWH and data lake technologies are blurring because cloud infrastructure (specifically, the separation of compute and storage) enables a convergence that was impossible in the on-premises environment. Today it is possible to apply SQL to data held in a data lake, and it's possible to run what is traditionally a Hadoop technology (e.g., Spark) against data stored in a DWH. In this section we will give you an introduction to how this convergence works and how it can be the basis for brand-new approaches that can revolutionize the way organizations are looking at the data; you'll get more details in Chapters 5 through 7.

Drawbacks of Data Marts and Data Lakes

Over the past 40 years, IT departments have come to realize that DWHs (actually data marts) are difficult to manage and can become very costly. Legacy systems that worked well in the past (such as on-premises Teradata and Netezza appliances) have proven to be difficult to scale, to be very expensive, and to pose a number of challenges related to data freshness. Additionally, they cannot easily provide modern capabilities such as access to AI/ML or real-time features without adding that functionality after the fact.

DWH users are frequently analysts who are embedded in a specific business unit. They may have ideas about additional datasets, analysis, data processing, and business intelligence functionality that would be very beneficial to their work. However, in a traditional company, they frequently do not have direct access to data owners, nor can they easily influence the technical decision makers who decide on datasets and tools. Additionally, because they do not have access to raw data, they are unable to test hypotheses or gain a deeper understanding of the underlying data.

Data lakes are not as simple or cost-effective as they may seem. While they can be scaled easily in theory, organizations often face challenges in planning and provisioning sufficient storage, especially if they produce highly variable amounts of data. Additionally, provisioning computational capacity for peak periods can be expensive, leading to competition for scarce resources between different business units.

On-premises data lakes can be fragile and require time-consuming maintenance. Engineers who could be developing new features are often relegated to maintaining data clusters and scheduling jobs for business units. The total cost of ownership is often higher than expected for many businesses. In short, data lakes do not create value, and many businesses find that the ROI is negative.

With data lakes, governance is not easily solved, especially when different parts of the organization use different security models. Then, the data lakes become siloed and segmented, making it difficult to share data and models across teams.

Data lake users typically are closer to the raw data sources and need programming skills to use data lake tools and capabilities, even if it is just to explore the data. In traditional organizations, these users tend to focus on the data itself and are frequently held at arm's length from the rest of the business. On the other hand, business users do not have the programming skills to derive insights from data in a data lake. This disconnect means that business units miss out on the opportunity to gain insights that would drive their business objectives forward to higher revenues, lower costs, lower risk, and new opportunities.

Convergence of DWHs and Data Lakes

Given these trade-offs, many companies end up with a mixed approach, where a data lake is set up to graduate some data into a DWH or a DWH has a side data lake for additional testing and analysis. However, with multiple teams fabricating their own data architectures to suit their individual needs, data sharing and fidelity gets even more complicated for a central IT team.

Instead of having separate teams with separate goals—where one explores the business and another knows the business—you can unite these functions and their data systems to create a virtuous cycle where a deeper understanding of the business drives exploration and that exploration drives a greater understanding of the business.

Starting from this principle, the data industry has begun shifting toward a new approach, *lakehouse* and *data mesh*, which work well together because they help solve two separate challenges within an organization:

- Lakehouse allows users with different skill sets (data analysts and data engineers) to access the data using different technologies.

- Data mesh allows an enterprise to create a unified data platform without centralizing all the data in IT—this way, different business units can own their own data but allow other business units to access it in an efficient, scalable way.

As an added benefit, this architecture combination also brings in more rigorous data governance, something that data lakes typically lack. Data mesh empowers people to avoid being bottlenecked by one team and thus enables the entire data stack. It breaks silos into smaller organizational units in an architecture that provides access to data in a federated way.

Lakehouse

Data lakehouse architecture is a combination of the key benefits of data lakes and data warehouses (see Figure 1-6). It offers a low-cost storage format that is accessible by various processing engines, such as the SQL engines of data warehouses, while also providing powerful management and optimization features.

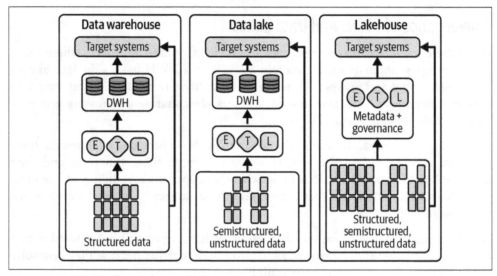

Figure 1-6. DWH, data lake, and lakehouse patterns

Databricks is a proponent of the lakehouse architecture because it was founded on Spark and needs to support business users who are not programmers. As a result, data in Databricks is stored in a data lake, but business users can use SQL to access it. However, the lakehouse architecture is not limited to Databricks.

DWHs running in cloud solutions like Google Cloud BigQuery, Snowflake, or Azure Synapse allow you to create a lakehouse architecture based around columnar storage that is optimized for SQL analytics: it allows you to treat the DWH like a data lake by also allowing Spark jobs running on parallel Hadoop environments to leverage the data stored on the underlying storage system rather than requiring a separate ETL process or storage layer.

The lakehouse pattern offers several advantages over the traditional approaches:

- Decoupling of storage and compute that enable:
  - Inexpensive, virtually unlimited, and seamlessly scalable storage
  - Stateless, resilient compute
  - ACID-compliant storage operations
  - A logical database storage model, rather than physical
- Data governance (e.g., data access restriction and schema evolution)
- Support for data analysis via the native integration with business intelligence tools
- Native support of the typical multiversion approach of a data lake approach (i.e., bronze, silver, and gold)
- Data storage and management via open formats like Apache Parquet and Iceberg
- Support for different data types in the structured or unstructured format
- Streaming capabilities with the ability to handle real-time analysis of the data
- Enablement of a diverse set of applications varying from business intelligence to ML

A lakehouse, however, is inevitably a technological compromise. The use of standard formats in cloud storage limits the storage optimizations and query concurrency that DWHs have spent years perfecting. Therefore, the SQL supported by lakehouse technologies is not as efficient as that of a native DWH (i.e., it will take more resources and cost more). Also, the SQL support tends to be limited, with features such as geospatial queries, ML, and data manipulation not available or incredibly inefficient. Similarly, the Spark support provided by DWHs is limited and tends to be not as performant as the native Spark support provided by a data lake vendor.

The lakehouse approach enables organizations to implement the core pillars of an incredibly varied data platform that can support any kind of workload. But what about the organizations on top of it? How can users leverage the best of the platform to execute their tasks? In this scenario there is a new operating model that is taking shape, and it is data mesh.

Data mesh

Data mesh is a decentralized operating model of tech, people, and process to solve the most common challenge in analytics—the desire for centralization of control in an environment where ownership of data is necessarily distributed, as shown in Figure 1-7. Another way of looking at data mesh is that it introduces a way of seeing data as a self-contained product rather than a product of ETL pipelines.

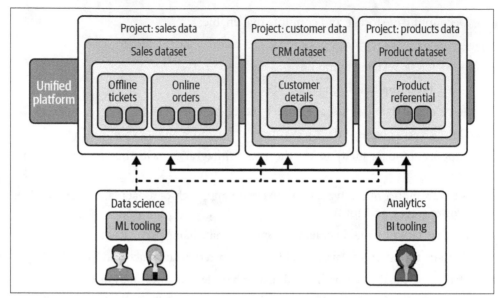

Figure 1-7. A data mesh unifies data access across the company, while retaining owner-ship of the data in distributed domains

Distributed teams in this approach own the data production and serve internal/external consumers through well-defined data schema. As a whole, data mesh is built on a long history of innovation from across DWHs and data lakes, combined with the scalability, pay-for-consumption models, self-service APIs, and close integration associated with DWH technologies in the public cloud.

With this approach, you can effectively create an on-demand data solution. A data mesh decentralizes data ownership among domain data owners, each of whom are held accountable for providing their data as a product in a standard way (see Figure 1-8). A data mesh also enables communication between various parts of the organization to distribute datasets across different locations.

In a data mesh, the responsibility for generating value from data is federated to the people who understand it best; in other words, the people who created the data or brought it into the organization must also be responsible for creating consumable data assets as products from the data they create. In many organizations, establishing a "single source of truth" or "authoritative data source" is tricky due to the repeated extraction and transformation of data across the organization without clear owner-ship responsibilities over the newly created data. In the data mesh, the authoritative data source is the data product (*https://oreil.ly/2WUaq*) published by the source domain, with a clearly assigned data owner and steward who is responsible for that data.

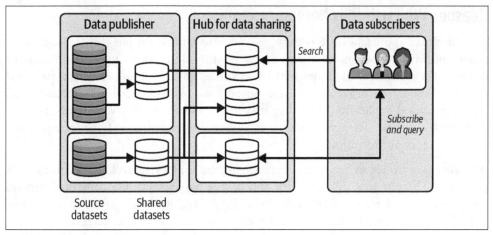

Figure 1-8. Data as a product

Having access to this unified view from a technology perspective (lakehouse) and from an organizational perspective (data mesh) means that people and systems get data delivered to them in a way that makes the most sense for their needs. In some cases this kind of architecture has to span multiple environments, generating, in some cases, very complex architecture. Let's see how companies can manage this challenge.

 For more information about data mesh, we recommend you read Zhamak Dehghani's book *Data Mesh: Delivering Data-Driven Value at Scale* (O'Reilly).

Hybrid Cloud

When designing a cloud data platform, it might be that one single environment isn't enough to manage a workload end to end. This could be because of regulatory constraints (i.e., you cannot move your data into an environment outside the organization boundaries), or because of the cost (e.g., the organization made some investments on the infrastructure that did not reach the end of life), or because you need a specific technology that is not available in the cloud. In this case a possible approach is adopting a hybrid pattern. A hybrid pattern is one in which applications are running in a combination of various environments. The most common example of hybrid pattern is combining a private computing environment, like an on-premises data center, and a public cloud computing environment. In this section we will explain how this approach can work in an enterprise.

Reasons Why Hybrid Is Necessary

Hybrid cloud approaches are widespread because almost no large enterprise today relies entirely on the public cloud. Many organizations have invested millions of dollars and thousands of hours into on-premises infrastructure over the past few decades. Almost all organizations are running a few traditional architectures and business-critical applications that they may not be able to move over to public cloud. They may also have sensitive data they can't store in a public cloud due to regulatory or organizational constraints.

Allowing workloads to transition between public and private cloud environments provides a higher level of flexibility and additional options for data deployment. There are several reasons that drive hybrid (i.e., architecture spanning across on-premises, public cloud, and edge) and multicloud (i.e., architecture spanning across multiple public cloud vendors like AWS, Microsoft Azure, and Google Cloud Platform [GCP], for example) adoption.

Here are some key business reasons for choosing hybrid and/or multicloud:

Data residency regulations
Some may never fully migrate to the public cloud, perhaps because they are in finance or healthcare and need to follow strict industry regulations on where data is stored. This is also the case with workloads in countries without a public cloud presence and a data residency requirement.

Legacy investments
Some customers want to protect their legacy workloads like SAP, Oracle, or Informatica on prem but want to take advantage of public cloud innovations like, for example, Databricks and Snowflake.

Transition
Large enterprises often require a multiyear journey to modernize into cloud native applications and architectures. They will have to embrace hybrid architectures as an intermediate state for years.

Burst to cloud
There are customers who are primarily on premises and have no desire to migrate to the public cloud. However, they have challenges of meeting business service-level agreements (SLAs) due to ad hoc large batch jobs, spiky traffic during busy periods, or large-scale ML training jobs. They want to take advantage of scalable capacity or custom hardware in public clouds and avoid the cost to scale up on-premises infrastructure. Solutions like MotherDuck, which adopt a "local-first" computing approach, are becoming popular.

Best of breed
> Some organizations choose different public cloud providers for different tasks in an intentional strategy to choose the technologies that best serve their needs. For example, Uber uses AWS (*https://oreil.ly/ajo8m*) to serve their web applications, but it uses Cloud Spanner on Google Cloud (*https://oreil.ly/gMwLu*) for its fulfillment platform. Twitter runs its news feed on AWS (*https://oreil.ly/5R4sy*), but it runs its data platform on Google Cloud (*https://oreil.ly/ubxTX*).

Now that you understand the reasons why you might choose a hybrid solution, let's have a look at the main challenges you will face when using this pattern; these challenges are why hybrid ought to be treated as an exception, and the goal should be to be cloud native.

Challenges of Hybrid Cloud

There are several challenges that enterprises face when implementing hybrid or multicloud architectures:

Governance
> It is difficult to apply consistent governance policies across multiple environments. For example, compliance security policies between on premises and public cloud are usually dealt with differently. Often, parts of the data are duplicated across on premises and cloud. Imagine your organization is running a financial report—how would you guarantee that the data used is the most recent updated copy if there are multiple copies that exist across platforms?

Access control
> User access controls and policies differ between on-premises and public cloud environments. Cloud providers have their own user access controls (called *identity and access management*, or IAM) for the services provided, whereas on-premises uses technologies such as local directory access protocol (LDAP) or Kerberos. How do you keep them synchronized or have a single control plane across distinct environments?

Workload interoperability
> When going across multiple systems, it is inevitable to have inconsistent runtime environments that need to be managed.

Data movement
> If both on-premises and cloud applications require access to some data, the two datasets must be in sync. It is costly to move data between multiple systems— there is a human cost to create and manage the pipeline, there may be licensing costs due to software used, and last but not least, it consumes system resources

such as computation, network, and storage. How can your organization deal with the costs from multiple environments? How do you join heterogeneous data that is siloed across various environments? Where do you end up copying the data as a result of the join process?

Skill sets

Having the two clouds (or on premises and cloud) means teams have to know and build expertise in two environments. Since the public cloud is a fast-moving environment, there is a significant overhead associated with upskilling and maintaining the skills of employees in one cloud, let alone two. Skill sets can also be a challenge for hiring systems integrators (SIs)—even though most large SIs have practices for each of the major clouds, very few have teams that know two or more clouds. As time goes on, we anticipate that it will become increasingly difficult to hire people willing to learn bespoke on-premises technologies.

Economics

The fact that the data is split between two environments can bring unforeseen costs: maybe you have data in one cloud and you want to make it available to another one, incurring egress costs.

Despite these challenges, a hybrid setup can work. We'll look at how in the next subsection.

Why Hybrid Can Work

Cloud providers are aware of these needs and these challenges. Therefore, they provide some support for hybrid environments. These fall into three areas:

Choice

Cloud providers often make large contributions to open source technologies. For example, although Kubernetes and TensorFlow were developed at Google, they are open source so that managed execution environments for these exist in all the major clouds and they can be leveraged even in the on-premises environments.

Flexibility

Frameworks such as Databricks and Snowflake allow you to run the same software on any of the major public cloud platforms. Thus, teams can learn one set of skills that will work everywhere. Note that the flexibility offered by tools that work on multiple clouds does not mean that you have escaped lock-in. You will have to choose between (1) lock-in at the framework level and flexibility at the cloud level (offered by technologies such as Databricks or Snowflake) and (2) lock-in at the cloud level and flexibility at the framework level (offered by the cloud native tools).

Openness

Even when the tool is proprietary, code for it is written in a portable manner because of the embrace of open standards and import/export mechanisms. Thus, for example, even though Redshift runs nowhere but on AWS, the queries are written in standard SQL and there are multiple import and export mechanisms. Together, these capabilities make Redshift and BigQuery and Synapse open platforms. This openness allows for use cases like Teads (*https://oreil.ly/avLkH*), where data is collected using Kafka on AWS, aggregated using Dataflow and BigQuery on Google Cloud, and written back to AWS Redshift (see Figure 1-9).

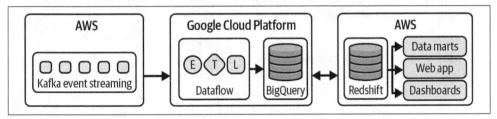

Figure 1-9. Hybrid analytics pipeline at Teads (figure based on an article by Alban Perillat-Merceroz and published in Teads Engineering: https://oreil.ly/PyJUv)

Cloud providers are making a commitment to choice, flexibility, and openness by making heavy investments in open source projects that help customers use multiple clouds. Therefore, multicloud DWHs or hybrid data processing frameworks are becoming reality. So you can build out hybrid and multicloud deployments with better cloud software production, release, and management—the way you want, not how a vendor dictates.

Edge Computing

Another incarnation of the hybrid pattern is when you may want to have computational power spanning outside the usual data platform perimeter, maybe to interact directly with some connected devices. In this case we are talking about *edge computing*. Edge computing brings computation and data storage closer to the system where data is generated and needs to be processed. The aim in edge computing is to improve response times and save bandwidth. Edge computing can unlock many use cases and accelerate digital transformation. It has many application areas, such as security, robotics, predictive maintenance, smart vehicles, etc.

As edge computing is adopted and goes mainstream, there are many potential advantages for a wide range of industries:

Faster response time

In edge computing, the power of data storage and computation is distributed and made available at the point where the decision needs to be made. Not requiring a round trip to the cloud reduces latency and empowers faster responses.

In preventive maintenance, it will help stop critical machine operations from breaking down or hazardous incidents from taking place. In active games, edge computing can provide the millisecond response times that are required. In fraud prevention and security scenarios, it can protect against privacy breaches and denial-of-service attacks.

Intermittent connectivity

Unreliable internet connectivity at remote assets such as oil wells, farm pumps, solar farms, or windmills can make monitoring those assets difficult. Edge devices' ability to locally store and process data ensures no data loss or operational failure in the event of limited internet connectivity.

Security and compliance

Edge computing can eliminate a lot of data transfer between devices and the cloud. It's possible to filter sensitive information locally and only transmit critical data model building information to the cloud. For example, with smart devices, watch-word processing such as listening for "OK Google" or "Alexa" can happen on the device itself. Potentially private data does not need to be collected or sent to the cloud. This allows users to build an appropriate security and compliance framework that is essential for enterprise security and audits.

Cost-effective solutions

One of the practical concerns around IoT adoption is the up-front cost due to network bandwidth, data storage, and computational power. Edge computing can locally perform a lot of data computations, which allows businesses to decide which services to run locally and which ones to send to the cloud, which reduces the final costs of an overall IoT solution. This is where low-memory binary deployment of embedded models in a format like Open Neural Network Exchange (ONNX), built from a modern compiled language like Rust or Go, can excel.

Interoperability

Edge devices can act as a communication liaison between legacy and modern machines. This allows legacy industrial machines to connect to modern machines or IoT solutions and provides immediate benefits of capturing insights from legacy or modern machines.

All these concepts allow architects to be incredibly flexible in the definition of their data platform. In Chapter 9 we will deep dive more into these concepts and we will see how this pattern is becoming a standard.

Applying AI

Many organizations are thrust into designing a cloud data platform because they need to adopt AI technologies—when designing a data platform, it is important to ensure that it will be future proof in being capable of supporting AI use cases. Considering the great impact AI is having on society and its diffusion within the enterprise environments, let's take a quick deep dive into how it can be implemented in an enterprise environment. You will find a deeper discussion in Chapters 10 and 11.

Machine Learning

These days, a branch of AI called *supervised machine learning* has become tremendously successful to the point where the term *AI* is more often used as an umbrella term for this branch. Supervised ML works by showing the computer program lots of examples where the correct answers (called *labels*) are known. The ML model is a standard algorithm (i.e., the exact same code) that has tunable parameters that "learn" how to go from the provided input to the label. Such a learned model is then deployed to make decisions on inputs for which the correct answers are not known.

Unlike expert systems, there is no need to explicitly program the AI model with the rules to make decisions. Because many real-world domains involve human judgment where experts struggle to articulate their logic, having the experts simply label input examples is much more feasible than capturing their logic.

Modern-day chess-playing algorithms and medical diagnostic tools use ML. The chess-playing algorithms learn from records of games that humans have played in the past,[2] whereas medical diagnostic systems learn from having expert physicians label diagnostic data.

Generative AI, a branch of AI/ML that has recently become extremely capable, is capable of not just understanding images and text but of generating realistic images and text. Besides being able to create new content in applications such as marketing, generative AI streamlines the interaction between machines and users. Users are able to ask questions in natural language and automate many operations using English, or other languages, instead of having to know programming languages.

In order for these ML methods to operate, they require tremendous amounts of training data and readily available custom hardware. Because of this, organizations adopting AI start out by building a cloud data/ML platform.

---

2 Recent ML systems such as AlphaGo (*https://oreil.ly/Garre*) learn by looking at games played between machines themselves: this is an advanced type of ML called *reinforcement learning*, but most industrial uses of ML are of the simpler supervised kind.

Uses of ML

There are a few key reasons for the spectacular adoption of ML in industry:

Data is easier.
It is easier to collect labeled data than to capture logic. Every piece of human reasoning has exceptions that will be coded up over time. It is easier to get a team of ophthalmologists to label a thousand images than it is to get them to describe how they identify that a blood vessel is hemorrhaging.

Retraining is easier.
When ML is used for systems such as recommending items to users or running marketing campaigns, user behavior changes quickly to adapt. It is important to continually train models. This is possible in ML, but much harder with code.

Better user interface.
A class of ML called *deep learning* has proven capable of being trained even on unstructured data such as images, video, and natural language text. These types of inputs are notoriously difficult to program against. This enables you to use real-world data as inputs—consider how much better the user interface of depositing checks becomes when you can simply take a photograph of a check instead of having to type all the information into a web form.

Automation.
The ability of ML models to understand unstructured data makes it possible to automate many business processes. Forms can be easily digitized, instrument dials can be more easily read, and factory floors can be more easily monitored because of the ability to automatically process natural language text, images, or video.

Cost-effectiveness.
ML APIs that give machines the ability to understand and create text, images, music, and video cost a fraction of a cent per invocation, whereas paying a human to do so would cost several orders of magnitude more. This enables the use of technology in situations such as recommendations, where a personal shopping assistant would be prohibitively expensive.

Assistance.
Generative AI can empower developers, marketers, and other white-collar workers to be more productive. Coding assistants and workflow copilots are able to simplify parts of many corporate functions, such as sending out customized sales emails.

Given these advantages, it is not surprising that a *Harvard Business Review* article (*https://oreil.ly/zhK6V*) found that AI generally supports three main business requirements:

- Automating business processes—typically automating back-office administrative and financial tasks
- Gaining insight through data analysis
- Engaging with customers and employees

ML increases the scalability to solve those problems using data examples and without needing to write custom code for everything. Then ML solutions such as deep learning allow solving these problems even when that data consists of unstructured information like images, speech, video, natural language text, etc.

Why Cloud for AI?

A key impetus behind designing a cloud data platform might be that the organization is rapidly adopting AI technologies such as deep learning. In order for these methods to operate, they require tremendous amounts of training data. Therefore, an organization that plans to build ML models will need to build a data platform to organize and make the data available to their data science teams. The ML models themselves are very complex, and training the models requires copious amounts of specialized hardware called *graphics processing units* (GPUs). Further, AI technologies such as speech transcription, machine translation, and video intelligence tend to be available as SaaS software on the cloud. In addition, cloud platforms provide key capabilities such as democratization, easier operationalization, and the ability to keep up with the state of the art.

Cloud Infrastructure

The bottom line is that high-quality AI requires a lot of data—a famous paper titled "Deep Learning Scaling Is Predictable, Empirically" (*https://oreil.ly/NEoxe*) found that for a 5% improvement in a natural language model, it was necessary to train twice as much data as was used to get the first result. The best ML models are not the most advanced ones—they are the ones that are trained on more data of high-enough quality. The reason is that increasingly sophisticated models require more data, whereas even simple models will improve in performance if trained on a sufficiently large dataset.

To give you an idea of the quantity of data required to complete the training of modern ML models, image classification models are routinely trained on one million images (*https://oreil.ly/l3yb2*) and leading language models are trained on multiple terabytes of data (*https://oreil.ly/vmOWR*).

As shown in Figure 1-10, this sort of data quantity requires a lot of efficient, bespoke computation—provided by accelerators such as GPUs and custom application-specific integrated circuits (ASICs) called *tensor processing units* (TPUs)—to harness this data and make sense of it.

Many recent AI advances can be attributed to increases in data size and compute power. The synergy between the large datasets in the cloud and the numerous computers that power it has enabled tremendous breakthroughs in ML. Breakthroughs include reducing word error rates in speech recognition (*https://oreil.ly/zDFuV*) by 30% over traditional approaches, the biggest gain in 20 years.

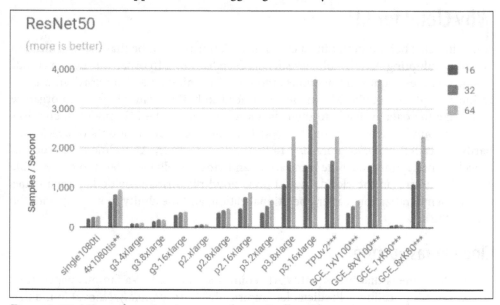

Figure 1-10. ML performance increases dramatically with greater memory, more processors, and/or the use of TPUs and GPUs (graph from AVP Project: https://oreil.ly/e18-t)

Democratization

Architecting ML models, especially in complex domains such as time-series processing or natural language processing (NLP), requires knowledge of ML theory. Writing code for training ML models using frameworks such as PyTorch, Keras, or TensorFlow requires knowledge of Python programming and linear algebra. In addition, data preparation for ML often requires data engineering expertise, and evaluating ML models requires knowledge of advanced statistics. Deploying ML models and monitoring them requires knowledge of DevOps and software engineering (often termed MLOps). Needless to say, it is rare that all these skills are present in every organization. Given this, leveraging ML for business problems can be difficult for a traditional enterprise.

Cloud technologies offer several options to democratize the use of ML:

ML APIs
Cloud providers offer prebuilt ML models that can be invoked via APIs. At that point, a developer can consume the ML model like any other web service. All they require is the ability to program against representational state transfer (REST) web services. Examples of such ML APIs include Google Translate, Azure Text Analytics, and Amazon Lex—these APIs can be used without any knowledge of NLP. Cloud providers provide generative models for text and image generation as APIs where the input is just a text prompt.

Customizable ML models
Some public clouds offer "AutoML," which are end-to-end ML pipelines that can be trained and deployed with the click of a mouse. The AutoML models carry out "neural architecture search," essentially automating the architecting of ML models through a search mechanism. While the training takes longer than if a human expert chooses an effective model for the problem, the AutoML system can suffice for lines of businesses that don't have the capability to architect their own models. Note that not all AutoML is the same—sometimes what's called AutoML is just parameter tuning. Make sure you are getting a custom-built architecture rather than simply a choice among prebuilt models, double-checking that there are various steps that can be automated (e.g., feature engineering, feature extraction, feature selection, model selection, parameter tuning, problem checking, etc.).

Simpler ML
Some DWHs (BigQuery and Redshift at the time of writing) provide the ability to train ML models on structured data using just SQL. Redshift and BigQuery support complex models by delegating to Vertex AI and SageMaker respectively. Tools like DataRobot and Dataiku offer point-and-click interfaces to train ML models. Cloud platforms make fine-tuning of generative models much easier than otherwise.

ML solutions
Some applications are so common that end-to-end ML solutions are available to purchase and deploy. Product Discovery on Google Cloud offers an end-to-end search and ranking experience for retailers. Amazon Connect offers a

ready-to-deploy contact center powered by ML. Azure Knowledge Mining provides a way to mine a variety of content types. In addition, companies such as Quantum Metric and C3 AI offer cloud-based solutions for problems common in several industries.

ML building blocks

Even if no solution exists for the entire ML workflow, parts of it could take advantage of building blocks. For example, recommender systems require the ability to match items and products. A general-purpose matching algorithm called *two-tower encoders* is available from Google Cloud. While there is no end-to-end back-office automation ML model, you could take advantage of form parsers to help implement that workflow quicker.

These capabilities allow enterprises to adopt AI even if they don't have deep expertise in it, thereby making AI more widely available.

Even if the enterprise does have expertise in AI, these capabilities prove very useful because you still have to decide whether to buy or build an ML system. There are usually more ML opportunities than there are people to solve them. Given this, there is an advantage to allowing noncore functionality to be carried out using prebuilt tools and solutions. These out-of-the-box solutions can deliver a lot of value immediately without needing to write custom applications. For example, data from a natural language text can be passed to a prebuilt model via an API call to translate text from one language to another. This not only reduces the effort to build applications but also enables non-ML experts to use AI. On the other end of the spectrum, the problem may require a custom solution. For example, retailers often build ML models to forecast demand so they know how much product to stock. These models learn buying patterns from a company's historical sales data, combined with in-house, expert intuition.

Another common pattern is to use prebuilt, out-of-the-box models for quick experimentation, and once the ML solution has proven its value, a data science team can build it in a bespoke way to get greater accuracy and hopefully more differentiation against the competition.

Real Time

It is necessary for the ML infrastructure to be integrated with a modern data platform because real-time, personalized ML is where the value is. As a result, speed of analytics becomes really important as the data platform must be able to ingest, process, and serve data in real time, or opportunities are lost. This is then complemented by the speed of action. ML drives personalized services, based on the customer's context, but has to provide inference before the customer context switches—there's a closing window for most commercial transactions within which the ML model needs to provide the customer with an option to act. To achieve this, you need the results of ML models to arrive at the point of action in real time.

Being able to supply ML models with data in real time and get the ML prediction in real time is the difference between preventing fraud and discovering fraud. To prevent fraud, it is necessary to ingest all payment and customer information in real time, run the ML prediction, and provide the result of the ML model back to the payment site in real time so that the payment can be rejected if fraud is suspected.

Other situations where real-time processing saves money are customer service and cart abandonment. Catching customer frustration in a call center and immediately escalating the situation is important to render the service effective—it will cost a lot more money to reacquire a customer once lost than to render them good service in the moment. Similarly, if a cart is at risk of being discarded, offering an enticement such as 5% off or free shipping may cost less than the much larger promotions required to get the customer back on the website.

In other situations, batch processing is simply not an effective option. Real-time traffic data and real-time navigation models are required for Google Maps to allow drivers to avoid traffic.

As you will see in Chapter 8, the resilience and autoscaling capability of cloud services is hard to achieve on premises. Thus, real-time ML is best done in the cloud.

MLOps

Another reason that ML is better in the public cloud is that operationalizing ML is hard. Effective and successful ML projects require operationalizing both data and code. Observing, orchestrating, and acting on the ML lifecycle is termed *MLOps*.

Building, deploying, and running ML applications in production entails several stages, as shown in Figure 1-11. All these steps need to be orchestrated and monitored; if, for example, data drift is detected, the models may need to be automatically retrained. Models have to be retrained on a constant basis and deployed, after making sure they are safe to be deployed. For the incoming data, you have to perform data preprocessing and validation to make sure there are no data quality issues, followed by feature engineering, followed by model training, and ending with hyperparameter tuning.

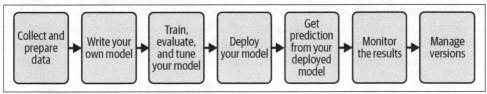

Figure 1-11. Stages of an ML workflow

In addition to the data-specific aspects of monitoring discussed, you also have the monitoring and operationalization that is necessary for any running service. A production application is often running continuously 24/7/365, with new data coming in regularly. Thus, you need tooling that makes it easy to orchestrate and manage these multiphase ML workflows and to run them reliably and repeatedly.

Cloud AI platforms such as Google's Vertex AI, Microsoft's Azure Machine Learning, and Amazon's SageMaker provide managed services for the entire ML workflow. Doing this on premises requires you to cobble together the underlying technologies and manage the integrations yourself.

At the time of writing this book, MLOps capabilities are being added at a breakneck pace to the various cloud platforms. This brings up an ancillary point, that with the rapid pace of change in ML, you are better off delegating the task of building and maintaining ML infrastructure and tooling to a third party and focusing on data and insights that are relevant to your core business.

In summary, a cloud-based data and AI platform can help resolve traditional challenges with data silos, governance, and capacity while enabling the organization to prepare for a future where AI capabilities become more important.

Core Principles

When designing a data platform, it can help to set down key design principles to adhere to and the weight that you wish to assign to each of these principles. It is likely that you will need to make trade-offs between these principles, and having a predetermined scorecard that all stakeholders have agreed to can help you make decisions without having to go back to first principles or getting swayed by the squeakiest wheel.

Here are the five key design principles for a data analytics stack that we suggest, although the relative weighting will vary from organization to organization:

Deliver serverless analytics, not infrastructure.
> Design analytics solutions for fully managed environments and avoid a lift-and-shift approach as much as possible. Focus on a modern serverless architecture to allow your data scientists (we use this term broadly to refer to data engineers, data analysts, and ML engineers) to keep their focus purely on analytics and move away from infrastructure considerations. For example, use automated data transfer to extract data from your systems and provide an environment for shared data with federated querying across any service. This eliminates the need to maintain custom frameworks and data pipelines.

Embed end-to-end ML.

Allow your organization to operationalize ML end to end. It is impossible to build every ML model that your organization needs, so make sure you are building a platform within which it is possible to embed democratized ML options such as prebuilt ML models, ML building blocks, and easier-to-use frameworks. Ensure that when custom training is needed, there is access to powerful accelerators and customizable models. Ensure that MLOps is supported so that deployed ML models don't drift and become no longer fit for purpose. Make the ML lifecycle simpler on the entire stack so that the organization can derive value from its ML initiatives faster.

Empower analytics across the entire data lifecycle.

The data analytics platform should be offering a comprehensive set of core data analytics workloads. Ensure that your data platform offers data storage, data warehousing, streaming data analytics, data preparation, big data processing, data sharing and monetization, business intelligence (BI), and ML. Avoid buying one-off solutions that you will have to integrate and manage. Looking at the analytics stack much more holistically will, in return, allow you to break down data silos, power applications with real-time data, add read-only datasets, and make query results accessible to anyone.

Enable open source software (OSS) technologies.

Wherever possible, ensure that open source is at the core of your platform. You want to ensure that any code that you write uses OSS standards such as standard SQL, Apache Spark, TensorFlow, etc. By enabling the best open source technologies, you will be able to provide flexibility and choice in data analytics projects.

Build for growth.

Ensure that the data platform that you build will be able to scale to the data size, throughput, and number of concurrent users that your organization is expected to face. Sometimes, this will involve picking different technologies (e.g., SQL for some use cases and NoSQL for other use cases). If you do so, ensure that the two technologies that you pick interoperate with each other. Leverage solutions and frameworks that have been proven and used by the world's most innovative companies to run their mission-critical analytics apps.

Overall, these factors are listed in the order that we typically recommend them. Since the two primary motivations of enterprises in choosing to do a cloud migration are cost and innovation, we recommend that you prioritize serverless (for cost savings and freeing employees from routine work) and end-to-end ML (for the wide variety of innovation that it enables).

In some situations, you might want to prioritize some factors over others. For startups, we typically recommend that the most important factors are serverless, growth, and end-to-end ML. Comprehensiveness and openness can be sacrificed for speed. Highly regulated enterprises might favor comprehensiveness, openness, and growth over serverless and ML (i.e., on premises might be necessitated by regulators). For digital natives, we recommend, in order, end-to-end ML, serverless, growth, openness, and comprehensiveness.

Summary

This was a high-level introduction to data platform modernization. Starting from the definition of the data lifecycle, we looked at the evolution of data processing, the limitations of traditional approaches, and how to create a unified analytics platform on the cloud. We also looked at how to extend the cloud data platform to be a hybrid one and to support AI/ML. The key takeaways from this chapter are as follows:

- The data lifecycle has five stages: collect, store, process, analyze/visualize, and activate. These need to be supported by a data and ML platform.

- Traditionally, organizations' data ecosystems consist of independent solutions that lead to the creation of silos within the organization.

- Data movement tools can break data silos, but they impose a few drawbacks: latency, data engineering resource bottlenecks, maintenance overhead, change management, and data gaps.

- Centralizing control of data within IT leads to organizational challenges. IT departments don't have necessary skills, analytics teams get poor data, and business teams do not trust the results.

- Organizations need to build a cloud data platform to obtain best-of-breed architectures, handle consolidation across business units, scale on-prem resources, and plan for business continuity.

- A cloud data platform leverages modern approaches and aims to enable data-led innovation through replatforming data, breaking down silos, democratizing data, enforcing data governance, enabling decision making in real time and using location information, and moving seamlessly from descriptive analytics to predictive and prescriptive analytics.

- All data can be exported from operational systems to a centralized data lake for analytics. The data lake serves as the central repository for analytics workloads and for business users. The drawback, however, is that business users do not have the skills to program against a data lake.

- DWHs are centralized analytics stores that support SQL, something that business users are familiar with.

- The data lakehouse is based on the idea that all users, regardless of their technical skills, can and should be able to use data. By providing a centralized and underlying framework for making data accessible, different tools can be used on top of the lakehouse to meet the needs of each user.

- Data mesh introduces a way of seeing data as a self-contained product. Distributed teams in this approach own the data production and serve internal/external consumers through well-defined data schema.

- A hybrid cloud environment is a pragmatic approach to meet the realities of the enterprise world such as acquisitions, local laws, and latency requirements.

- The ability of the public cloud to provide ways to manage large datasets and provision GPUs on demand makes it indispensable for all forms of ML, but deep learning and generative AI in particular. In addition, cloud platforms provide key capabilities such as democratization, easier operationalization, and the ability to keep up with the state of the art.

- The five core principles of a cloud data platform are to prioritize serverless analytics, end-to-end ML, comprehensiveness, openness, and growth. The relative weights will vary from organization to organization.

Now that you know where you want to land, in the next chapter, we'll look at a strategy to get there.

CHAPTER 2

Strategic Steps to Innovate with Data

The reason your leadership is providing the funds for you to build a data platform is very likely because they want the organization to innovate. They want the organization to discover new areas to operate in, to create better ways of operating the business, or to serve better-quality products to more customers. Innovation of this form typically happens through better understanding of customers, products, or the market. Whether your organization wants to reduce user churn or acquire new users or predict the repair cycle of a product or identify whether a lower-cost alternative will be popular, the task starts with data collection and analysis. Data is needed to analyze the current state of the business, identify shortcomings or opportunities, implement ways to improve upon the status quo, and measure the impact of those changes. Often, business unit–specific data has to be analyzed in conjunction with other data (both from across the organization and with data from suppliers and marketplaces). When building a data platform, it is important to be intentional and keep the ultimate "why" (of fostering innovation) firmly in mind.

In this chapter, you will learn the seven strategic steps to take when you are building a platform to foster innovation, why these steps are essential, and how to achieve them using present-day cloud technologies. Think of these steps as forming a pyramid (as depicted in Figure 2-1), where each step serves as the foundation for the steps that follow.

In this chapter, we will crystallize the concepts that underlie all the steps but defer details on their implementation to later chapters. For example, while we will describe the concept of breaking down silos in this chapter, we'll describe the architecture of the analytics hub or data mesh approaches to do so in Chapters 5, 6, and 7.

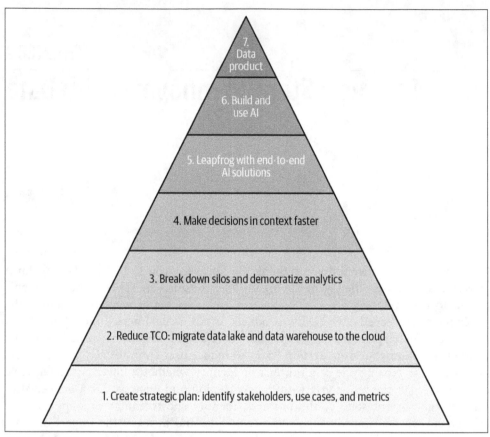

Figure 2-1. The seven-step journey we suggest to build a cloud data and AI platform

Step 1: Strategy and Planning

For the final six steps to be successful, you need to first formulate a strategic plan wherein you identify three main components:

Goals
What are the ambitions that the organization has when it comes to making the best use of data? It is important to dig deeper and identify goals that go beyond cost savings. Specifically, it is important to identify the decisions that will be made using the data and the metrics by which you can know the transformation has been successful.

Stakeholders
Who are the people in the organization who have the mandate to sponsor and drive deeper transformations? It is important to ensure that you bring together all these stakeholders—in our experience, IT projects tend to be underresourced

and always in imminent risk of failure, whereas business-driven projects have longer-term executive support and funding. Business projects also have a higher return on investment.

Change management process

How do you effectively cascade and communicate the approach to the entire organization to get sponsorship of the final users?

This strategic planning needs to be periodically revisited. Are the goals still the same? Are there new stakeholders who need to be briefed? Is there discontent brewing in the ranks?

Let's look at these three components one by one.

Strategic Goals

You should be clear-headed about your goals when building a data and AI/ML platform. Very often, stakeholders will frame goals in terms of the limitations of the current platform. For example, the goal might be stated as "We want to be able to create monthly statements for our three million customers within three hours" if your current most painful problem is that reporting workloads cause cascading outages. However, you don't want your goal in building a platform to be narrowly defined by a single use case. Instead, you want to start from a clear-headed view of the strategic goals you want to achieve.

Design your system based on the strategic direction of the business. What is the desired turnaround time for shipping information to be provided for new purchases? What is the anticipated growth in customer numbers? Will the mix of customers who arrive via mobile versus via brokers change over time? What is the expected headcount in the IT team? Does the business wish to enable field personnel to make more decisions? Do you want to send out monthly statements, or do you want to dynamically generate reports of historical activity on demand? How do we plan to make money from this reporting? Will we change our business practices based on these results? What do reports need to provide to support our current business in the field? The inability of the current platform to support these needs will naturally fall out from these strategic concerns, but this allows you to holistically frame the requirements of the system instead of being tied down by a single use case and old ways of thinking. This also helps you communicate the need for the system to nontechnical executives.

If possible, get numeric estimates for these strategic business goals over the next two to three years to help you make cost-effective decisions. For example, it can be tempting to simply say, "Queries should run as fast as possible," but that is a recipe for building an overengineered and costly system. Instead, if you know that you will have, at peak, 1,500 concurrent queries each processing 100 GB of data that need to take less than 10 seconds to run, you can choose technology that achieves your goal without breaking the bank. This also works in reverse. Knowing that the business is acquiring customers at a 60% year-over-year basis, it might be clear that the clickstream dataset is poised to be on the order of 1 TB/day. This will prevent you from making shortsighted decisions that need to be unwound.

This is often limited by the time horizon over which you can foresee business growth. It is also subject to real-world events. For example, the COVID-19 pandemic of 2020 upended many businesses' plans and accelerated a move toward digital and omnichannel experiences. Sometimes, you build a system that has to be scrapped and rebuilt, but you can minimize how often this happens by thinking expansively about contingencies.

Although the details may differ, we find that the strategic goals identified at most organizations ultimately require the following of their data platform:

Reduce the cost of operating the data and AI platform.
    In particular, linearly growing IT costs with growth in dataset sizes can be unsustainable.

Increase the speed of innovation by accelerating the time to get value from new projects.
    Experimenting on new ideas should not face months-long delays procuring machines, installing software, getting access to datasets, etc.

Democratize insights from data.
    Enable domain experts and people in the field to interact with the data directly and gain insights.

Incorporate predictive analytics, not just descriptive analytics, into decision making.
    For example, rather than simply measuring the amount of material used last week, predict the amount of material needed over the following week based on the amounts used in the recent past.

The relative prioritization varies between businesses (as it should). Many startups and digital natives emphasize speed of innovation and flexibility to grow, whereas many mature enterprises emphasize cost over flexibility. For example, a startup might use a petabyte-scale DWH even though its data is small because it expects to see 10x annual growth. A more mature business might choose to use batch processing because it is less expensive than stream processing. These different starting points impact the type of innovation and growth possible—the petabyte-scale DWH might allow the startup to target recommendations based on every payment transaction as they happen, whereas the more mature business might only send recommendation emails daily, and only to customers who made large orders.

Identify Stakeholders

A solid definition of the strategy starts with the correct requirements gathering. To do that successfully, it is incredibly important to identify the right people within the organization who are able to understand the needs and effectively collaborate across all the different business units to reduce the risk of choosing the wrong approach and solution. But who are the right people?

Are we talking about people coming from the business (e.g., CEO or chief financial officer [CFO]), or is it better to rely on the IT team (e.g., CIO, CTO, chief data officer [CDO], etc.)? Well, it really depends on the organization. We have seen many different approaches, but the one common theme is that this kind of transformation journey usually has the highest rate of success when supported directly by the business. Why? Many times, the IT organization may be mandated only with keeping things running and reducing costs year over year. If your stakeholders are only in IT, their incentives are very different than if your group of stakeholders includes people from BUs who need to develop new products, reach more customers, or fundamentally change the business.

By making the definition of a new data platform more than just a pure IT activity, you can raise the visibility of the transformation and ensure that the new platform allows the organization to solve so many business problems that were not addressable before (e.g., real-time analysis).

Even within the area of the company that supports the initiative, it is crucial to have full commitment from all the people involved. But these may be very busy people with insufficient time and expertise to spend on this transformation project. Therefore, another key question to ask is: does the company have enough internal people (with the right skills and experience) to support the initiative? Or do you need to get someone outside the company to steer the project in the right direction? It is not just a matter of technical knowledge but also a matter of leadership and management to ensure that the design and implementation of the data platform are successful and that the business outcomes are positive.

Change Management

Once you have identified the goals and the people who should steer toward the objectives, next you must define a strategy for the change management. Organizations can have the most ambitious goals supported by the most influential people, but they will have tremendous difficulty implementing the project if there is no clear mission to effectively cascade the message down the chain.

When embracing a project like data-driven transformation, we have seen so many companies forgetting to put the focus on the *cultural aspect* of the transformation and treating it as a merely technological project. Business users, and employees who will leverage the data platform in general, should be ready to embrace the change, and this can be achieved only via adequate processes and the right skills.

As shown in Figure 2-2, change management is an intersection among people, technology, and process:

People and technology

It is essential to develop a comprehensive training program to enable employees to utilize the new resources that are made available to them within the organization. This can be done either by the company itself (internally delivered) or by a partner (externally delivered). The more emphasis organizations place on upskilling their workforce, the more successful they will be in achieving their overall business goals.

People and process

It is always a matter of leadership. Leaders within the company have to foster the overall message; when people are enthused by leadership (and this is another link to the fact that stakeholders are super important!), the level of adoption increases. We have seen so many projects failing because of the lack of proper support from the same people who launched the initiative. It is important that leaders work on several internal campaigns to properly spread the message across the company, helping people to embrace the change. Some common questions to ask are: How are the teams structured? Have they got executive sponsorship? How are cloud projects budgeted, governed, assessed?

Process and technology

This is related to the ability of the organization to take advantage of adoption of cloud native services for scaling. Some common questions are: What is the extent to which the organization abstracts away the infrastructure with managed and serverless cloud services? What is the level of implementation of the automation processes and the programmable infrastructure code that runs through it? Automation is a critical asset for success because from one side it reduces the human effort, and in parallel it helps with making low-risk and frequent changes that are the key ingredients for innovation.

Success requires all three elements to work together cohesively. Many organizations have achieved this by setting up a dedicated group of people called the *Center of Excellence* (CoE) whose goal is to set the direction and drive the company in the direction of a people-process-technology harmony. We will revisit this concept with a concrete example in Chapter 12.

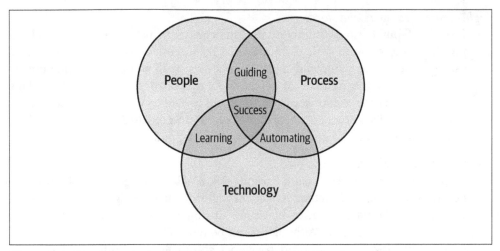

Figure 2-2. People, process, and technology working together toward success

Step 2: Reduce Total Cost of Ownership by Adopting a Cloud Approach

The first step for most enterprises, after creating the strategy, is to define (*and find*) a budget. Moving your enterprise DWH and data lakes to the cloud can save you a considerable amount of the cost of a legacy implementation. Let's look at why this is and how you can set yourself up for maximum savings.

Why Cloud Costs Less

Migrating data to the cloud can save you money due to several factors:

Reduction in operating costs

On premises, your company bears the entire cost to operate the system, and much of the maintenance is done manually. Cloud providers (who we will call hyperscalers), on the other hand, have built incredibly cost-efficient ways to manage large clusters of machines. Amazon, for example, brings their expertise running one of the world's largest and most reliable websites in a very low-margin business to provide cloud infrastructure at a very low cost. Similarly, Google runs nine services that have to be run very efficiently because over a billion users of each of these services (like Search, Gmail, and YouTube) use them for free. Users of the public cloud benefit from the low cost due to the high degree of automation built into the operation of cloud services. The majority of cloud services do not require maintenance because most of the activities (e.g., hardware maintenance, security checks, packages updates, etc.) are managed automatically under the hood.

Right-sizing of compute and storage

Instead of purchasing equipment that matches anticipated peak usage, cloud providers allow you to scale computational resources according to demand and usage. For example, you could start your systems small and increase the number of machines as the number of reports to be created grows over time. This benefit applies both to services from the cloud providers (such as Amazon EMR, Google Cloud Dataproc, and Azure HDInsight) and to third-party tools such as Databricks or Teradata Vantage that run on top of cloud infrastructure.

Autoscaling of workloads

Many cloud services (e.g., Azure Cosmos DB, AWS Aurora, Google Cloud Composer, Snowflake, and Actian Avalanche) allow you to assign more machines during peak hours and fewer machines during off-hours. Note that we said fewer machines, not zero. Although it can be tempting to completely shut down services during off-hours, consider whether you really want to retain that brick-and-mortar model. Your company's website, hopefully, is not shut down at night. Your backend systems should not be, either. Retaining the ability to service the occasional urgent request at night tends to pay off in dramatic fashion.

Serverless workloads

A few modern cloud services (e.g., BigQuery on Google Cloud Platform, Athena on AWS, Azure Functions) are serverless—you get to submit code and the system takes care of executing it for you. Think of a serverless system as an autoscaling cluster that is shared among all the hyperscaler's customers. Thus, serverless systems bring the cost benefits of operating cloud infrastructure all the way up the stack. Because labor tends to be the most expensive line item on an IT budget, serverless cloud services lead to the most cost-effective solutions. Note that many vendors position their autoscaling services as "serverless," so you should verify that the service in question is truly serverless—you get the cost benefits of serverless only if it is multitenant. If the cluster belongs to you, you will need to manage the cluster (for example, find out who runs what jobs on the cluster and when), and so you are not getting the labor cost advantage that accrues to serverless solutions.

Now that you have a better understanding of why cloud may cost less, let's have a look at how to estimate the amount of savings you may achieve.

How Much Are the Savings?

In Figure 2-3, we have shown the results of a proof of concept (PoC) we carried out on a real-world data lake. We first moved the workload as-is to the cloud, then put it on autoscaling infrastructure, and finally modernized it. We measured what the cloud costs would be. Because this was a PoC, the systems were not run long enough in these configurations to measure personnel costs to operate these systems.

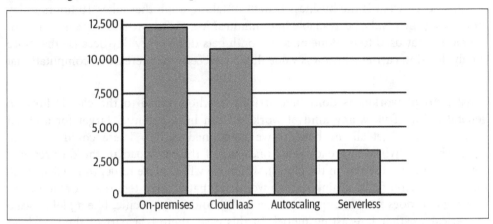

Figure 2-3. Monthly cost (in USD) of operating a 100-node data lake; personnel costs to operate the system not included

Actual savings will vary, of course, depending on the specific details of your platform and workload. As a ballpark estimate, simply moving a workload as-is to the cloud tends to provide a savings of about 10%. Adding right-sizing tends to add an additional 5%. Autoscaling tends to add a 40% savings, and serverless tends to tack on an additional 30%. If you take advantage of all these savings—for example, by changing a workload that uses Hive on premises to using a serverless solution on the cloud—the cost savings can be as high as 95%. It is essential to analyze the source workload before migrating it to the cloud. In some cases, a pure lift-and-shift migration may not be beneficial because the workload was developed to leverage specific hardware features of the on-premises environment. In these cases, it is important to evaluate updating the code (when possible) to modernize the workload and make it able to leverage autoscaling and serverless capabilities.

When Does Cloud Help?

Adding fuel to all of this is basic cloud economics. Ignoring the impact of pricing discounts, it costs the same to run a job on 10 machines for 10 hours as it does to run the job on 100 machines for 1 hour or to run the job on 1,000 machines for 6 minutes. The ability to give you access to 1,000 "warm" instances for 6 minutes out of a multitenant cluster is what makes serverless so cost-effective. Of course, it is not just cost—what is the business benefit of taking a job that takes 10 hours today and having the results be available in 6 minutes? Very often, what happens is that an operation that used to be done once a month gets done every day because the more timely decision carries a business value that far exceeds the increase in computational cost.

What kind of workloads don't benefit from a whole move to the cloud? From a general point of view, any kind of workload can be a potential target for a cloud environment to get all the benefits we mentioned earlier. There could be some cases where a hybrid approach (e.g., one part of the workload in the on-premises environment and the rest in the cloud), which we will explore in depth in Chapter 9, may have a better fit: let's think about a workload that is consistent (i.e., does not need to grow and does not have spikes), large scaled, and very specific, like a global-scale numerical weather forecasting model. In this case, there is a part of the workload that requires specialized hardware (e.g., shared memory, high-speed interconnects), which obviates the immediate hardware cost advantage of the cloud, and specialized operations personnel who understand weather models, and it experiences almost the same load day in and day out. This part can be retained on premises while having other collateral elements (e.g., data backup) that can immediately benefit from a cloud adoption.

Ephemeral and spiky workloads tend to benefit the most from a cloud move, mostly by reducing the need to spend valuable time doing resource provisioning. Ephemeral and spiky workloads will also benefit from autoscaling and the cloud economics of pay-for-what-you-use. So, when prioritizing a cloud move based on cost, start with the ephemeral and spiky workloads.

Additionally, the risk associated with employee turnover is reduced with cloud computing since the technology stack is well known and enterprise support is available. With bespoke data centers, on the other hand, your IT department may have you by the network cables!

Step 3: Break Down Silos

Once you have migrated all your data to the cloud, you can start to look at how to get more value from it. One of the best ways to start getting value from data is to break down data silos. In other words, avoid having multiple, disjointed, and sometimes invisible datasets. We are now in the third level of the Figure 2-1 pyramid.

Breaking down data silos involves striking the right balance between decentralization and value. Decentralization is good because data quality reduces the farther away from the domain experts the data gets. So you have to give domain experts control over the data. Don't centralize data in IT. At the same time, remember that you get the greatest AI/ML value by combining data that you have across your organization and even data shared by partners. Breaking silos between different parts of the organization is key.

How do you square this circle? How do you allow different parts of the organization to maintain control of their data but provide access to the data to anyone who's allowed to do so? We explore how in the following section.

Unifying Data Access

What will not work is to have each team put its data on a cluster and then manage access to that cluster. Instead, centralize data on the cloud. Note that a centralized storage location does not mean a centralized ownership structure. For example, the data could be stored on Azure Blob Storage, but every department could put "their" data in "their" bucket.

Access to data should be managed through the cloud provider's IAM. Avoid the temptation of carrying over on-premises authentication mechanisms like LDAP or Kerberos to the cloud. If you need to maintain a hybrid infrastructure, map on-premises Kerberos roles to Cloud IAM. If you are using software that needs its own authentication mechanism (e.g., MySQL), use an authentication proxy to avoid proliferation of login mechanisms. Avoid using software that provides neither IAM nor proxies to IAM. Having data and insights locked in will cause you a lot of heartache in the long term, whatever that software's near-term benefits.

If you are multicloud, ensure that you standardize on a SaaS single sign-on (SSO) authentication mechanism such as Okta and then map the Okta authentication to each of the clouds' IAMs. An alternative approach, if you have a "main" cloud, is to federate that cloud's IAM with others: for example, you might federate Google Cloud Identity to use Azure Active Directory if Azure is your main cloud but you wish to have some data workloads on Google Cloud.

Make sure that access to data is auditable based on the actual user making the request, not through service accounts that break the link back to an individual user. Because privacy and government regulations on access to data continue to become stricter, avoid getting locked into any software that operates in their own cloud project or reads data in an opaque way.

What this means is that each department would manage their data and classify their data. For example, they could tag some of the columns in their DWH as containing financial data. The data governance policy might be that the only people allowed to view financial data are people in accounting and vice presidents and above. This policy is enforced by the IT department (not the data owner) using cloud IAM.

Don't fall into the temptation of centralizing the control of data to break down silos. Data quality reduces the further away from the domain experts you get. You want to make sure that domain experts create datasets and own buckets. This allows for local control, but access to these datasets will be controlled through Cloud IAM roles and permissions. The use of encryption, access transparency, and masking/dynamic techniques can help ensure org-wide security even if the responsibility of data accuracy lies with the domain teams.

Choosing Storage

Where should you store the data?

Store structured and semistructured data in a location that is optimized for SQL analytics. Google BigQuery, AWS Redshift, Azure Synapse, Actian Avalanche, Snowflake, etc., are good choices. These tools allow you to centralize the data and still have different datasets managed by different teams but as part of the same larger DWH.

Another option is to store the structured or semistructured data in an open format such as Parquet using a distributed table format like Apache Iceberg or Databricks Delta Lake on top of a cloud blob store like AWS S3. While you may take a bit of a performance hit in SQL analytics when you store data in these open formats (as opposed to native storage mechanisms like Capacitor in BigQuery), the lower cost of storage and the flexibility to support non-SQL analytics (such as ML) might make this a worthwhile trade-off.

Unstructured data should be stored in a format and location that is optimized for reading from a variety of computational engines—Spark, Beam, TensorFlow, PyTorch, etc. Aim to use standard cloud-friendly formats such as Parquet, Avro, TensorFlow Records, and Zarr and store the files on Google Cloud Storage, Azure Blob Storage, or AWS S3. Comma-separated values (CSV) and JavaScript Object Notation (JSON) are human readable and relatively easy to process, and so have their place as well.

If the data is held by a fully managed service, make sure that you have direct, live access to the data without having to go through its query interface. When using Databricks, for example, you have the option to store data as Apache Parquet files on any cloud storage. BigQuery, as another example, offers a Storage API to directly read the columnar data instead of going through its query interface or exporting data.

Our recommendation to choose the storage layer based on type of data might seem surprising. Shouldn't you store "raw" data in a data lake and "clean" data in a DWH? As mentioned in Chapter 1, data lakes and DWHs are converging, and it doesn't make sense to treat them separately any more. Instead, you want to think about the characteristics of the data and the type of processing that you will want to do on the data. Some of your "raw" data, if it is structured, will be in Redshift/BigQuery, and some of your processed data, if unstructured, will reside in a blob storage service.

Typically, each analytics dataset or bucket will be in a single cloud region (or multi-region such as EU or US). We term such a storage layer a *distributed data layer* to avoid getting sidetracked by the lake versus warehouse debate.

Encourage teams to provide wide access to their datasets ("default open"). Data owners control access and are responsible for classifying the data subject to org-wide data governance policies. Specialized teams may also have the ability to tag datasets (for privacy, etc.). Permissions to their datasets are managed by the data owners. Upskill your workforce so that they are discovering and tagging datasets and building integration pipelines to continually increase the breadth and coverage of your distributed data layer.

Semantic Layer

One collateral effect you may experience when you build a democratized data culture is that you may start to see analytics silos. The same variable may be called by different column names in different parts of the organization. Each time a key performance indicator (KPI) is calculated is one more opportunity for it to be calculated in a wrong or inconsistent way. So encourage data analytics teams to build a semantic layer[1] (so that vocabularies can be standardized and KPIs can be computed once and reused everywhere else) and apply governance through it—see Figure 2-4.

---

1 A layer of abstraction that provides a consistent way to understand data. It translates complex information into familiar business terms such as product, customer, or revenue to offer a unified, consolidated view of data across the organization.

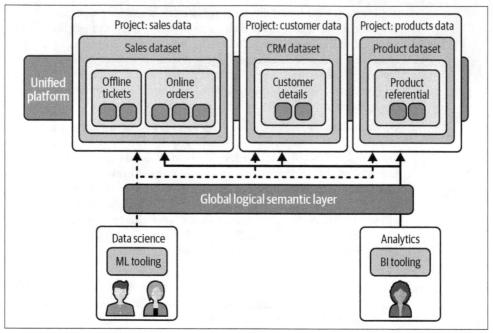

Figure 2-4. Global logical semantic layer to guarantee unified KPIs and definitions across the different domains

Tools like Looker, Informatica, Collibra, AtScale, and Cube can help define and standardize the semantic layer. Using such tools has the advantage of being multi-cloud and spanning between on premises and cloud. Thus, you can standardize your data governance across all your environments. On the cloud, the actual queries are carried out by the underlying DWH, so there is no data duplication when using these tools to create dashboards.

Do not make copies of data. Extracts and copies increase security risk, make data dependencies hard to track, and decrease the timeliness of analysis. Establish a lightweight semantic layer and bring compute to the single source of data.

 Regardless of where you store the data, you should bring computational resources to that data. For example, you might store your data on Azure Blob Storage as Parquet files and use Databricks or HDInsight to process the data using Spark. Treat compute and storage as separate, and ensure that you mix and match according to workload. For example, your structured data can be in BigQuery, but you can choose to do your processing using SQL in Big-Query, Java/Python Apache Beam in Cloud Dataflow, or Spark on Cloud Dataproc.

There is also a trend toward providing consistent control panes across different environments. Google's BigQuery Omni, for example, allows you to process data in AWS S3 buckets, Azure Blob Storage, and MySQL from the BigQuery interface. Tools like Informatica, Collibra, Looker, etc., provide a consistent interface to data in different clouds and on-prem environments.

As you have seen, removing silos is a key step in unlocking the power of the data because it enables better visibility and better collaboration among teams. Let's see now how you can move into the next steps to leverage this amount of data at your disposal in an even faster way.

Step 4: Make Decisions in Context Faster

The value of a business decision decreases with latency and distance. For example, suppose you are able to approve a loan in one minute or in one day. The one-minute approval is much, much more valuable than the one-day turnaround. Similarly, if you are able to make a decision that takes into account spatial context (whether it is based on where the user currently lives or where they are currently visiting), that decision is much more valuable than one devoid of spatial context. Therefore, an important modernization goal of your platform should be that you can do geographic information systems (GIS), streaming, and ML on data without making copies of the data. The principle of the previous section, of bringing compute to the data, should apply to GIS, streaming, and ML as well.

Batch to Stream

In many of the organizations that we work with, the size of data has been increasing between 30% and 100% year on year. Due to the power of compounding, this translates to planning for a 4x to 32x data growth over the next five years.

One of the counterintuitive aspects of a dramatic increase in data volumes is that it starts to make sense to process the data *more* frequently the larger the data volume gets. For example, suppose a business was creating a daily report based on its website traffic and this report took two hours to create. If the website traffic grows by 4x, the report will take eight hours to create unless the business puts four times the number of machines on the job. Rather than do this, an approach that makes the reports more timely is to compute statistics on six hours of data four times a day and aggregate these reports to create daily reports that are updated four times a day, as shown in Figure 2-5. The computational cost of both these approaches is nearly the same, yet the second approach can bring considerable business benefits. Extrapolate this approach, and it makes sense to have a constantly updating dashboard—you can see 24-hour aggregates that are up-to-the-minute. As data volumes increase, many businesses have this conversation and change from batch data processing to stream processing.

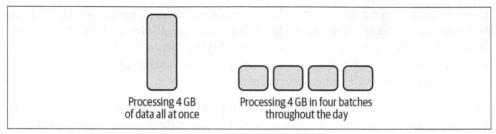

Processing 4 GB
of data all at once

Processing 4 GB in four batches
throughout the day

Figure 2-5. Spreading out processing can lead to lower latencies, fewer spikes, and less computational overhead

Contextual Information

Another key element of speeding up decision making is automating it. As data quality increases, or as the business changes its focus to its long tail of customers, there is an increasing need to cut down friction in the user experience. A frequent, expert user of your products will put up with a lot more than an occasional, less sophisticated user. Being able to catch frustrated users and provide them contextual help becomes important.

Real-time, location-based visualizations are increasingly how decisions get made. In many cases, these visualizations are built into the application that the user is using. For example, Shopify provides vendors with graphs and charts that depict how their store is performing. To do this at scale, the graphics are actually embedded into the website, rather than being a standalone dashboard product. It is a best practice to ensure that location information is part of your data schema, whether it is the location of a store or the location of a delivery truck. So if your schema includes an address, make sure the schema requires that the address be geocoded and made to be in canonical form. It is very difficult to retroactively add clean geographic information to datasets.

Cost Management

While few technology executives would quibble with the preceding, streaming has the reputation of being expensive to implement, monitor, and maintain over time.[2] How can you enable real-time decision making without breaking your budget?

First, do not build two systems, one for batch and the other for streaming. Instead, treat batch processing as a special case of streaming. Software tools like Apache Flink and Apache Beam (even Spark Structured Streaming) make this possible. Second,

---

2 Please be advised that switching from batch processing to streaming processing is not necessarily more expensive. In fact, it may save you money in the long run because you do not need to reprocess the same data multiple times a day with multiple batch runs. You can process it in real time instead.

do not custom-build monitoring, observability, late arrival, scaling, and so on. Flink and Beam are open source technologies, but to execute them, leverage fully managed services such as Kinesis Data Analytics on AWS or Cloud Dataflow on GCP—this is because the skill to manage and troubleshoot streaming infrastructure is quite rare.

The alternate approach is to treat stream processing as a special case of batch (or vice versa per Flink's philosophy). People who do this try to do micro-batching, by processing tiny bits of data as quickly as possible. This kind of approach can work when very fresh data, but not necessarily real time, is needed. It means that it is not acceptable to wait an hour or a day for batch processing to run, but at the same time it is not important to know what happened in the last few seconds.

Next, land the streaming data into a DWH or storage tier that provides the latest information to readers (and is capable of handling them at scale). In other words, as long as you can land the data in real time, all analytics on the data will reflect the latest information without any further effort on your part.

Now that you have seen how we can leverage up-to-date and context-related information, let's have a look at how to infuse AI/ML to have a better understanding of the data.

Step 5: Leapfrog with Packaged AI Solutions

One of the most exciting developments in technology in the 2010s was the rise of deep learning, a branch of AI. AI encompasses the class of problems where a computer can be used as a decision-making tool. Commonly, AI systems were built by programming computers to think or act like humans. To do so, the thought process of experts had to be carefully encoded into rules that the computers could follow. Because humans often cannot precisely explain their judgment, such expert systems rarely performed very well.

ML is a class of AI techniques where, instead of capturing human logic, the ML "model" is shown a large number of correct decisions and the model is expected to infer how to make a correct decision in the future. Because collecting data can be easier than capturing logic, ML was able to solve a wide range of problems. However, the data usually had to be structured data, of the sort held in relational databases. In the mid-2010s, a set of techniques called deep learning achieved prominence. These techniques, which employed "deep neural networks," were capable of understanding unstructured data like images, speech, video, natural language text, etc. That, in turn, has led to the development of technology like Google Photos (i.e., ability to search pictures using natural language queries) or Alexa (i.e., interaction via NLP). In the enterprise, too, deep learning has enabled organizations to extract information from unstructured data like product catalogs and user reviews. Prebuilt generative

AI solutions are becoming available for enterprise use cases such as content creation, customer experience, coding copilots, and other workflow assistants.

Because AI is getting more mature, it is no longer necessary to invest considerable engineering time into building AI capabilities in your organization. Instead, you can leverage the benefits of AI through the many AI solutions that you can buy or customize. These fall into a few categories: predictive analytics, understanding and generating data, personalization, and packaged solutions.

Predictive Analytics

ML models are trained from examples of correct decisions. An enterprise DWH is often a great source of such training examples. For example, suppose you are in the business of buying used cars, repairing them, and selling them. You would like to create a system to estimate the cost of repairing a vehicle bought at auction. It is clear that the historical data you have of your business is a good source of what the repair costs actually were for vehicles that you purchased and fixed up. In other words, the correct answers for historical data are present in the data in your DWH (see Figure 2-6) and can be used to train an ML model. The trained ML model can then be used to predict the cost of repairing vehicles that subsequently come up for auction.

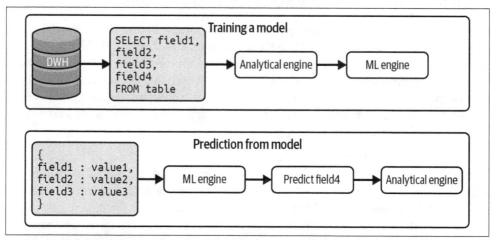

Figure 2-6. The enterprise DWH is a source of training examples for ML models

Problems like detecting a fraudulent transaction or estimating when a machine is going to fail, whether an ad will be clicked on, how many items will be sold, whether a customer will make a purchase, and so on are examples of predictive analytics problems. These problems can be trained by teaching the model to predict one value in the historical record based on the other factors that have also been captured.

Understanding what factors affect something like the repair cost and bringing all the data in the organization that bears upon this estimate into the DWH are prerequisites to successfully do predictive analytics. Once you have built an enterprise DWH, there are a large number of prebuilt forecasting solutions available to create the necessary model. Indeed, DWHs such as AWS Redshift and Google BigQuery provide the ability to train custom ML models without moving the data out of the DWH by connecting to AWS SageMaker and Google Cloud Vertex AI respectively.

Understanding and Generating Unstructured Data

Problems like identifying eye disease from retinal images, detecting an illegal left turn from a traffic camera, transcribing text from videos, and identifying abusive language in reviews are examples of using ML models to interpret unstructured data: images, videos, or natural language.

Deep learning has revolutionized the understanding of unstructured data, with each successive generation of models lowering the error rate to the point that products like question answering in Google Home, Smart Reply in Gmail, and photograph retrieval in Google Photos are highly accurate.

Unlike with predictive analytics, it is rarely necessary to create and train models to understand unstructured data. Instead, prebuilt models like Azure Vision API, Google Video Intelligence API, and AWS Comprehend can be used as-is. Use these APIs to enrich your data. For example, even with no ML knowledge, a developer can use Google's NLP API to extract the sentiment of reviews and add the sentiment as an extra column in your DWH.

What if the label provided by these prebuilt models is insufficient for your use case? Perhaps the image recognition API returns a response indicating that the image contains a screw, but you want the API to return a value that it is Item #BD-342-AC in your catalog. Even in that case, it is not necessary to train models from scratch. AutoML models (i.e., a standard ML model for a problem space such as image recognition that can be trained with custom data) such as those from Google Cloud, Azure, H2O.ai, DataRobot, etc., are customizable by simply fine-tuning them on your own data, often with as few as a dozen examples of each type. AutoML models exist for images, video, and natural language. Use them to get high-quality customized APIs that work for your problem.

Besides interpreting unstructured data, AI techniques also exist to generate it. Called generative AI (we'll discuss this further in Chapter 10), it can be used to generate text, images, speech, music, and videos. Here, too, prebuilt ("foundational") models exist that can already solve a wide variety of problems (called *zero-shot learning*). These are available through APIs from both cloud vendors (Azure OpenAI, Vertex AI) and independents (such as OpenAI, Anthropic, Midjourney, Cohere, etc.).

In many enterprise use cases, it is necessary to integrate the data and ML platforms to the generative AI models to "ground" the models in reality. For example, it is possible to customize the behavior of foundational generative AI models by just passing in a few examples (called *few-shot learning*) and crafting an appropriate input (called a *prompt*). These examples can be obtained from the data platform. Frameworks such as Hugging Face and LangChain offer open source solutions to specific problems like question answering based on enterprise documents. This involves retrieving the appropriate documents, again from a data platform through a vector similarity search, and running the chain on the ML platform. Sometimes, these are available as fully managed solutions on the cloud (e.g., Google Enterprise Search). Finally, it is possible to fine-tune these foundational models for specific tasks (called *supervised fine-tuning*), and the cloud providers offer this capability through their ML platforms.

Personalization

Rather than provide the exact same product to all users, ML offers the opportunity to provide a more tailored experience. Problems such as customer segmentation, targeting, and product recommendations fall into the category of personalization.

Personalization is driven by the historical behavior of your customers. For example, if you are a retailer, you might recommend products to users based on other people's behavior ("People who bought this item also bought..."), based on their own purchase history, or based on item similarity. All this information is present in your enterprise DWH (or at least, it can be). Therefore, you can power recommendation engines off your storage engine.

And indeed, Google BigQuery ML has a recommendation module, and Google's Recommendations AI operates off BigQuery data. Similarly, recommendation modules in Azure Machine Learning operate off Azure Synapse.

In all three categories of AI considered in this section, it is possible to stand up a quick prototype in a matter of hours to days. The models all exist; the data requirements are not onerous, and you can train ML models with a single click or single SQL query.

Packaged Solutions

In addition to the individual ML models and techniques discussed in the previous sections, always be on the lookout for packaged solutions that solve domain-specific problems in a turnkey way.

For example, conversational AI that interacts via natural language can accurately handle common, routine questions like finding out store hours of operation or requesting a restaurant reservation. Conversational AI is now capable of populating the screen of a call center support agent with suggested answers to the customer's question. Such solutions are readily integrable into an enterprise's telephone system.

Solutions like order to cash, inventory management, shelf-out identification, etc., are ready to integrate into your business. Doubtless, by the time you are reading this, many more packaged and turnkey solutions will be available. We encourage you to leapfrog the limitations of what you can realistically achieve with your current technology stack by adopting these packaged solutions.

Step 6: Operationalize AI-Driven Workflows

The last stage of your data platform strategy is to go beyond simple predictions and decisions to automating end-to-end workflows. You want to be able to solve business problems in a fully automated and autonomous way. For example, you don't want to merely predict when a machine will fail next; you want to schedule maintenance for the machine before it fails. In fact, you want to do this optimally so that your operating cost is lower, machines last longer, and your repair facility is not overwhelmed. To achieve all this, you must first of all understand what level of automation you want to have within your organization (e.g., fully automated or just assistance?), and then you need to focus on building a data culture to build a path toward your desired goal. Last but not least, you need to reinforce your data scientists team that is the fuel for the realization of your AI desires.

Identifying the Right Balance of Automation and Assistance

In our experience, many organizations make many decisions in a one-off way. If they used a data-driven approach and invested in making those data-driven decisions more systematically, they would reap hefty dividends.

Such systematic automation is one reason to break down silos, gain a consolidated view of data, and make prescriptive recommendations—as depicted in Figure 2-7, this is the logical end station of the data transformation journey. As the data maturity of an enterprise deepens, leadership needs to encourage the movement of the enterprise from one stage to the next.

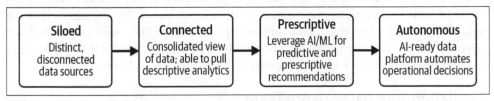

Figure 2-7. Increasing data maturity of an enterprise

To achieve this increasing maturity, it is necessary for both executives and staff to be clear-headed about what the final goal is. Is it full automation of decisions? Is it AI-guided decision making? In other words, are humans out of the loop? Or are they "over" the loop?

Consider, for example, the difference in the way navigation instructions are generated by Google Maps and by your nation's air traffic control system. The former is an example of humans out of the loop. It is fully automated. In the air traffic control case, the system provides guidance, but it is a human who gives the final navigation instructions to landing aircraft. Of course, in both cases, humans receive and act on the navigation instructions.

The right balance of automation versus assistance is something that organizations usually settle on after a fair bit of experimentation. It varies from industry to industry and from organization to organization. The relative mix is often one of the ways that different businesses in the same industry compete with one another. As such, this is usually something that is led by product management, not engineering.

Building a Data Culture

It will be necessary for the organization to build applications and systems to achieve the end goal, whether the goal is full automation or to provide assistance to experts. Building such a system will require the organization to inculcate a data culture.

It is not enough to simply put in place an analytics data platform. It is also necessary to change the culture of the organization to one where data-driven experiments are the norm and successful experiments get operationalized and scaled.

Building a data culture (*https://oreil.ly/yVykJ*) is key to unlocking innovation because you will enhance data literacy within the organization, spreading the knowledge needed to read and work with the data. Just because you have built a platform that enables data silos to be broken doesn't mean that they will be. Just because decisions can be made in a data-driven manner does not mean that old heuristics will be easily discarded.

Successful organizations undertake a transformation program that involves providing training on data tools (such as business intelligence dashboards and embedded analytics) to their entire creative workforce. They seek to change the way employees are rewarded, to encourage risk taking and entrepreneurship. They seek to put in place ways to measure everything that is important to the business. Finally, they are looking to equip their workforce with data tools so that they can effect change.

Populating Your Data Science Team

There are several roles that your data platform will need to enable for your organization to realize value from its data and AI investments: data engineers, data scientists, ML engineers, developers, and domain experts. Unless all these groups are actively collaborating on your data platform, you cannot say that you have built a future-ready data platform.

Data engineers ingest, prepare, and transform data. They use ETL tools to land the data in the DWH. They monitor the data pipelines to ensure that the pipelines are running correctly and not corrupting the data feeds.

Data scientists carry out data analytics to help decision makers gain visibility into how the business is performing, answer hypotheticals, model outcomes, and create innovative models. A key decision maker here is the product management team. Data science teams do analysis that helps inform product managers on ROI of different items on the product roadmap. For example, a data scientist in an agricultural technology company might provide answers to questions about the yield per acre of different seeds and how it depends on the soil type. They might answer hypotheticals such as the anticipated profits if the product mix at a store were to be changed to have more of one seed than another. They might also model answers to questions such as the ROI of improving availability in smaller stores. Finally, data scientists may break down a business strategy, such as creating personalized harvest planning, into component models and build them.

Once a model is created, it needs to be run routinely. ML engineers encapsulate the entire workflow in an ML pipeline and then ensure that it is executed in such a way that it can be monitored. Models are monitored both for resilience (Is the model running? Is it handling all the users requesting predictions?) and for accuracy (Are the results correct?). Models tend to drift over time. Sometimes this is because the environment itself changes (a new type of pest starts to affect a certain type of seed, so its yield estimates are no longer valid), and sometimes it is because users adapt to the model (farmers start to plant more soybeans than corn in response to price changes of the corresponding seed varieties, and this changes the demand for certain types of fertilizers). ML engineers look for such drift and retrain the model with new data. This is called MLOps.

Deployed models are available as APIs. Developers invoke the models and depict their results in the applications that end users use.

Domain experts, also known as business analysts, employ predictive analytics to enable data-driven decision making. Data scientists observe the decisions that experts make, and they look at ways to speed up the decision making by breaking down data silos that prevent this data from being accessed routinely. They use packaged AI solutions to enrich the data, and thus they continue the cycle of data-powered innovation.

Step 7: Product Management for Data

To maximize the leverage you get from data, apply product management principles.[3] A few years ago, what many executives meant by "treating data as a product" was that they wanted to monetize their data directly, such as by selling it on a data marketplace. However, today such marketplaces tend to mostly contain data created by companies that specialize in aggregating data across many sources (e.g., retail footfall, credit card receipts, product reviews). Few companies have found success monetizing their first-party data.

So what does it mean today when a typical business aspires to treat data as a product?

Applying Product Management Principles to Data

Our preferred way to think about this is to combine the desired outcome and the process to get there. The desired outcome is that your organization will maximize the leverage it gets from its data by treating it as a product, and here the characteristics highlighted by the definitions above (usefulness, standardization, governance) are important. We take an expansive view of what a data product is—datasets qualify, but so do data pipelines, dashboards, data-reliant applications, and ML models.

Desired outcomes are valuable only when accompanied by a path to get there. To treat data as a product, apply product management principles when conceiving and building data products. What product management principles? (1) Have a product strategy, (2) be customer-centric, (3) do lightweight product discovery, and (4) focus on finding market fit. We recommend adopting 10 data practices (see Figure 2-8) aligned to these principles.

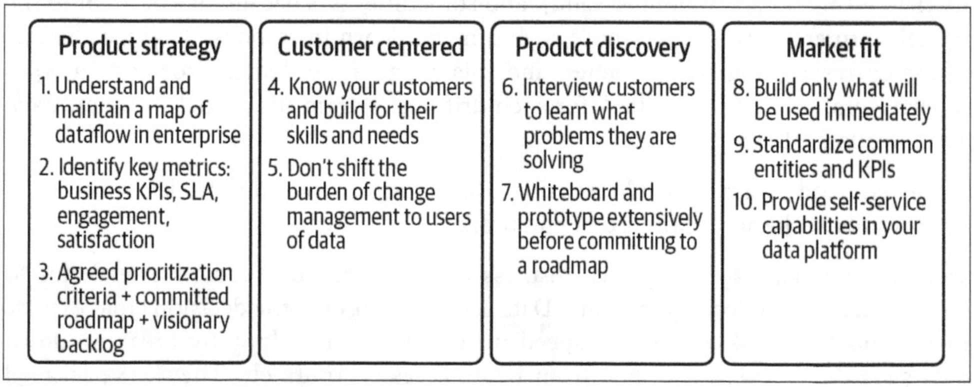

Product strategy	Customer centered	Product discovery	Market fit
1. Understand and maintain a map of dataflow in enterprise	4. Know your customers and build for their skills and needs	6. Interview customers to learn what problems they are solving	8. Build only what will be used immediately
2. Identify key metrics: business KPIs, SLA, engagement, satisfaction	5. Don't shift the burden of change management to users of data	7. Whiteboard and prototype extensively before committing to a roadmap	9. Standardize common entities and KPIs
3. Agreed prioritization criteria + committed roadmap + visionary backlog			10. Provide self-service capabilities in your data platform

Figure 2-8. Product managing data

---

3 This section is based on the LinkedIn post "How to Treat Data as a Product" (*https://oreil.ly/VvwDi*) by one of the authors of this book.

1. Understand and Maintain a Map of Data Flows in the Enterprise

One key job of a product manager is simplification. Treating data as a product means that the data product team maintains a high-level model of data flows in the business that can be easily communicated for discoverability. You need to maintain this map at multiple levels of granularity.

Imagine that you have an ecommerce site. At the highest level, for the ecommerce site, it might be:

- Web traffic
- Product catalog
- Web content
- Orders
- Inventory
- Customer survey

At the next level of granularity, web traffic might be broken down into session data, page data, etc. Capture how each dataset is collected, how it is processed, what roles can access it and how, whether personally identifiable information (PII) or other attributes are present, what quality assurances are made, etc. Also capture the production use cases for each dataset. As you go from higher levels of granularity to lower levels, the mapping starts to include details of your data platform implementation. It starts to become a data catalog.

2. Identify Key Metrics

A data catalog is simply a record of what currently exists. It does not capture why the data is important or whether the data is fit for purpose (unless you leverage ad hoc tags to do that). It doesn't tell you what needs to be improved. An important part of your data product strategy is to get alignment across the enterprise on your key metrics—what you will measure, how you will measure it, and what the target number for the metric is (goals will change over time). The universe of metrics that you track should include:

Business KPIs
   What business outcomes need to be enabled by data?

SLA
   What is the data availability? Data quality? Refresh rate?

Engagement

How widely and how often is the data used across the company?

Satisfaction

How satisfied are customers (could be internal) with what data is available and how easy it is to use?

For the hypothetical ecommerce site introduced in the previous step, the business outcomes might involve increasing customer lifetime value, increasing free-tier conversions, etc. The SLA for the inventory displayed to internal purchasers (for restocking) might be that it's available 99.99% of the time, at an hourly refresh, and is maintained to be above the next week's predicted sales. You might want the inventory predictions to be used not only by internal purchases but also by logistics teams and incorporated into dashboards. And you might have a measure of how often the predicted inventory amounts are overridden.

3. Agreed Criteria, Committed Roadmap, and Visionary Backlog

The data catalog is a record of what currently exists. The metrics capture what your goals are. Neither of these explains where you are going next.

It is important to adapt the product vision over time based on customer feedback, stakeholder input, and market conditions. During all this, your stakeholders will ask you for features and timelines and expect you to keep your commitments. To handle change and user feedback, you need three things:

- Prioritization criteria are what stakeholders agree on beforehand—this enables transparency and buy-in across the org on the product roadmap.

- The product roadmap itself is informed by a process of product discovery so that the team can avoid agreeing to timelines in the absence of information and prototyping.

- Things that you think are important but are yet to be roadmapped will be captured in a product backlog. Typically, the product backlog consists of customer problems that need to be solved (not features that have to be built). In many ways, the backlog (not the roadmap) forms your longer-term product vision. Organize the backlog to tell a clear story.

The roadmap needs to be high commitment—you should be able to commit to the timelines and features on the roadmap. A great way to do this is to get agreement on prioritization criteria, do product discovery, and maintain a product backlog.[4]

---

4 Please note that a product roadmap is a living document that is subject to change based on market and business requirements.

Recalling that one of our hypothetical data products (see previous step) is inventory predictions for the upcoming week, we need to agree on how we measure how good the predictions are. Is it that we rarely run out? That we minimize the costs of procuring and storing the items? Is the running out at the warehouse level? Or at the company level? These form the prioritization criteria. If someone asks you to customize the inventory model for perishable goods, is it worth doing? You will initially add it to a product backlog. Then you'll do product discovery to determine the ROI of doing such a project—this will include the cost of increasing/decreasing refrigeration at the warehouses, for example. Only when you know the value will you add this to your product roadmap.

4. Build for the Customers You Have

Too often, data teams get caught up in technology slogans: they only provide APIs, or insist that everyone publishes data into their enterprise DWH, or expect conformance to a single dictionary.

Take a leaf out of product management and develop a deep knowledge of who your customers are. What are they building? A mobile app or a monthly report? What do they know? SQL or Java? What tools do they use? Dashboards or TensorFlow? Do they need alerts whenever the data changes? Do they need moving averages of the data in real time? Do they care about test coverage?

Then, serve data in ways that your target customers can use it. For example, you might serve the data in a DWH (to data analysts), make it accessible via APIs (to developers), publish it in feature stores (to data scientists), or provide a semantic layer usable in dashboards (to business users).

If the hypothetical inventory prediction data product that we are using as our example will be leveraged by internal purchasers who are business users, the predictions will have to be served in the application that is used for ordering replenishments. So the predictions will likely have to be accessible via an API for the application developers to use.

5. Don't Shift the Burden of Change Management

Change and conflict are inevitable. The suppliers of data will change formats; the consumers of data will have new needs; the data velocity will change; the same data might be provided in multiple channels; your customers will move to an alternate supplier due to cost. These are not solely the problem of the team that makes the changes or the team that uses the data.

A big part of treating data as a product is to ensure that users of data are not stuck with change management responsibilities. As much as possible, make sure to evolve schema and services so that changes are transparent to downstream users.

When backward-incompatible change inevitably happens, version the changes and work with stakeholders to move them from older versions of the data to newer versions. This might involve creating a migration team whose job is to move the enterprise from one version to the next.

What's true of change management is also true of security. Make sure to build safeguards for PII and compliance instead of shifting the burden to users of your data products.

Suppose our hypothetical inventory prediction data product is customized to include predictions of perishable goods. If this involves requesting additional information on the items being sold, you will have to take on the responsibility of ensuring that your item catalog is enhanced for all existing items. This data engineering work is part of the scoping of the project, and it feeds into the ROI of whether that work is worth doing.

6. Interview Customers to Discover Their Data Needs

How do you evolve the product backlog, prioritize needs, and add to the roadmap? An important discipline is to ensure that you are constantly talking to customers and discovering what data they need to solve the problems that they are encountering. What shortcomings of the current data products are they having to work around? These problems feed into your product backlog, for you to prioritize and solve.

It is important that before any new data product idea enters the product roadmap that the need for the product has been validated by potential (internal or external) customers. Building on spec ("build it and they will come") is extremely risky. Much safer is to build implementations of ideas that have already been validated with customers.

How do you do that?

7. Whiteboard and Prototype Extensively

Whiteboard the design of the data product with customers who want it. This ensures that what you land on in the data platform will meet their needs in terms of quality, completeness, latency, etc. Walk through potential uses of data with them before you build any data pipelines or transformations.

One of the best tools here is a prototype. Many use cases of data can be validated by building a minimum viable prototype. What do we mean? If the sales team believes that building a customer data platform will help them cross-sell products, validate this by picking up a set of records from the individual products' sales pipelines, doing the match manually, and trying to cross-sell the resulting customers.

We recommend using a prototype, plus interviews with potential users of the final product, to scope the problem in terms of:

- What needs to be built: identify everything, from data pipelines to user interfaces that are needed for the project to succeed
- The ROI that you can expect in terms of business KPIs

Do this before you write any code. It's only when you have a clear idea of what needs to be built and the expected ROI that you should add the project to your roadmap. Until then, keep the problem in your backlog.

In the case of our hypothetical inventory predictions data product, you would have validated the input schema and how the predictions will be used with the key product users, checked how much more refrigeration warehouses can accommodate, etc. You'll do this before you write any code, perhaps by doing the predictions in a spreadsheet and game-playing the whole set of scenarios for a wide variety of products.

8. Build Only What Will Be Used Immediately

Prioritize going to production quickly over having all the necessary features built. This means that you should be using agile, iterative processes to build only the datasets, data pipelines, analytics, etc., that are immediately required. Don't focus on developing too many features that don't have a significant impact: the effort you're putting in won't be worth it.

Use the product backlog to capture future needs. Build those capabilities only after you have identified customers who will use those features and can give you feedback in whiteboarding/prototyping sessions.

9. Standardize Common Entities and KPIs

Provide canonical, enriched datasets for common entities and KPIs that will be standard across the business. Usually, these enriched entities power a large number of high-ROI use cases (e.g., customer data platform, content management platform) or are required for regulatory/compliance purposes (e.g., the way to calculate taxes).

Typically, you'll have only a handful of these standardized datasets and metrics because such enrichment requires significant collaboration across business units and reduces their release velocity.

10. Provide Self-Service Capabilities in Your Data Platform

You have to balance flexibility and standardization in a way that fits your organization. Do not go overboard with the previous step (of standardization). Do not build centralized datasets that have everything anyone could ever want. Instead, enable teams to be self-sufficient. This is the microservices principle as applied to data.

One way to achieve this balance is to provide small, self-contained datasets that customers can customize by joining with other datasets in domain-specific ways. Often, this is implemented as a data mesh, with each business unit responsible for the quality of the datasets that it publishes into a shared analytics hub.

Summary

In this chapter you have understood more about the process that organizations should put in place to innovate with data. The key takeaways from this chapter are as follows:

- Create a strategic plan by identifying key business goals, gathering the right stakeholders, and setting in place change management across the enterprise. Ensure that your set of stakeholders includes the business units that will most benefit from the data platform if they were to adopt it.

- Reduce total cost of ownership by moving to the cloud. When doing so, do not try to replicate the technology choices you made on premises. Instead, select technologies that autoscale, separate compute and storage, embrace NoOps, and allow you to power all sorts of applications without data movement.

- Break down data silos so that data from across the organization can be joined together. It is important to ensure that each individual department controls its data and is responsible for its quality. However, all the data is available on a uniform platform to enable cross-organization access.

- Make decisions in context faster by streaming data into your DWH in real time and ensuring that data access always reflects the latest data. The data tables should, wherever relevant, include contextual metadata such as location information.

- Take advantage of customizable and adaptable AI models so you don't have to build bespoke AI models. These help regardless of whether your need is for predictive analysis, understanding unstructured data, or personalization. Predictive analytics and personalization can be driven from your data platform. Unstructured data can be added to your data platform by processing it using prebuilt AI models.

- Expand beyond one-off ML models and into automating entire workflows. This step is often led by product management, and analysis here often informs the product roadmap.

- Build a culture of innovation by hiring and staffing teams that consist of data engineers, data scientists, ML engineers, developers, and business analysts.

- Use product management principles to formulate your data product strategy: be customer-centric, discover products through whiteboarding and prototyping, and find the right balance between standardization and flexibility.

In this chapter, we discussed a strategy for how to build an innovative data organization. In the next chapter, we'll focus on a key aspect you have to keep in mind when designing your data analytics platform: skills that existing employees currently possess or will need to pick up.

CHAPTER 3

Designing Your Data Team

When designing a data platform, there are several technical aspects to take into consideration: performance, cost, operational overhead, operational excellence, integration of new analytical and ML approaches, etc. However, these technical aspects will fall to the wayside if you don't address the culture of the company—new technologies require a willingness from employees to change their mental models and ways of working. Another key aspect to keep in mind is the skills that existing employees currently possess and will need to pick up. In some cases, employees who learn new skills and change their way of working will end up in a different role than the role they had before the data platform was in place.

In this chapter, we explore how organizations can plan and orchestrate these changes in mental models, workflows, technical skills, and roles. Every organization is unique, and so building a data platform will involve devising a granular plan for each division and employee in it. In this chapter, we describe what such a granular plan would look like for different types of organizations.

Classifying Data Processing Organizations

Organizations can succeed by employing different strategies based on their talent. There is no universal "best" approach. A sports team with a strong defense should play to their strengths and focus on defense, not try to copy the offense of a team with skilled offensive players. Similarly, if your organization has a strong team of data analysts, it should focus on its people rather than attempting to transform into an organization full of data engineers.

Decide on the best strategy for your organization based on the skills of your workforce and the complexity of your use cases. Do you need a small but highly capable (and expensive) group of data engineers? Or should you leverage a large and already present workforce of data analysts to enrich and transform data that can be acted on? How much domain knowledge do these workers need? Would training the current workforce to carry out higher-value work be realistic? Or should you invest in generative AI or no-code tools and make such foundational pieces of technology available to the larger workforce?

The best technology approach will also vary within the organization—the composition of the workforce will vary between the sales team and the factory floor. So the granular plan involves detailing the best technology approach for each business unit. Technology-wise, the plan will also make choices between an approach based on standard ETL (hard skills on ETL tools required) and a modern one based on ELT (more general SQL skills required).

Consider the traditional persona value chain as sketched in Figure 3-1. You can see that every data user in an organization has a small and specialized set of technical skills. If an organization wants to increase the scope of its data analysis team, it also has to scale the size of its data engineering and data science teams to make sure enough people have the right technical skills to support the data analysts.

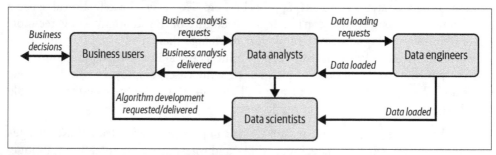

Figure 3-1. Data processing: traditional persona value chain

The new paradigms provided by the public cloud have opened up new possibilities for how data processing, data analysis, and algorithm development are done. Cloud technologies make new ways of working now possible—they allow analysts to carry out batch or real-time data processing tasks that used to be managed by data engineers while also allowing them to experiment with off-the-shelf data science solutions. Additionally, the potential scope of any given persona—the skills they have and the duties they are responsible for—has increased. As data technology becomes more accessible, data workers are able to take on new tasks and address the data value chain without the bottlenecks associated with the traditional persona value chain. This is leading to a convergence of skills across roles, allowing existing teams to more easily scale to additional responsibilities. The distinction between data analysts focused on solving problems using an ELT approach with SQL code and data engineers/data scientists more aligned with an ETL approach and general-purpose code (e.g., Python, Java, Scala, etc.) is becoming less clear. Blended approaches (as depicted in Figure 3-2) are becoming more common because they can take advantage of the best of both ETL and ELT patterns. The majority of the organizations we see today fall into this blended model, though the balance of roles and how much of the data processing has to be done via either ETL or ELT vary depending on the type of the organization.

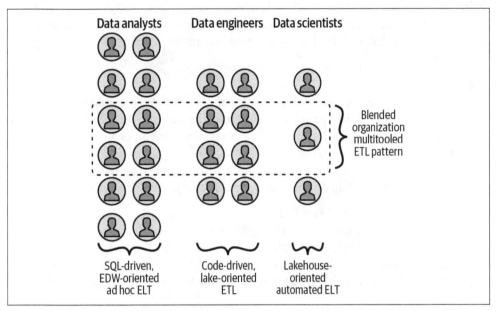

Figure 3-2. Data processing: persona framework

In simpler terms, data workers are now able to do more with the data they have, and they are able to do it more efficiently. This is because the technology is more accessible and because data workers are able to blend their skills with those of other data professionals. This is leading to a more efficient and effective way of processing data.

Organizations can be broadly classified under three types: *data analysis driven*, *data engineering driven*, and *data science driven*. In the following sections, we will cover an idealized way of building a data processing organization for each of these types. In reality, companies will consist of different divisions or business units that fall into these categories, and so they will find themselves applying all the strategies. Some teams will be a combination of roles, and so the transformation will involve a blended approach. As you consider the different types of users who will be part of your data team, remember what you learned in Chapter 2: "To maximize the leverage you get from data, apply product management principles." You should always use product management principles to develop your data product strategy, be customer-centric, discover products through whiteboarding and prototyping, and find the right balance between standardization and flexibility.

Data Analysis–Driven Organization

A data analysis–driven organization is one in which data analysts play a central role in decision making. It is important to note that whether an organization is analyst driven is not a black-and-white issue but rather a spectrum of overlapping characteristics:

Mature industry
These organizations are well-known and established businesses with well-established (and perhaps outdated) systems. The industry in which they operate is typically mature and stable. The primary work involves human analysis of a variety of products or situations. Canonical examples of data analysis–driven organizations are the merchandising units of retailers (e.g., Walmart) and commercial loan processing divisions of large banks (e.g., JPMorgan Chase).

Enterprise DWH (EDW) and batch ETL
In technical terms, the central information hub is an EDW that has been built over time with a high level of technical debt and legacy technology. The transformation of data within the DWH is carried out through scheduled ETL processes such as nightly batches. This batch process adds to the latency of serving the data.

Business intelligence
The majority of data professionals in the organization are accustomed to answering business questions by running SQL queries against a centralized DWH, creating reports and dashboards using BI tools, and using spreadsheets to access similar data. As a result, the internal talent pool is most comfortable with SQL, BI tools, and spreadsheets.

Note that even in mature industries such as retail and finance, emerging digital organizations (ecommerce and fintech) may seek to capture the fastest-growing digital areas and customer segments with the greatest potential. Such digital natives may have a different workforce composition than established players (e.g., Etsy versus Walmart; Paytm versus JPMorgan Chase); we wouldn't put digital natives in the same category as established players.

Now that you have a clearer view of what we mean by analysis-driven organizations, let's discuss the main levers to pull for the transformation.

The Vision

To democratize the use of a cloud data platform in an analysis-driven organization, analysts should be able to do advanced analytics through familiar interfaces such as spreadsheets, SQL, and BI tools. This means providing easy-to-use tools for bringing data into the target system and seamless connectivity to analysis and visualization tools.

This was once common practice with traditional EDWs. Data was enriched, transformed, and cleansed using SQL, and ETL tools were used to orchestrate the process. Similarly, materialized views and user-defined functions can be used to enrich, transform, and cleanse data in a modern DWH.

However, this assumes that the analyst already has access to all the data sources. Creating complex ingestion pipelines used to be costly and often cumbersome. Therefore, data pipelines were managed outside of the DWH due to resource and cost constraints.

This is no longer the case with new cloud DWHs. The role of ingestion is now simply to bring data close to the cloud, and the transformation and processing part moves back to the cloud EDW. This leads to data being staged in a storage bucket or on a messaging system before being ingested into the cloud EDW.

All of this not only reduces the time required to make data available but also frees up data analysts to focus on looking for data insights using tools and interfaces that they are used to. Therefore, in the new world, ELT should replace ETL tooling—data analysts can use SQL orchestration tools such as dbt or Dataform to string together SQL statements to carry out ELT. Ingesting data directly from a source or staging area allows analysts to exploit their key SQL skills and also increases the timeliness of the data they receive. They don't need to wait for a swamped data engineering team to implement ETL pipelines.

In conclusion, the best way to scale the use of a cloud data platform is to provide analysts with easy-to-use tools (such as dbt) and interfaces (such as Excel or Tableau) that they can easily become proficient in. This will enable them to do advanced analytics without having to wait for data engineering teams to implement complex ETL pipelines.

Once the data is available in the cloud EDW, it is time to begin the analysis. In the past, much data analysis was done using spreadsheets, but spreadsheets often struggle to handle the volume of data that needs to be analyzed in the new world. Even though Google Sheets and Excel have capabilities to connect live to DWHs, it is still somewhat clunky. We recommend that analysts be provided access to create visualizations and reports using modern BI tools that are capable of handling large datasets (e.g., Power BI, Tableau, or Looker).

The Personas

The main roles in the data departments of analysis-driven organizations are data analysts, business analysts, and data engineers.

Data analysts

Data analysts receive, understand, and fulfill requests from the business and make sense of the relevant data. Data analysts aim to meet the information needs of their organizations. They are responsible for the logical design and maintenance of data. Some of their tasks may include creating layouts and designs for tables to meet business processes as well as reorganizing and transforming data sources. Additionally, they are responsible for generating reports and insights that effectively communicate trends, patterns, or predictions that the business requests.

To build the mission for the analysis-driven organizations, it is necessary to expand the experience and skill set of the data analyst community in two ways. First, it is critical to promote the trend of data analysts learning about the business. Data analysts need to acquire a deep knowledge of business domains. Second, data analysts need to acquire the technical skills to analyze and depict data regardless of its volume or size. Fortunately, this is now possible using SQL and BI tools. The expansion of the skills of data analysts into the business and into big data is depicted in Figure 3-3.

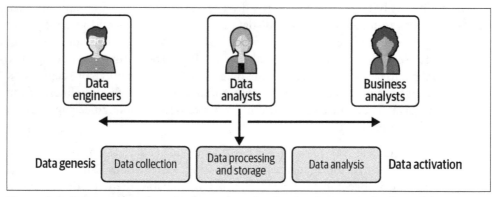

Figure 3-3. Data analyst domain expansions for the development of a data-driven strategy

Business analysts

Business analysts are domain experts who use data to act on analytical insights.

Cloud-based DWHs and serverless technologies have expanded the responsibilities of business analysts into what was traditionally the realm of domain experts. This is because analysts can now focus on adding value to the business by analyzing data, rather than wasting time on administrative and technical management tasks. Additionally, the volume and type of data that can be stored in a DWH is no longer a limitation, so analysts can now go deeper into the business to find insights.

The DWH can function as both a landing area for data and a system of record for both structured and semistructured data. This means that business analysts have all the data they need to analyze in one place. Overall, cloud-based DWHs and serverless technologies have made it possible for business analysts to be more productive and to add more value to the business.

While business analysts can do no-code and low-code ML models, they will struggle with more complex workflows that involve ML or natural language text. They will also not have the skills to implement sophisticated data science algorithms such as for ranking or recommendations. Therefore, you will still need a data science team if your activation needs are more complex.

Data engineers

Data engineers focus on the downstream data pipeline and the first phases of data transformation, such as loading and integrating new sources. They also manage data governance and data quality processes.

In an analysis-driven organization, the number of data engineers will be small because the data analyst teams will be largely self-sufficient and capable of building simple data pipelines and ML models. Analysis-driven organizations embrace the concept of ELT rather than traditional ETL. The main difference is that the common data processing tasks are handled after the data is loaded to the DWH. ELT makes extensive use of SQL logic to enhance, cleanse, normalize, refine, and integrate data and make it ready for analysis. There are several benefits of such an approach: it reduces time to act, data is loaded immediately, and it is made available to multiple users concurrently. Therefore, a change management strategy for such an organization has to focus on aspects such as SQL, views, functions, scheduling, etc.

Even in an analysis-driven organization, data engineering teams generally control extraction of data from source systems. While this can be made easier through the use of SQL-based tools, enabling data analysts to do some of that work, you still need a solid data engineering team. There are batch jobs that would still require creating data pipelines and that would be more suitable for ETL. For example, bringing data from a mainframe to a DWH would require additional processing steps: data types need to be mapped, COBOL books need to be converted, and so on.

In addition, for use cases like real-time analytics, the data engineering teams will configure the streaming data sources such as Pub/Sub or Kafka topics or Kinesis

Data Streams. The way that you deal with generic tasks is still the same—they can be written as generic ETL pipelines and then reconfigured by the analysts. For example, applying data quality validation checks from various source datasets to the target environment will follow a template set up by a data engineer.

The Technological Framework

There are three fundamental principles underlying the high-level reference architecture for an analysis-driven organization:

SQL as a standard
Technology should be tailored to the current organizational culture. Components that offer a SQL interface should be prioritized, regardless of where they are in the data processing pipeline.

From EDW/data lake to a structured data lake
Information systems infrastructure and its data should be integrated to expand the possibilities of analytical processing on new and diverse data sources. This may involve merging a traditional DWH with a data lake to eliminate silos (more on the lakehouse architecture in Chapter 7).

Schema-on-read first approach
Due to the low cost of storage, your organization no longer needs to impose rigid rules on data structures before data is received. Moving away from a schema-on-write to a schema-on-read model allows for real-time access to data. Data can be kept in its raw form and then transformed into the schema that will be most useful. Additionally, the data platform can manage the process of keeping these copies in sync (for example, using materialized views, change data capture, etc.). Therefore, do not be afraid to keep multiple copies of the same data assets.

Combining these principles, we can define a high-level architecture like the one shown in Figure 3-4. This informational architecture satisfies the three principles listed above and supports a few key data analysis patterns:

- The "traditional" BI workloads, such as creating a dashboard or report
- An ad hoc analytics interface that allows for the management of data pipelines through SQL (ELT)
- Enabling data science use cases with ML techniques
- Real-time streaming of data into the DWH and processing of real-time events

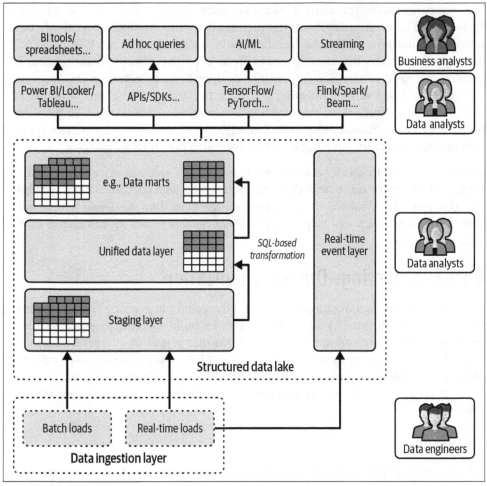

Figure 3-4. A high-level informational architecture for the analysis-driven organization

The first two patterns are quite similar to the traditional SQL data warehousing world, but the last two present innovations in the form of SQL abstractions for more advanced analytical patterns. In the realm of ML, Redshift ML or BigQuery ML allows data analysts to execute ML models on data stored in the DWH using standard SQL queries. SQL streaming extensions such as Dataflow and KSQL enable aggregating data streams with unbounded, real-time sources such as Pub/Sub or Kafka. This technology enables a world of possibilities, even without the need to invest in new profiles and/or roles.

Data preparation and transformation are key considerations when choosing between ELT and ETL for an analysis-driven organization. ELT should be used whenever possible, as it allows data to be transformed in the structured data lake using SQL. This approach offers the same functionality as extensive data integration suites but without the need to sacrifice data quality or operations monitoring. Products such as dbt bring a software engineering approach to data modeling and building data workflows; dbt effectively allows building ELT workflows similar to ETL workflows built by code, but instead using SQL. This allows data analysts (who are not systems programmers) to carry out reliable and sophisticated data transformations.

In simpler terms, ELT is a better option than ETL for analysis-driven organizations because it allows for more flexibility and control over data transformation. Additionally, dbt provides a software engineering approach to data modeling and building data workflows, which can help to improve the reliability and sophistication of data transformations.

Data Engineering–Driven Organization

An engineering-driven organization is focused on data integration. There are companies (e.g., Plaid in fintech) whose business is to build integration pipelines for an entire industry. More commonly, this is a team that is part of a larger business. For example, an investment firm might have a team whose job is to discover, reformat, and ingest financial (e.g., stock market, companies' SEC filings, etc.) and alternative (e.g., credit card spend, e-receipts, retail footfall, etc.) data from a large number of vendors.

The Vision

When your data transformation needs are complex, you need data engineers to play a central role in the company's data strategy to ensure that you can build reliable systems cost-effectively. Data engineers are at the crossroads between data owners and data consumers.

The business data owner is the designated point of contact for business teams that know the business and provide data for the data architecture. Data consumers are focused on extracting insights from the different data available in the architecture. Here you typically find data science teams, data analysts, BI teams, etc. These groups sometimes combine data from different business units and produce artifacts (ML models, interactive dashboards, reports, and so on). For deployment, they require the help of the data engineering team so that data is consistent and trusted.

Data engineers have the following responsibilities:

- Transporting data and enriching data while building integrations between analytical systems and operational systems (as in the real-time use cases).

- Parsing and transforming messy data coming from business units and external suppliers into meaningful and clean data, with documented metadata.

- Applying DataOps—that is, functional knowledge of the business plus software engineering methodologies applied to the data lifecycle. This includes monitoring and maintenance of data feeds.

- Deploying ML models and other data science artifacts analyzing or consuming data.

Building complex data engineering pipelines is expensive but enables increased capabilities:

Enrichment
Data engineers create processes to collect data from different sources and combine it to create a more valuable dataset. This data can then be used to make better decisions.

Training datasets
The quality of ML models is largely driven by the data used to train those models. By bringing in data from multiple sources and unifying them into datasets ready for training ML models, data engineers can increase the productivity of data science teams.

Unstructured data
When the ML models need to use unstructured data (such as review text or images), there are special challenges. Such data usually doesn't follow a strict schema as a traditional DWH would use. In addition, it needs to be scrubbed of PII (such as telephone numbers in chat transcripts) and unsafe-for-work content (especially images) and transformed (e.g., using embeddings).

Productionization
Data engineering work is also required to productionize and get value from ad hoc data science work. Without data engineering, data scientists will be stuck carrying out experiments and producing applications that work for specific use cases but are rarely productionized or generalized.

Real-time analytics
Applications such as anomaly detection and fraud prevention require immediate responses. In such use cases, data consumers need to process information as data arrives on the fly. They have to do so with low latency. This type of real-time analytics requires transformation done outside of the target DWH.

All the preceding usually requires custom applications or state-of-the art tooling. In reality, there are very few organizations whose engineering capabilities excel to such a degree that they can truly be called engineering organizations. Many fall into what we call a blended organization (see Figure 3-2).

The Personas

Data engineers develop and optimize all the processes needed to get access to the data and the solutions needed to perform related analysis and generate reports.

Knowledge

The data engineering role requires a deep understanding of databases and programming languages, along with certain business skills to work across departments. Regardless of the size of the organization they are working in, data engineers need to have some standard skills to be successful. The most valuable knowledge includes:

Data warehousing and data lake solutions
Cloudera Data Platform, Oracle Exadata, Amazon RedShift, Azure Synapse, Google BigQuery, Snowflake, Databricks, Hadoop ecosystem, etc., where data engineers can handle huge volumes of data.

Database systems
Database systems like SQL and NoSQL. They should know how to work on and manipulate RDBMSs for information storage and retrieval.

ETL tools
Both traditional tools such as Informatica and Ab Initio and modern frameworks such as Apache Beam, Spark, and Kafka.

Programming languages
Python, Java, Scala.

Data structures and algorithms
Data structures and algorithms allow organizing and storing data for easy access and manipulation, making this an essential skill for data engineers.

Automation and scripting
Data engineers should be able to write scripts to automate repetitive tasks since they have to deal with such huge amounts of data (e.g., bash, PowerShell, Hashi-Corp Terraform, Ansible, etc.).

Container technology
The de facto standard for moving data projects to production. Projects developed on a local machine can be "shipped" to a staging and production cluster

(typically) with no issues. Data pipelines and ML models are reproducible and can run anywhere in the same fashion.

Orchestration platforms
Because of the proliferation of solutions and tools that need to be integrated to perform data engineering tasks, orchestration tools like Apache Airflow have become mandatory.

Certifications measure a data engineer's knowledge and proficiency against vendor and/or industry benchmarks, confirming that the individual has the necessary expertise to contribute to your enterprise data strategies. Examples are AWS Certified Data Analytics, Cloudera Certified Professional (CCP) Data Engineer, Google Professional Data Engineer, and Microsoft Certified: Azure Data Engineer Associate.

Responsibilities

Data engineers are responsible for making sure that the data generated and needed by different business units gets ingested into the architecture. This job requires two disparate skills: functional knowledge and data engineering/software development skills. This skill set is often described using the term *DataOps* (which evolved from DevOps methodologies developed within the past decades but applied to data engineering practices).

Data engineers have another responsibility, too. They must help with the deployment of artifacts produced by the data consumers. Typically, the data consumers do not have the deep technical skills and knowledge to take the sole responsibility for deployment of their artifacts. This is also true for highly sophisticated data science teams. So data engineers must add other skills under their belt: ML and business intelligence platform knowledge. Let's clarify this point: we don't expect data engineers to become ML engineers. ML engineering is the process of deploying ML models developed by data scientists into live production systems. Data engineers, on the other hand, build the infrastructure that others use to work on data, such as data storage and data transportation. Data engineers need to understand ML to ensure that the data delivered to the first layer of a model (the input) is correct. They will also become key when delivering that first layer of data in the inference path, as here the data engineering skills around scale, high availability, etc., really need to shine.

By taking the responsibility of parsing and transforming messy data from various business units, or for ingesting in real time, data engineers allow the data consumers to focus on creating value. Data scientists and other types of data consumers are abstracted away from data encodings, large files, legacy systems, and complex message queue configurations for streaming. The benefits of concentrating that knowledge in a highly skilled data engineering team are clear, notwithstanding that other teams (business units and consumers) may also have their data engineers to work as interfaces with other teams. More recently, we've even seen squads created with members of the business units (data product owners), data engineers, data scientists, and other roles. This effectively creates complete teams with autonomy and full responsibility over a data stream, from the incoming data down to the data-driven decisions that impact the business.

The Technological Framework

The data engineering team already requires a wide range of skills. Do not make their job more difficult by expecting them to also maintain the infrastructure where they run data pipelines. Data engineers should focus on how to clean, transform, enrich, and prepare the data, rather than on how much memory or how many cores their solution may require.

Reference architectures

The ingestion layer is made up of Kinesis, Event Hubs, or Pub/Sub for real-time data and S3, Azure Data Lake, or Cloud Storage for batch data (see Figures 3-5, 3-6, and 3-7). It does not need any preallocated infrastructure. All of these solutions can be used for a variety of cases since they can automatically scale up to meet the demands of the input workload.

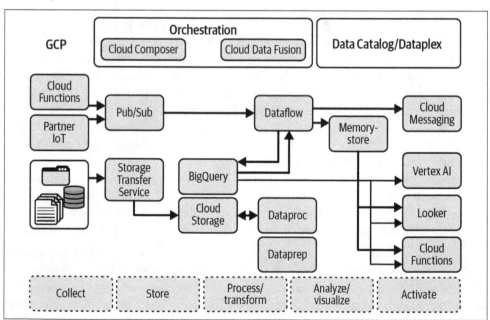

Figure 3-5. Example data engineering–driven architecture on Google Cloud

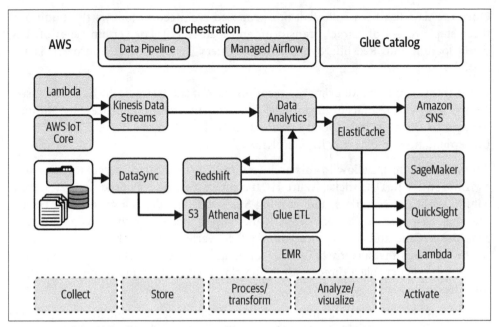

Figure 3-6. Example data engineering–driven architecture on AWS

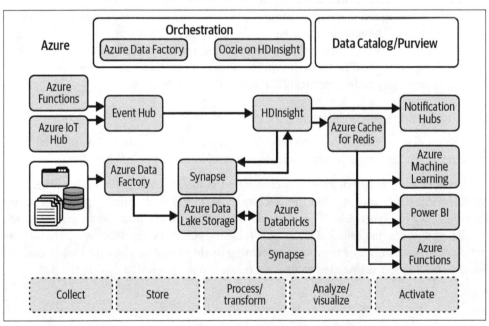

Figure 3-7. Example data engineering–driven architecture on Azure

Once the data has been collected, our proposed architecture follows the traditional three-step process of extract, transform, and load (ETL). For certain types of files, direct loading into Redshift, Synapse, or BigQuery (using an ELT approach) is also feasible.

In the transform layer, we primarily recommend Apache Beam as the data processing component because of its unified model for batch and streaming processing. Runners for Apache Beam include Cloud Dataflow on GCP and any managed Flink or Spark implementation on the other hyperscalers.

An alternative to Dataflow in this architecture is using a Spark-based solution such as Amazon EMR, Databricks, Azure HDInsight, or Google Dataproc. However, these solutions are not serverless, and running Spark clusters idle is a major cost. Having said that, there are also serverless Spark alternatives that are provided as part of AWS SageMaker/Glue and as a service with GCP Serverless Spark. The main use case is for those teams that already have large amounts of code in Spark or Hadoop. These Spark solutions enable a direct path to the cloud without having to review all those pipelines.

Another alternative for data processing is a codeless environment for creating data pipelines using a drag-and-drop interface, such as that provided by AWS Glue, Azure Data Factory, or GCP Data Fusion. Traditional ETL tools such as Informatica, Ab Initio, and Talend also run in serverless mode in the cloud with underlying Kubernetes clusters. Some of these tools use either Hadoop/Spark solutions or similar proprietary compute engines behind the scenes, so everything we have mentioned earlier applies also to the case of the ETL tools. If your team prefers to create data pipelines without having to write any code, graphical ETL tools are the right choice.

Benefits of the reference architecture

The reference architectures presented in Figures 3-5, 3-6, and 3-7 are based on a preference for serverless NoOps technologies and streaming pipelines.

By using serverless technology, you eliminate the maintenance burden from the data engineering team and provide the necessary flexibility and scalability for executing complex and/or large jobs. For example, scalability is essential when planning for traffic spikes during Black Friday for retailers. Using serverless solutions allows retailers to look into how they are performing during the day. They no longer need to worry about resources needed to process massive data generated during the day.

The reference architectures give the data engineering team the possibility to write fully custom code for the data pipelines. This may be because the parsing requirements can be complex and no off-the-shelf solution may work. In streaming, the team may want to implement complex business logic at a low latency. However, the team should try to reuse code by creating reusable libraries and by using technologies such as Dataflow templates. This brings the best of both worlds (reuse and rewrite) while saving precious time that can be dedicated to higher-impact code rather than common I/O tasks.

The reference architectures presented have another important feature: the possibility to transform existing batch pipelines to streaming.

Data Science–Driven Organization

A data science–driven organization is an entity that maximizes the value from the data available to create a sustainable competitive advantage. To do so, the organization leans on automated algorithms that often (but not always!) employ ML. Rather than rely on one-off reports and analytics as an analysis-driven organization would, a science-driven organization attempts to make decisions in an automated way. For example, a bank that is data analysis driven would have data analysts assess each commercial loan opportunity, build an investment case, and have an executive sign off on it. A data science–driven fintech, on the other hand, would build a loan approval system that makes decisions on the majority of loans using some sort of automated algorithm.

The Vision

A science-driven organization is one that extracts the maximum value from its data and uses ML and analytics to gain a sustainable competitive advantage. When building such a data science team, there are some principles that should be followed:

Adaptability
A platform must be adaptable enough to accommodate all types of users. For instance, while some data scientists/analysts are more inclined to create their own models, others may prefer to use no-code solutions or conduct analyses in SQL. This also encompasses the availability of a variety of ML and data science tools such as TensorFlow, R, PyTorch, Beam, or Spark. The platform should also be open enough to function in multicloud and on-premises environments while supporting open source technology when possible to avoid lock-in effects. Finally, resources should never become a bottleneck, as the platform must be able to scale quickly to meet an organization's needs.

Standardization

Standardization increases a platform's efficiency by making it easier to share code and technical artifacts. This improves communication between teams and boosts their performance and creativity. Standardization also enables data science and ML teams to work in a modular fashion, which is essential for efficient development. Standardization can be achieved by using standard connectors to connect to source/target systems. This avoids "technical debt," which is common in ML and data science workflows.

Accountability

Data science and ML use cases often involve sensitive topics such as fraud detection, medical imaging, or risk calculation. As a result, it is critical that a data science and ML platform helps to make these workflows as transparent, explainable, and secure as possible. Openness is linked to operational excellence. Collecting and monitoring metadata during all phases of the data science and ML workflows is essential to create a "paper trail" that allows you to ask questions such as:

- Which data was used to train the model?
- Which hyperparameters were used?
- How is the model performing in production?
- Did any form of data drift or model skew occur during the last period?

In addition, a science-driven organization must have a thorough understanding of its models. While this is less of a problem for traditional statistical methods, ML models (such as deep neural networks) are much more opaque. A platform must provide simple tools for analyzing such models to use them with confidence. Finally, a mature data science platform must provide all the security measures to protect data and artifacts while managing resource usage on a granular level.

Business impact

According to McKinsey (*https://oreil.ly/O_MZs*), many data science projects fail to progress beyond the pilot or proof-of-concept stage. As a result, it is more important to anticipate or measure the business impact of new initiatives and choose ROI than to chase the latest cool solution. Therefore, it is critical to identify when to buy, build, or customize ML models and connect them together in a single integrated stack. For example, using an out-of-the-box solution by calling an API rather than building a model after months of development would help you achieve a higher ROI and demonstrate greater value.

Activation

The ability to operationalize models by embedding analytics into the tools used by end users is key to achieve scaling in providing services to a broad set of users. The ability to send small batches of data to the service and have it return your predictions in the response allows developers with little data science expertise to use models. In addition, it is important to facilitate seamless deployment and monitoring of edge inferences and automated processes with flexible APIs. This allows you to distribute AI across your private and public cloud infrastructure, on-premises data centers, and edge devices.

Building a science-driven organization comes with several socio-technical challenges. Often an organization's infrastructure is not flexible enough to react to a fast-changing technological landscape. A platform also needs to provide enough stand-ardization to foster communication between teams and establish a technical "lingua franca." Doing so is key to allowing modularized workflows between teams and establishing operational excellence. In addition, securely monitoring complex data science and ML workflows is often too opaque.

A science-driven organization should be built on a technical platform that is highly adaptable in terms of technological openness. Hence, it is critical to enable a wide set of personas and provide technological resources in a flexible and serverless manner. Whether to buy or build a solution is one of the key drivers of realizing ROI for the organization, and this will define the business impact any AI solution would make. At the same time, enabling a broad number of users allows activating more use cases. Finally, a platform needs to provide the tools and resources to make data science and ML workflows open, explanatory, and secure to provide the maximum form of accountability.

The Personas

Teams in data science–driven organizations are made up of a variety of people with different skills and experience. However, most teams include four core roles: data engineers, ML engineers, data scientists, and analysts. It is important to note that these roles are not always clearly defined and can overlap to some extent. An effective organizational structure will allow for collaboration and the full utilization of all team members' skills:

Data engineers

Data engineers are responsible for developing data pipelines and ensuring that the data meets all quality standards. This includes cleaning, merging, and enriching data from multiple sources to turn it into information that can be used for downstream analytics.

ML engineers

ML engineers create and oversee complete ML models. While ML engineers are the rarest of the four personas, they become essential once an organization intends to run critical business workflows in production.

Data scientists

Data scientists are a bridge between data and ML engineers. Together with business stakeholders, they translate business needs into testable hypotheses, ensure that value is derived from ML workloads, and create reports to demonstrate the value of data.

Data analysts

Data analysts provide business insight and ensure that the data-driven solutions that the business is seeking are implemented. They answer ad hoc questions and provide regular reports that analyze both historical and recent data.

There are various arguments for whether a company should establish centralized or decentralized data science teams. There are also hybrid models, such as a federated organization in which data scientists are embedded in a centralized organization. As a result, it is more important to focus on how to address these socio-technical challenges using the principles described before.

The Technological Framework

We strongly recommend standardizing on the ML pipelines infrastructure of your public cloud provider (i.e., Vertex AI on Google Cloud, SageMaker on AWS, or Azure Machine Learning on Azure) rather than cobbling together one-off training and deployment solutions. The reference architecture (see Figure 3-8) consists of an ML pipeline to automate experimentation and training. The trained model is deployed in a pipeline where many of the training steps are repeated through containerization. Use a feature store when features will be too expensive to compute on demand or have to be injected server side. Deploy models to endpoints.

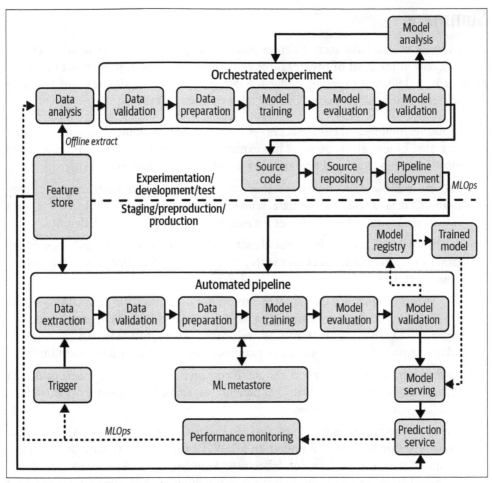

Figure 3-8. Make data science experimentation repeatable and deployments robust using the ML pipeline product available in the public cloud

Summary

In this chapter, you have seen different ways of designing your data team to ensure their success in the kind of organization you are in. The best approach is to find the right mix of skills and experience that will complement your existing team and help you achieve your business goals. The key takeaways are as follows:

- Cloud technologies facilitate access to new ways of working. The potential surface area of any given persona has expanded. Data workers are now able to do more with the data they have, and they are able to do it more efficiently.

- You can build a data culture whether your organization consists mostly of data analysts, data engineers, or data scientists. However, the path toward a data culture and required technologies for each organization type are different.

- Determine which organizational classification is right for you and then begin establishing the vision, personas with related skills, and technological framework to support it.

- The vision of what a data platform should do also varies. In an analysis-driven organization, it should democratize access to data. In an engineering-driven organization, it's about ensuring reliability cost-effectively. In a science-driven organization, it should confer competitive advantage via business impact.

- Analysis-driven organizations should focus on SQL skills, engineering-driven organizations on ETL and DataOps capabilities, and science-driven organizations on MLOps and AI capabilities.

- The recommended architecture for an analysis-driven organization is a data warehouse (or lakehouse founded on a DWH); for an engineering-driven organization, it is a data lake (or lakehouse founded on a data lake); and for a science-driven organization, it is an ML pipelines architecture connected to a lakehouse. These will be covered in Chapters 5 through 7.

The following chapter will offer you a general technological migration framework that you can apply to migrate from a legacy environment to a modern cloud architecture.

CHAPTER 4

A Migration Framework

Unless you are at a startup, it is rare that you will build a data platform from scratch. Instead, you will stand up a new data platform by migrating things into it from legacy systems. In this chapter, let's examine the process of migration—all the things that you should do when making your journey to a new data platform. We will first present a conceptual model and possible framework you should follow when modernizing the data platform. Then, we will review how an organization can estimate the overall cost of the solution. We will discuss how to ensure that security and data governance are in place even while the migration is going on. Finally, we'll discuss schema, data, and pipeline migration. You'll also learn about options for regional capacity, networking, and data transfer constraints.

Modernize Data Workflows

Before you start creating a migration plan, you should have a comprehensive vision of why you are doing it and what you are migrating toward.

Holistic View

Data modernization transformation should be considered holistically. Looking at this from a bird's-eye perspective, we can identify three main pillars:

Business outcomes
> Focus on the workflows that you are modernizing and identify the business outcomes those workflows drive. This is critical to identify where the gaps are and where the opportunities sit. Before making any technology decisions, limit the migration to use cases that align with the business objectives identified by leadership (typically over a time horizon of two to three years).

Stakeholders

Identify the persons or roles (some of these teams may not yet exist) who will potentially gain access to the data. Your goal with data modernization is to democratize data access. Therefore, these teams will need to become data literate and proficient in whatever tools (SQL, Python, dashboards) the modernization end-state technologies expect them to use.

Technology

You'll have to define, implement, and deploy data architecture, modeling, storage, security, integration, operability, documentation, reference data, quality, and governance in alignment with business strategy and team capabilities.

Make sure you are not treating migration as a pure IT or data science project but one where the technological aspect is just a subset of a larger organizational change.

Modernize Workflows

When you think about a modernization program, your mind naturally gravitates to the pain you are experiencing with the tools you have. You decide that you want to upgrade your database and make it globally consistent and scalable, so you modernize it to Spanner or CockroachDB. You decide that you want to upgrade your streaming engine and make it more resilient and easier to run, so you pick Flink or Dataflow. You decide you are done tuning clusters and queries on your DWH, so you modernize to BigQuery or Snowflake.

These are all great moves. You should definitely upgrade to easier-to-use, easier-to-run, much more scalable, much more resilient tools whenever you can. However, if you do only like-for-like tool changes, you will end up with just incremental improvements. You will not get transformational change from such upgrades.

To avoid this trap, when you start your data modernization journey, force yourself to think of workflows, not technologies. What does it mean to modernize a data workflow? Think about the overall task that the end user wants to do. Perhaps they want to identify high-value customers. Perhaps they want to run a marketing campaign. Perhaps they want to identify fraud. Now, think about this workflow as a whole and how to implement it as cheaply and simply as possible.

Next, approach the workflow from first principles. The way to identify high-value customers is to compute total purchases for each user from a historical record of transactions. Figure out how to make such a workflow happen with your modern set of tools. When doing so, lean heavily on automation:

Automated data ingest

Do not write bespoke ELT pipelines. Use off-the-shelf ELT tools such as Datastream or Fivetran to land the data in a DWH. It is so much easier to transform on the fly, and capture common transformations in materialized views, than it is to write ETL pipelines for each possible downstream task. Also, many SaaS systems will automatically export to S3, Snowflake, BigQuery, etc.

Streaming by default

Land your data in a system that combines batch and streaming storage so that all SQL queries reflect the latest data (subject to some latency). Same with any analytics—look for data processing tools that handle both streaming and batch using the same framework. In our example, the lifetime value calculation can be a SQL query. For reuse purposes, make it a materialized view. That way, all the computations are automatic, and the data is always up to date.

Automatic scaling

Any system that expects you to prespecify the number of machines, warehouse sizes, etc., is a system that will require you to focus on the system rather than the job to be done. You want scaling to be automatic, so that you can focus on the workflow rather than on the tool.

Query rewrites, fused stages, etc.

You want to be able to focus on the job to be done and decompose it into understandable steps. You don't want to have to tune queries, rewrite queries, fuse transforms, etc. Let the modern optimizers built into the data stack take care of these things.

Evaluation

You don't want to write bespoke data processing pipelines for evaluating ML model performance. You simply want to be able to specify sampling rates and evaluation queries and be notified about feature drift, data drift, and model drift. All these capabilities should be built into deployed endpoints.

Retraining

If you encounter model drift, you should retrain the model 9 times out of 10. This should be automated as well. Modern ML pipelines will provide a callable hook that you can tie directly to your automated evaluation pipeline so you can automate retraining as well.

Continuous training

Model drift is not the only reason you might need to retrain. You want to retrain when you have a lot more data. Maybe when new data lands in a storage bucket. Or when you have a code check-in. Again, this can be automated.

Once you land on the need for a fully automated data workflow, you are looking at a pretty templatized setup that consists of a connector, DWH, and ML pipelines. All of these can be serverless, so you are basically looking at just configuration, not cluster management.

Of course, you will be writing a few specific pieces of code:

- Data preparation in SQL
- ML models in a framework such as TensorFlow or PyTorch
- Evaluation query for continuous evaluation

The fact that we can come down to such a simple setup for each workflow explains why an integrated data and AI platform is so important.

Transform the Workflow Itself

You can make the workflow itself much more efficient by making it more automated using the modern data stack. But before you do that, you should ask yourself a key question: "Is this workflow necessary to be precomputed by a data engineer?"

Because that's what you are doing whenever you build a data pipeline—you are precomputing. It's an optimization, nothing more.

In many cases, if you can make the workflow something that is self-serve and ad hoc, you don't have to build it with data engineering resources. Because so much is automated, you can provide the ability to run any aggregation (not just lifetime value) on the full historical record of transactions. Move the lifetime value calculation into a declarative semantic layer to which your users can add their own calculations. This is what a tool like Looker, for example, will allow you to do. Once you do that, you get the benefits of consistent KPIs across the org and users who are empowered to build a library of common measures. The ability to create new metrics now lies with the business teams, where this capability belongs in the first place.

A Four-Step Migration Framework

You can apply a standardized approach to many of the situations you might encounter in the process of building your data platform. This approach is, for the most part, independent of the size and the depth of the data platform—we have followed it both for modernizing the DWH of a small company and for developing a brand-new data architecture for a multinational enterprise.

This approach is based on the four main steps shown in Figure 4-1:

1. *Prepare and discover.*
   All stakeholders should conduct a preliminary analysis to identify the list of workloads that need to be migrated and current pain points (e.g., inability to scale, process engine cannot be updated, unwanted dependencies, etc.).

2. Assess and plan.

Assess the information collected in the previous stage, define the key measures of success, and plan the migration of each component.

3. Execute.

For each identified use case, decide whether to decommission it, migrate it entirely (data, schema, downstream and upstream applications), or offload it (by migrating downstream applications to a different source). Afterward, test and validate any migration done.

4. Optimize.

Once the process has begun, it can be expanded and improved through continuous iterations. A first modernization step could focus only on core capabilities.

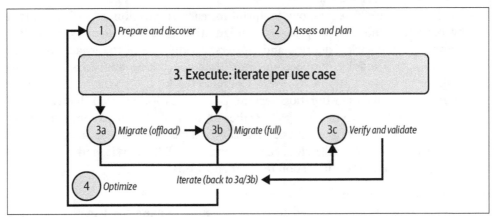

Figure 4-1. Four-step migration framework

Let's go through each of these steps in turn.

Prepare and Discover

The first step is to prepare and discover. This involves defining the scope of the migration and collecting all the information related to the workloads/use cases that will be migrated. It includes analyzing a wide range of inputs from multiple stakeholders across the enterprise, such as business, finance, and IT. Ask those stakeholders to:

- List all use cases and workloads, with their associated priorities, that are relevant to the migration. Make sure they include compliance requirements, latency sensitivities, and other relevant information.

- Explain the expected benefits that they can get with the new system (e.g., query performance, amount of data they are able to handle, streaming capabilities, etc.).

- Suggest solutions available on the market that could meet the business needs.

- Perform an initial TCO analysis to estimate the value of the migration.

- Identify needs around training and recruiting to build a capable workforce.

You can use questionnaires to collect these insights from application owners, data owners, and selected final users.

Assess and Plan

The second step is to assess the collected data and plan all the activities that need to be done to accomplish the identified goals. This involves:

1. Assessment of the current state
Analyze the current technology footprint for each application, workflow, or tool by collecting and analyzing server configurations, logs, job activity, data flow mapping, volumetrics, queries, and clusters. As the size of the legacy footprint increases, this activity may become very time-consuming and error-prone. So look for tools (such as SnowConvert, CompilerWorks, AWS Schema Conversion Tool, Azure Database Migration Service, Datametica Raven, etc.) that can automate the entire process, from data gathering to analysis and recommendation. These tools can provide workload breakdown, dependencies mapping, complexity analysis, resource utilization, capacity analysis, SLA analysis, end-to-end data lineage, and various optimization recommendations.

2. Workload categorization
Use the information collected through the questionnaire used in the "Prepare and Discover" step, along with the in-depth insights from the assessment phase, to categorize and select the approach for all the identified workloads into one of the following options:

Retire
The workload will initially remain on prem and will eventually be decommissioned.

Retain
The workload will remain on prem due to technical constraints (e.g., it runs on dedicated hardware) or for business reasons. This may be temporary until the workload can be refactored, or possibly moved to a colocation facility where data centers need to be closed and services can't be moved.

Rehost

The workload will be migrated into the cloud environment, leveraging its infrastructure as a service (IaaS) capabilities. This is often known as a "lift and shift."

Replatform

The workload (or part of it) will be partially changed to improve its performance or reduce its cost and then moved to the IaaS; this is often known as "move and improve." Optimize after doing a lift and shift experience, generally starting with containerization.

Refactor

The workload (or part of it) will be migrated to one or more cloud fully managed platform as a service (PaaS) solutions (e.g., BigQuery, Redshift, Synapse).

Replace

The workload will be completely replaced by a third-party off-the-shelf or SaaS solution.

Rebuild

The workload is completely rearchitected using cloud fully managed solutions and reimplemented from scratch. This is where you rethink your application and plan how to leverage the best of the cloud native services.

3. *Workload clusterization*

Cluster the workloads that will not be retired/rebuilt into a series of groups based on their relative business value and the effort needed to migrate them. This will help to identify a prioritization you can follow during the migration. For example:

- *Group 1*: high business value, low effort to migrate (Priority 0—quick wins)
- *Group 2*: high business value, high effort to migrate (Priority 1)
- *Group 3*: low business value, low effort to migrate (Priority 2)
- *Group 4*: low business value, high effort to migrate (Priority 3)

In Figure 4-2 you can see an example of clusterization where workloads have been divided into groups based on the described prioritization criteria. In each group, workloads can have different migration approaches.

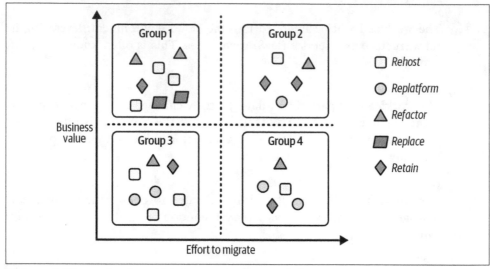

Figure 4-2. Example of workload categorization and clusterization

Throughout this process, we recommend that you adhere to the following practices:

Make the process measurable.
Ensure that stakeholders are agreed on and can evaluate the results of the modernization using some business KPIs.

Start with minimum viable product (MVP) or proof of concept (PoC).
Break down large jobs into smaller tasks and ensure that standard templates exist for any work you are about to undertake. If not, conduct a PoC and use that as a template going forward. Be on the lookout for quick wins (Priority 0 workloads) that can be leveraged not only as an example for the other transformations but also as a demonstration to leadership of the impact that such modernization might introduce.

Estimate the overall time needed to complete all the activities.
Create a holistic project plan (working with vendors or consultants if necessary) to define the time, cost, and people needed for workload transformation.

Overcommunicate at milestones.
Ensure that stakeholders understand the plan, how long it will take, and what the key components are. Make sure to deliver value and instill confidence along the way with completed cloud projects that people in the organization can actually start to use. Try to identify milestones and send out an ad hoc communication recapping details about the work that has been done.

Now that you have a good understanding of the tasks you need to complete to prepare for your next migration, let's take a look at how you should go about doing so.

Execute

For each workload, you now have a plan. Specifically, you know what will be migrated (the entirety of the workload or just a part), where it will be migrated (IaaS, PaaS, or SaaS), how you are going to migrate (rehost, replatform, rebuild, etc.), how you are going to measure success, what templates you are going to follow, how much time it's going to take, and what milestones you are going to communicate at. To turn the plan into reality, we recommend that you set up a landing zone, migrate to it, and validate the migrated tasks.

Landing zone

First you have to build what is called the *landing zone*—the target environment where all the workloads will reside. This activity can assume different levels of complexity based on your current configuration, but at the bare minimum you will need to:

- Define the target project and related organization (e.g., Google Cloud organization hierarchy)
- Set up a new identity management solution or integrate with a legacy or third-party one (e.g., Azure Active Directory or Okta)
- Configure the authorization (e.g., AWS IAM) and auditing systems (e.g., Azure security logging and auditing)
- Define and set up the network topology and related configuration

Once the landing zone is ready, it is time for you to start the migration.

Migrate

It is generally advisable to split a migration into multiple phases, or iterations, unless the number of workloads you have to migrate is very small. This will allow you to gain experience and confidence in how to proceed and deal with challenges and errors as you migrate a subset of the workloads at a time.

For each workload, you may have to consider:

Schema and data migration
Depending on the use case, you may need to translate the data model or simply transfer the data.

Query transpile
In some cases, you may need to translate queries from your source system to the target system. If the target system does not support all extensions, you may need to refactor the queries. You can leverage tools such as Datametica Raven or generative AI to reduce the manual effort involved.

Data pipelines migration

Data pipelines form the core part of a data workload that prepares the data for analysis. We will see possible approaches to dealing with such migrations in "Schema, Pipeline, and Data Migration" on page 113.

Business application migration

Once you have migrated the data, you need to migrate the applications that enable users to interact with the data.

Performance tuning

If the migrated workload is not performing as expected, you have to troubleshoot it and fix it. Perhaps the target solution has not been properly configured, the data model you define does not allow you to leverage all the capabilities of the target platform, or there is an issue in the transpiling process.

It is essential to use infrastructure as code tools like Ansible or Terraform, as they can automate as much of the deployment infrastructure management as possible, speeding up the tests and execution of each iteration.

Validate

Once the workload has been migrated, you have to double-check if everything has been completed successfully. Verify that your workload performance, running cost, time to access data, etc., are all aligned with your identified KPIs. Validate that all the results you get are compliant with your expectations (e.g., query results are the same as in the legacy environment). Once you are sure that results are aligned with your needs, it is time to move to the second use case, and then to the third until you have migrated everything. If possible, parallelize later iterations to speed up the overall process.

It is always a good idea at the end of each workload to note eventual issues you may have and the time needed to complete all the activities and related lessons learned to improve the process in the subsequent workloads.

Optimize

The last step of the framework is optimization. Here, you won't focus on the performance of every single migrated component. Instead, you will consider the new system as a whole and identify potential new use cases to introduce to make it even more flexible and powerful. You should reflect on what you got from the migration (e.g., unlimited scalability, enhanced security, increased visibility, etc.) and what you would potentially do as a next step (e.g., expand the boundaries of data collection to the edges, develop some better synergies with suppliers, start monetizing proper data, etc.). You can start from the information gathered at the "Prepare and Discover" step, figure out where you are in your ideal journey, and think about additional next steps.

It is a never-ending story because innovation, like business, never sleeps, and it will help organizations become better and better at understanding and leveraging their data.

Now that you have a better understanding of how to approach a migration by leveraging the four-step migration framework, let us delve into how to estimate the overall cost of the solution.

Estimating the Overall Cost of the Solution

You have just seen a general migration framework that can help organizations define the set of activities that they need to carry out to modernize a data platform. The first question that the CTO, CEO, or CFO may ask is: "What is the total cost we will have to budget for?" In this section, we will review how organizations generally approach this challenge and how they structure their work to get quotes from vendors and third-party suppliers. Always keep in mind that it is not just a matter of the cost of technology—there are always people and process costs that have to be taken into consideration.

Audit of the Existing Infrastructure

As you've seen, everything starts with an evaluation of the existing environment. If you do not have a clear view of the current footprint, you will surely have challenges in correctly evaluating the pricing of your next modern data platform. This activity can be carried out in one of three ways:

Manually by the internal IT/infrastructure team
>Many organizations maintain a configuration management database (CMDB), which can be a file or a standard database that contains all pivotal information about hardware and software components used within the organization. It is a sort of snapshot of what is currently running within the organization and the related underlying infrastructure, highlighting even the relationships between components. CMDBs can provide a better understanding of the running costs of all the applications and help with shutting down unnecessary or redundant resources.

Automatically by the internal IT/infrastructure team
>The goal is exactly the same described in the previous point but with the aim to leverage software that helps collect information in an automatic way (data related to the hardware, applications running on servers, relationship between systems, etc.). These kinds of tools (e.g., StratoZone, Cloudamize, CloudPhysics, etc.) usually generate suggestions related to the most common target cloud hyperscalers (e.g., AWS, Google Cloud, and Azure), such as the size of machines

and optimization options (e.g., how many hours per day a system should be up and running to carry out its task).

Leveraging a third-party player
Consulting companies and cloud vendors have experienced people and automation tools to perform all the activities to generate the CMDB and the detailed reports described in the first two options. This is what we recommend if your organization typically outsources IT projects to consulting companies.

Request for Information/Proposal and Quotation

While this is the only migration you may do, and so you have to learn as you go along, consulting companies do this for a living and are usually far more efficient at handling migration projects. Verify, of course, that the team assigned to you does have the necessary experience. Some SIs may even execute assessments and provide cost estimates as an investment if they see a future opportunity.

Identifying the best partner or vendor to work with during the modernization journey can be a daunting task. There are a lot of variables to consider (the knowledge, the capabilities, the cost, the experience), and it may become incredibly complicated if not executed in a rigorous way. This is why organizations usually leverage three kinds of questionnaires to collect information from potential SIs:

Request for information (RFI)
Questionnaire used to collect detailed information about vendors'/possible partners' solutions and services. It has an *educational* purpose.

Request for proposal (RFP)
Questionnaire used to collect detailed information about how vendors/partners will leverage their products and services to solve a specific organization problem (in this case, the implementation of the modern data platform). It serves to *compare* results.

Request for quotation (RFQ)
Questionnaire used to collect detailed information about pricing of different vendors/possible partners based on specific requirements. It serves to quantify and standardize pricing to facilitate future comparisons.

Your organization probably has policies and templates on how to do this. Talk to your legal or procurement department. Otherwise, ask a vendor to show you what they commonly use.

Once you have received all the responses from all the vendors/potential partners, you should have all the information to pick the best path forward. In some cases, especially when the problem to solve can be incredibly fuzzy (e.g., real-time analysis that can have multiple spikes during even a single day), it is challenging even for the vendors/potential partners to provide clear details about costs. This is why sometimes vendors will ask to work on a PoC or MVP to gain a better understanding of how the solution works in a real use case scenario and facilitate the definition of the final pricing.

Proof of Concept/Minimum Viable Product

The design and the development of a new data platform can be challenging because the majority of the organizations want to leverage a data platform migration opportunity to have something more than a mere lift and shift—they want to add new features and capabilities that were not available in the old world. Because this is new to them, organizations (and therefore vendors) may not have a complete understanding of the final behavior and, most importantly, of the final costs the platform will incur.

To address this challenge, organizations typically ask selected vendors or potential partners to implement an initial mock-up of the final solution (or a real working solution but with limited functionality) as the first step after analyzing the RFP response. This mock-up allows stakeholders to experience how the final solution will behave so that they can determine whether any scoping changes are necessary. The mock-up also makes cost estimation much easier, although it is important to note that we are always talking about estimates, rather than concrete pricing. It is practically impossible to have clear and final defined pricing when adopting a cloud model, especially if you want to leverage elasticity. Elasticity, which is one of the main benefits of the cloud, can only be experienced in production.

There are three ways to approach the idea of the mock-up:

Proof of concept
> Build a small portion of the solution to verify feasibility, integrability, usability, and potential weaknesses. This can help estimate the final price. The goal is not to touch every single feature that will be part of the platform but instead to verify things that may need to be redesigned. When working with streaming pipelines, for example, it is a good practice to create a PoC by randomly varying the amount of data to be processed. This will allow you to see how the system scales and provide you with better data for estimating the final production cost.

Minimum viable product
> The goal of an MVP is to develop a product with a very well-defined perimeter having all the features implemented and working like a real, full product that can be deployed in a production environment (e.g., a data mart implemented on a new DWH and connected to a new business intelligence tool to address a very specific use case). The main advantage of MVPs is to get feedback from real users quickly, which helps the team improve the product and produce better estimations.

Hybrid
> Initially, the team will develop a general PoC with a broader perimeter but with a limited depth (e.g., an end-to-end data pipeline to collect data needed to train an ML algorithm for image classification), and then, based on the first results and cost evaluation, the focus will move to the development of an MVP that can be seen as the first step toward the implementation of the full solution.

Now that you know how to estimate cost, let us delve into the first part of any migration—setting up security and data governance.

Setting Up Security and Data Governance

Even as the ownership and control of the data move to business units, security and governance remain a centralized concern at most organizations. This is because there needs to be consistency in the way roles are defined, data is secured, and activities are logged. In the absence of such consistency, it is very difficult to be compliant with regulations such as "the right to be forgotten" (*https://oreil.ly/xweT4*), whereby a customer can request that all records pertaining to them be removed.

In this section, we'll discuss what capabilities need to be present in such a centralized data governance framework. Then, we'll discuss the artifacts that the central team will need to maintain and how they come together over the data lifecycle.

Framework

There are three risk factors that security and governance seek to address:

Unauthorized data access
> When storing data in a public cloud infrastructure, it is necessary to protect against unauthorized access to sensitive data, whether it is company-confidential information or PII protected by law.

Regulatory compliance
> Laws such as the General Data Protection Regulation (GDPR) and Legal Entity Identifier (LEI) limit the location, type, and methods of data analysis.

Visibility
> Knowing what kinds of data exist in the organization, who is currently using the data, and how they are using it may be required by people who supply your organization with data. This requires up-to-date data and a functional catalog.

Given these risk factors, it is necessary to set up a comprehensive data governance framework that addresses the full life of the data: data ingestion, cataloging, storage, retention, sharing, archiving, backup, recovery, loss prevention, and deletion. Such a framework needs to have the following capabilities:

Data lineage
> The organization needs to be able to identify data assets and record the transformations that have been applied to create each data asset.

Data classification
> We need to be able to profile and classify sensitive data so that we can determine what governance policies and procedures need to apply to each data asset or part thereof.

Data catalog
> We need to maintain a data catalog that contains structural metadata, lineage, and classification and permits search and discovery.

Data quality management
> There needs to be a process for documenting, monitoring, and reporting of data quality so that trustworthy data is made available for analysis.

Access management
> This will typically work with Cloud IAM to define roles, specify access rights, and manage access keys.

Auditing
> Organizations and authorized individuals from other organizations such as regulatory agencies need to be able to monitor, audit, and track activities at a granular level required by law or industry convention.

Data protection
> There needs to be the ability to encrypt data, mask it, or delete it permanently.

To operationalize data governance, you will need to put in place a framework that allows these activities to take place. Cloud tools such as Dataplex on Google Cloud and Purview on Azure provide unified data governance solutions to manage data assets regardless of where the data resides (i.e., single cloud, hybrid cloud, or multi-cloud). Collibra and Informatica are cloud-agnostic solutions that provide the ability to record lineage, do data classification, etc.

In our experience, any of these tools can work, but the hard work of data governance is not in the tool itself but in its operationalization. It is important to establish an operating model—the processes and procedures for data governance—as well as a council that holds the various business teams responsible for adhering to these processes. The council will also need to be responsible for developing taxonomies and ontologies so that there is consistency across the organization. Ideally, your organization participates in and is in line with industry standards bodies. The best organizations also have frequent and ongoing education and training sessions to ensure that data governance practices are adhered to.

Now that we have discussed what capabilities need to be present in a centralized data governance framework, let's enumerate the artifacts that the central team will need to maintain.

Artifacts

To provide the above capabilities to the organization, a central data governance team needs to maintain the following artifacts:

Enterprise dictionary

This can range from a simple paper document to a tool that automates (and enforces) certain policies. The enterprise dictionary is a repository of the information types used by the organization. For example, the code associated with various medical procedures or the necessary information that has to be collected about any financial transaction is part of the enterprise dictionary. The central team could provide a validation service to ensure that these conditions are met. A simple example of an enterprise dictionary that many readers are familiar with is the address validation and standardization APIs provided by the US Postal Service. These APIs are often used by businesses to ensure that any address stored in any database within the organization is in a standard form.

Data classes

The various information types within the enterprise dictionary can be grouped into data classes, and policies related to each data class can be defined in a consistent way. For example, the data policy related to customer addresses might be that the zip code is visible to one class of employees but that information that is more granular is visible only to customer support personnel actively working on a ticket for that customer.

Policy book

A policy book lists the data classes in use at the organization, how each data class is processed, how long data is retained, where it may be stored, how access to the data needs to be controlled, etc.

Use case policies

Often, the policy surrounding a data class depends on the use case. As a simple example, a customer's address may be used by the shipping department fulfilling the customer order but not by the sales department. The use cases may be much more nuanced: a customer's address may be used for the purpose of determining the number of customers within driving distance of a specific store, but not for determining whether a specific customer is within driving distance of a specific store.

Data catalog

This is a tool to manage the structural metadata, lineage, data quality, etc., associated with data. The data catalog functions as an efficient search and discovery tool.

Beyond the data-related artifacts listed above, the central organization will also need to maintain an SSO capability to provide a unique authentication mechanism throughout the organization. Because many automated services and APIs are accessed through keys, and these keys should not be stored in plain text, a key management service is often an additional responsibility of the central team.

As part of your modernization journey, it is important to also start these artifacts and have them in place so that as data is moved to the cloud, it becomes part of a robust data governance framework. Do not postpone data governance until after the cloud migration—organizations that do that tend to quickly lose control of their data.

Let's now look at how the framework capabilities and artifacts tie together over the life of data.

Governance over the Life of the Data

Data governance involves bringing together people, processes, and technology over the life of the data.

The data lifecycle consists of the following stages:

1. Data creation

This is the stage where you create/capture the data. At this stage, you should ensure that metadata is also captured. For example, when capturing images, it is important to also record the times and locations of the photographs. Similarly, when capturing a clickstream, it is important to note the user's session ID, the page they are on, the layout of the page (if it is personalized to the user), etc.

2. Data processing

When you capture the data, then you usually have to clean it, enrich it, and load it into a DWH. It is important to capture these steps as part of a data lineage. Along with the lineage, quality attributes of the data need to be recorded as well.

3. Data storage

You generally store both data and metadata in a persistent store such as blob storage (S3, GCS, etc.), a database (Postgres, Aurora, AlloyDB, etc.), a document DB (DynamoDB, Spanner, Cosmos DB, etc.), or a DWH (BigQuery, Redshift, Snowflake, etc.). At this point, you need to determine the security requirements for rows and columns as well as whether any fields need to be encrypted before being saved. This is the stage at which data protection is front and center in the mind of a data governance team.

4. Data catalog

You need to enter the persisted data at all stages of the transformation into the enterprise data catalog and enable discovery APIs to search for it. It is essential to document the data and how it can be used.

5. Data archive

You can age off older data from production environments. If so, remember to update the catalog. You must note if such archiving is required by law. Ideally, you should automate archival methods in accordance with policies that apply to the entire data class.

6. Data destruction

You can delete all the data that has passed the legal period that it is required to be retained. This too needs to be part of the enterprise's policy book.

You have to create data governance policies for each of these stages.

People will execute these stages, and those people need to have certain access privileges to do so. The same person could have different responsibilities and concerns at different parts of the data lifecycle, so it is helpful to think in terms of "hats" rather than roles:

Legal
Ensures that data usage conforms to contractual requirements and government/industry regulations

Data steward
The owner of the data, who sets the policy for a specific item of data

Data governor
Sets policies for data classes and identifies which class a particular item of data belongs to

Privacy tsar
Ensures that use cases do not leak personally identifiable information

Data user
Typically a data analyst or data scientist who is using the data to make business decisions

Now that we have seen a possible migration and security and governance framework, let's take a deep dive into how to start executing the migration.

Schema, Pipeline, and Data Migration

In this section, we will take a closer look at patterns you can leverage for schema and pipeline migrations and challenges you have to face when transferring the data.

Schema Migration

When starting to move your legacy application into the new target system, you might need to evolve your schema to leverage all the features made available by the target system. It is a best practice to first migrate the model as-is into the target system connecting the upstream (data sources and pipelines that are feeding the system) and downstream (the scripts, procedures, and business applications that are used to process, query, and visualize the data) processes and then leverage the processing engine of the target environment to perform all the changes. This approach will help ensure that your solution works in the new environment, minimizing the risk of downtime and allowing you to make changes in a second phase.

You can usually apply the *facade pattern* here—a design method to expose to the downstream processes a set of views that mask the underlying tables to hide the complexity of the eventually needed changes. The views can then describe a new schema that helps with leveraging ad hoc target system features, without disrupting the upstream and downstream processes that are then "protected" by this abstraction layer. In case this kind of approach cannot be followed, the data has to be translated and converted before being ingested into the new system. These activities are generally performed by data transformation pipelines that are under the perimeter of the migration.

Pipeline Migration

There are two different strategies you can follow when migrating from a legacy system to the cloud:

You are offloading the workload.
  In this case, you retain the upstream data pipelines that are feeding your source system, and you put an incremental copy of the data into the target system. Finally, you update your downstream processes to read from the target system. Then you can continue the offload with the next workload until you reach the end. Once completed, you can start fully migrating the data pipeline.

You are fully migrating the workload.
  In this case, you have to migrate everything in the new system (all together with the data pipeline), and then you deprecate the corresponding legacy tables.

Data that feeds the workload needs to be migrated. It can come from various data sources, and it could require particular transformations or joins to make it usable. In general, there are four different data pipeline patterns:

ETL
> All the transformation activities, along with the data collection and data ingestion, will be carried out by an ad hoc system that comes with a proper infrastructure and a proper programming language (the tool can make interfaces programmable with standard programming languages available, anyway).

ELT
> Similar to ETL but with the caveat that all the transformations will be performed by the process engine where the data will be ingested (as we have seen in the previous chapters, this is the preferred approach when dealing with modern cloud solutions).

Extract and load (EL)
> This is the simplest case, where the data is already prepared and it does not require any further transformations.

Change data capture (CDC)
> This is a pattern used to track data changes in the source system and reflect them in the target one. It usually works together with an ETL solution because it stores the original record before making any changes to the downstream process.

As you saw in the previous section, you could identify different approaches for different workloads' migration. The same methodology can be applied to the data pipelines:

Retire
> The data pipeline solution is not used anymore because it is referred to an old use case or because it has been superseded by a new one.

Retain
> The data pipeline solution remains in the legacy system because it can potentially be retired very soon, so it is not financially viable to embark on a migration project. It may also be the case that there are some regulation requirements that inhibit data movement outside the corporate boundaries.

Rehost
> The data pipeline solution is lifted and shifted into the cloud environment leveraging the IaaS paradigm. In this scenario, you are not introducing any big modification except at the connectivity level, where an ad hoc networking configuration (usually a virtual private network, or VPN) might need to be set up to enable communication between the cloud environment and the on-premises world. If the upstream processes are outside the corporate perimeter

(e.g., third-party providers, other cloud environments, etc.), a VPN might not be needed since the communication can be established in a secure way leveraging other technologies, like authenticated REST APIs, for example. Before proceeding, it is necessary to validate with the cloud vendor if there is any technology limitation in the underlying system that prevents the correct execution of the solution and to double-check eventual license limitations.

Replatform

In this scenario, part of the data pipeline solution is transformed before the migration to benefit from features of the cloud, such as a PaaS database or containerization technology. Considerations on the connectivity side highlighted in the "rehost" description are still valid.

Refactor

The pipeline solution will be migrated to one or more cloud fully managed PaaS solutions (e.g., Amazon EMR, Azure HDInsight, Google Cloud Dataproc, Databricks). When dealing with this approach, it is a best practice to readopt the same iterative approach you are adopting for the entire migration:

- Prepare and discover the jobs and potentially organize them by complexity.
- Plan and assess the possible MVP to be migrated.
- Execute the migration and evaluate the result against your defined KPIs.
- Iterate with all the other jobs until the end.

Considerations on the connectivity side highlighted in the preceding "rehost" description are still valid.

Replace

The pipeline solution will be completely replaced by a third-party off-the-shelf or SaaS solution (e.g., Fivetran, Xplenty, Informatica, etc.). Considerations on the connectivity side highlighted in the "Rehost" section are still valid.

Rebuild

The pipeline solution is completely rearchitected using cloud fully managed solutions (e.g., AWS Glue, Azure Data Factory, Google Cloud Dataflow). Considerations on the connectivity side highlighted in the "Rehost" section are still valid.

During the migration phase, especially in the integration with the target system, you might find that your data pipeline solution is not fully compatible with the identified target cloud solution right out of the box. You could need a connector, usually called a *sink*, that enables the communication between the data pipeline solution (e.g., the ETL system) and the target environment. If the sink for that solution does not exist, you may be able to generate a file as output of the process and then ingest the data in the following step. This approach will introduce extra complexity to the process, but it is a viable temporary solution in case of emergency (while waiting for a connector from the vendor).

Data Migration

Now that you have your new schema and pipelines ready, you are ready to start migrating all your data. You should focus on thinking about how to deal with data transfer. You may want to migrate all your on-premises data into the cloud, even dusty old tapes (maybe one day someone will require that data). You may face the reality that a single FTP connection over the weekend will not be enough to accomplish your task.

Planning

Data transfer requires planning. You need to identify and involve:

Technical owners
> People who can provide access to the resources you need to perform the migration (e.g., storage, IT, networking, etc.).

Approvers
> People who can provide you with all the approvals you need to get access to the data and to start the migration (e.g., data owners, legal advisors, security admin, etc.).

Delivery
> The migration team. They can be people internal to the organization if available or people belonging to third-party system integrators.

Then you need to collect as much information as you can to have a complete understanding of what you have to do, in which order (e.g., maybe your migration team needs to be allowlisted to a specific network storage area that contains the data you want to migrate), and the possible blockers that you might encounter. Here is a sample of questions (not exhaustive) that you should be able to answer before proceeding:

- What are the datasets you need to move?
- Where does the underlying data sit within the organization?
- What are the datasets you are allowed to move?
- Is there any specific regulatory requirement you have to respect?
- Where is the data going to land (e.g., object store versus DWH storage)?

- What is the destination region (e.g., Europe, Middle East, and Africa, UK, US, etc.)?
- Do you need to perform any transformation before the transfer?
- What are the data access policies you want to apply?
- Is it a one-off transfer, or do you need to move data regularly?
- What are the resources available for the data transfer?
- What is the allocated budget?
- Do you have adequate bandwidth to accomplish the transfer, and for an adequate period?
- Do you need to leverage offline solutions (e.g., Amazon Snowball, Azure Data Box, Google Transfer Appliance)?
- What is the time needed to accomplish the entire data migration?

Once you know the attributes of data you are migrating, you need to consider two key factors that affect the reliability and performance of the migration: capacity and network.

Regional capacity and network to the cloud

When dealing with cloud data migration, typically there are two elements that need to be considered carefully: the regional capacity and the quality of the network connectivity to the cloud.

A cloud environment is not infinitely scalable. The reality is that the hardware needs to be purchased, prepared, and configured by the cloud providers in the regional location. Once you have identified the target architecture and the resources that are needed to handle the data platform, you should also file a capacity regional plan with your selected hyperscaler to be sure the data platform will have all the hardware needed to meet the usage and the future growth of the platform. They will typically want to know the volume of the data to be migrated and that will be generated once in the cloud, the amount of compute you will need to crunch the data, and the number of interactions you will have with other systems. All these components will serve as an input to your hyperscalers to allow them to be sure that the underlying infrastructure will be ready from day zero to serve all your workloads. In case of stockouts (common if your use case involves GPUs), you may have to choose the same service but in another region (if there are not any compliance/technology implications) or leverage other compute-type services (e.g., IaaS versus PaaS).

The network, even if it is considered a commodity nowadays, plays a vital role in every cloud infrastructure: if the network is slow or it is not accessible, parts of your organization can remain completely disconnected from their business data (this is true even when leveraging an on-premises environment). When designing the cloud platform, some of the first questions you need to think about are: How will my organization be connected to the cloud? Which partner am I going to leverage to set up the connectivity? Am I leveraging standard internet connection (potentially with a VPN on top of it), or do I want to pay for an extra dedicated connection that will ensure better reliability? All these topics are generally discussed in the RFI/RFP questionnaires, but they should also be part of one of the very first workshops you have with the vendor/partner that you've selected to design and implement the platform.

There are three main ways to get connected to the cloud:

Public internet connection

Leveraging public internet networks. In this case, organizations usually leverage a VPN on top of the public internet protocol to protect their data and to guarantee an adequate level of reliability. Performance is strictly related to the ability of the organization to be close to the nearest point of presence of the selected cloud hyperscalers.

Partner interconnect

This is one the typical connections organizations may leverage for their production workloads, especially when they need to have guaranteed performance with high throughput. This connection is between the organization and the selected partner that then takes care of the connection with the selected hyperscalers. Leveraging the pervasiveness of the telco providers, organizations can set up high-performance connections with an affordable price.

Direct interconnect

This is the best connection possible, where the organization connects directly (and physically) with the network of the cloud provider. (This can be possible when both of the parties have routers in the same physical location.) Reliability, throughput, and general performance are the best, and pricing can be discussed directly with the selected hypervisors.

For more details of how to configure these three connectivity options, see the documentation at Azure (*https://oreil.ly/x34sr*), AWS (*https://oreil.ly/fNZOg*), and Google Cloud (*https://oreil.ly/j4V7J*).

Typically, during a PoC/MVP phase, the public internet connection option is chosen because it is faster to set up. In production, the partner interconnect is the most common, especially when the organization wants to leverage a multicloud approach.

Transfer options

To choose the way that you will transfer data to the cloud, consider the following factors:

Costs

Consider the following potential costs involved in the transfer of data:

Networking

You may need to enhance your connectivity before proceeding with the data transfer. Maybe you do not have adequate bandwidth to support the migration and you need to negotiate with your vendor to add additional lines.

Cloud provider

Uploading data to a cloud provider tends to be free, but if you are exporting data not only from your on-premises environment but also from another hyperscaler, you might be charged an *egress cost* (which usually has a cost per each GB exported) and potentially a read cost as well.

Products

You may need to purchase or rent storage appliances to speed up the data transfer.

People

The team who will carry out the migration.

Time

It's important to know the amount of data you have to transfer and the bandwidth you have at your disposal. Once you know that, you will be able to identify the time needed to transfer the data. For example, if you have to transfer 200 TB of data and you have only 10 Gbps bandwidth available, you will need approximately two days to complete your transfer.[1] This assumes that the bandwidth is fully available for your data transfer, which may not be the case. If during your analysis you discover that you need more bandwidth, you might need to work with your internet service provider (ISP) to request an increase or determine the time of day when such bandwidth is available. It may also be the right time to work with your cloud vendor to implement direct connection. This prevents your data from going on the public internet and can provide a more consistent throughput for large data transfers (e.g., AWS Direct Connect, Azure ExpressRoute, Google Cloud Direct Interconnect).

---

1 There are several services freely available on the web that can help you with this estimation exercise—for example, Calculator.net's bandwidth calculator (*https://oreil.ly/wL8OC*).

Offline versus online transfer

In some cases, an online transfer is infeasible because it will take too long. In such cases, select an offline process leveraging storage hardware. Cloud vendors offer this kind of service (e.g., Amazon Snowball data transfer, Azure Data Box, Google Transfer Appliance), which is particularly useful for data transfers from hundreds of terabytes up to petabyte scale. You order a physical appliance from your cloud vendor that will have to be connected to your network. Then you will copy the data, which will be encrypted by default, and you will request a shipment to the closest vendor facility available. Once delivered, the data will be copied to the appropriate service in the cloud (e.g., AWS S3, Azure Blob Storage, Google Cloud Storage) and will be ready to be used.

Available tools

Once you have cleared out all the network dynamics, you should decide how to handle data upload. Depending on the system you might want to target (e.g., blob storage, DWH solution, database, third-party application, etc.), you generally have the following options at your disposal:

Command-line tools

Tools (e.g., AWS CLI, Azure Cloud Shell, or Google Cloud SDK) that will allow you to interact with all the services of the cloud provider. You can automate and orchestrate all the processes needed to upload the data into the desired destination. Depending on the final tool, you may have to pass by intermediate systems before being able to upload data to the final destination (e.g., passing by blob storage first before ingesting data into the DWH), but thanks to the flexibility of the various tools, you should be able to easily implement your workflows—for example, leveraging bash or PowerShell scripts.

REST APIs

These will allow you to integrate services with any applications you may want to develop—for example, internal migration tools that you have already implemented and leveraged or brand-new apps that you may want to develop for that specific purpose.

Physical solutions

Tools for offline migration as discussed in the preceding description of offline versus online transfer.

Third-party commercial off-the-shelf (COTS) solutions

These could provide more features like network throttling, custom advanced data transfer protocols, advanced orchestration and management capabilities, and data integrity checks.

Migration Stages

Your migration will consist of six stages (see Figure 4-3):

1. Upstream processes feeding current legacy data solutions are modified to feed the target environment.

2. Downstream processes reading from the legacy environment are modified to read from the target environment.

3. Historical data is migrated in bulk into the target environment. At this point, the upstream processes are migrated to also write to the target environment.

4. Downstream processes are now connected to the target environment.

5. Data can be kept in sync between the legacy and target environments, leveraging CDC pipelines until the old environment is fully dismissed.

6. Downstream processes become fully operational, leveraging the target environment.

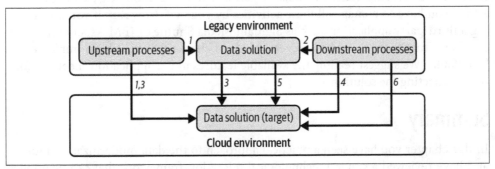

Figure 4-3. Data migration strategy

There are some final checks that you should perform to ensure you don't hit bottlenecks or data transfer issues:

Perform a functional test.
    You need to execute a test to validate that your entire data transfer migration is working correctly. Ideally, you'd execute this test during the execution of your MVP, selecting a considerable amount of data, leveraging potentially all the tools that you might want to use during the entire migration. The goal of this step is mainly to verify you can operate your data transfer correctly while at the same time surface potential project-stopping issues, such as the inability to use the tools (e.g., your workforce is not trained or you do not have adequate support from your system integrator) or networking issues (e.g., network routes).

Perform a performance test.
> You need to verify that your current infrastructure can handle migration at scale. To do so, you should identify a large sample of your data (generally between 3% and 5%) to be migrated to confirm that your migration infrastructure and solution correctly scale according to the migration needs and you are not surfacing any specific bottlenecks (e.g., slow source storage system).

Perform a data integrity check.
> One of the most critical issues you might encounter during a data migration is that the data migrated into the target system is deleted because of an error or is corrupted and unusable. There are some ways to protect your data from that kind of risk:
>
> - *Enable versioning and backup* on your destination to limit the damage of accidental deletion.
> - *Validate your data* before removing the source data.

If you are leveraging standard tools to perform the migration (e.g., CLIs or REST APIs), you have to manage all these activities by yourself. However, if you are adopting a third-party application such as Signiant Media Shuttle or IBM Aspera on Cloud, it is likely that there are already several kinds of checks that have been implemented by default. (We suggest reading the available features in the application sheet carefully before selecting the solution.)

Summary

In this chapter you have seen a practical approach to the data modernization journey and have reviewed a general technological migration framework that can be applied to any migration, from a legacy environment to a modern cloud architecture. The key takeaways are as follows:

- Focus on modernizing your data workflow, not just upgrading individual tools. Choosing the right tool for the right job will help you reduce costs, get the most out of your tools, and be more efficient.

- A possible data migration framework can be implemented in four steps: prepare and discover, assess and plan, execute, and optimize.

- Prepare and discover is a pivotal step where you focus on defining the perimeter of the migration and then on collecting all the information related to the various workloads/use cases that you've identified to be migrated.

- Assess and plan is the step where you define and plan all the activities that need to be done to accomplish the identified goal (e.g., categorization and clusterization of the workloads to be migrated, definition of KPIs, definition of a possible MVP, and definition of the migration plan with related milestones).

- Execute is the step where you iteratively perform the migration, improving the overall process at each iteration.

- Optimize is the step where you consider the new system as a whole and identify potential new use cases to introduce to make it even more flexible and powerful.

- Understanding the current footprint and what will be the total cost of the final solution is a complex step that can involve multiple actors. Organizations usually leverage RFI, RFP, and RFQ to get more information from vendors/potential partners.

- Governance and security remain a centralized concern at most organizations. This is because there needs to be consistency in the way roles are defined, data is secured, and activities are logged.

- The migration framework has to work in accordance with a very well-defined governance framework that is pivotal throughout the entire life of data.

- When migrating schema of your data, it might be useful to leverage a pattern like the facade pattern to make the adoption of target solution features easier.

- Connectivity and securing regional capacity are critical when utilizing cloud solutions. Network configuration, bandwidth availability, cost, people, tools, performance, and data integrity are the main points that have to be clarified for every workload.

In the four chapters so far, you have learned why to build a data platform, a strategy to get there, how to upskill your workforce, and how to carry out a migration. In the next few chapters, we will delve into architectural details, starting with how to architect modern data lakes.

CHAPTER 5

Architecting a Data Lake

A data lake is the part of the data platform that captures raw, ungoverned data from across an organization and supports compute tools from the Apache ecosystem. In this chapter, we will go into more detail about this concept, which is important when designing modern data platforms. The cloud can provide a boost to the different use cases that can be implemented on top of it, as you will read throughout the chapter.

We will start with a recap of why you might want to store raw, ungoverned data that only supports basic compute. Then, we discuss architecture design and implementation details in the cloud. Even though data lakes were originally intended only for basic data processing, it is now possible to democratize data access and reporting using just a data lake—because of integrations with other solutions through APIs and connectors, the data within a data lake can be made much more fit for purpose. We will finally take a bird's-eye perspective on a very common way to speed up analysis and experimentation with data within an organization by leveraging data science notebooks.

Data Lake and the Cloud—A Perfect Marriage

Data helps organizations make better decisions, faster. It's the center of everything from applications to security, and more data means more need for processing power, which cloud solutions can provide.

Challenges with On-Premises Data Lakes

Organizations need a place to store all types of data, including unstructured data (images, video, text, logs, binary files, web content). This was the main reason that enterprises adopted data lakes. Initially, enterprises believed that data lakes were just pure raw storage.

Business units wanted to extract insights and value from the data stored by IT departments, rather than simply storing it. Thanks to the evolution of the Hadoop ecosystem, data lakes enabled organizations capable of doing big data analytics to go beyond the mere concept of storage offload. Data lakes brought advanced analytics and ML capabilities within reach. Hadoop and related technologies jump-started a massive adoption of data lakes in the 2010s.

However, companies have struggled to get a sufficient return on investment from their data lake efforts because of drawbacks around TCO, scalability, governance, and agility. The resource utilization and overall cost of managing an on-premises data lake can become unmanageable. Resource-intensive data and analytics processing often leads to missed SLAs. Data governance and security issues can lead to compliance concerns. Analytics experimentation is slowed due to the time required to provision resources.

With estimates that by 2025, 80% of organizations' data will be unstructured (*https:// oreil.ly/KxCbZ*), the on-premises world is no longer able to provide adequate environments at an affordable price. Cloud solutions, as you saw in Chapter 2, allow organizations to first reduce the TCO and then build a platform for innovation because people within the company can focus on business value instead of hardware management.

Benefits of Cloud Data Lakes

The cloud paradigm is hugely beneficial for data lakes because:

- It is not necessary to store all data in an expensive, always-on Hadoop Distributed File System (HDFS) cluster. Object storage solutions (e.g., AWS S3, Azure Blob Storage, or Google Cloud Storage) are fully managed, infinitely scalable, and a fraction of the cost.

- Hadoop clusters, which provide not only storage capabilities but even processing compute power, can be created on demand in a short amount of time (a few minutes or seconds), generating an immediate cost saving due to the fact that they do not need to be always on. These Hadoop clusters can read/write data directly from object storage—even though such data access is slower than reading/writing to HDFS, the cost savings of having ephemeral clusters can make the overall trade-off worthwhile.

- Hyperscalers usually offer capabilities to leverage less-expensive virtual machines (VMs), called *spot instances* or *preemptible instances*, for worker nodes. These VMs have the drawback that they can be evicted by the system at any time (generally with a 30-to-60-second notice), but they can easily be substituted with new ones thanks to the underlying Hadoop technology that is worker-node-failure tolerant. Thanks to this approach, additional costs can be saved.

- Nowadays, the majority of the Hadoop services available on hyperscalers are fully managed and offered in PaaS mode (even though you can build your own Hadoop cluster leveraging a pure IaaS service). PaaS means that you do not need to manage by yourself all the VMs needed for master and worker nodes but that you can instead focus on building processing to extract value from the data.

- On-premises Hadoop clusters tend to generate data silos within the organization because of the fact that the HDFS pools were not designed to be prone to data sharing. The fact that instead in the cloud we can have an effective separation between storage (i.e., data in object storage that can be injected in any HDFS cluster) and compute (i.e., VMs created on demand) gives organizations better flexibility in handling the challenges in data governance.

Cloud is the perfect habitat for data lakes because it addresses all the challenges with on-premises data lakes: TCO, scalability, elasticity, and consistent data governance.

The market is strongly investing in data lakes and especially in the cloud-based ones. Amazon EMR, Azure Data Lake, and Google Cloud Dataproc are available on the hyperscalers. Databricks (the developer behind the open source Spark engine that is part of all major Hadoop distributions) has built a complete multicloud data platform that offers not only storage and compute but also a full set of features to handle the entire data lifecycle.

Next, let's look at the design and implementation details of a data lake on the cloud.

Design and Implementation

The design of a data lake depends on whether you need streaming, how you will do data governance, what Hadoop capabilities you use, and which hyperscaler you are building on. Let's take these one by one.

Batch and Stream

When analyzing data workloads, the first question to answer is the age of the data to be processed: is it data that has been stored for some time, or is it data that has just arrived in the system? Based on the answer, choose between the two main approaches to data processing: batch and streaming. Batch processing has been the dominant approach for over 20 years, but streaming has become increasingly popular in recent years, especially with the advent of the cloud. Streaming processing is better suited for handling large amounts of data in real time, while batch processing is better for processing large amounts of data offline.

Whether batch or stream, there are four storage areas in a data lake:

Raw/Landing/Bronze
    Where raw data is collected and ingested directly from source systems.

Staging/Dev/Silver
> Where more advanced users (e.g., data engineers, data scientists) process the data to prepare it for final users.

Production/Gold
> Where the final data used by production systems is stored.

Sensitive (optional)
> Where sensitive data resides. It is connected to all other stages and facilitates data access governance to ensure compliance with company and government regulations.

In 2014, two new architectures were proposed to allow both batch and stream processing at scale: Lambda (by Nathan Marz) and Kappa (by Jay Kreps). The Lambda architecture (shown in Figure 5-1) uses separate technology stacks for the *batch layer* that spans all the (historical) facts and the *speed layer* for the real-time data.

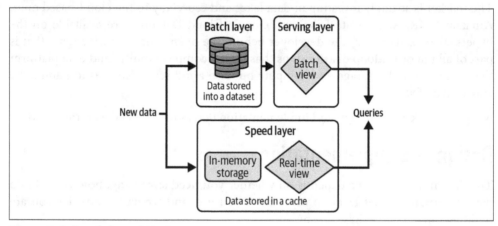

Figure 5-1. Lambda architecture

New data ingested into the system is stored both in a persistent dataset (*batch layer*) and in a volatile cache (*speed layer*). The first one is then indexed and made available to the serving layer for the *batch views* while the second is exposed by the speed layer via *real-time views*. Both datasets (persistent and volatile) can be queried in parallel or disjointly to answer the needed question. This architecture is generally deployed in a Hadoop environment where HDFS can be leveraged as a batch layer while technologies like Spark, Storm, or Beam can be used for the speed layer. Hives can then finally be the solution for the implementation of the serving layer, for example.

In the Kappa architecture (shown in Figure 5-2), you can perform both real-time and batch processing with a single technology stack (e.g., Beam/Spark). The core is the streaming architecture. First, the event streaming platform stores the incoming data. From there, a stream processing engine processes the data in real time, making data available for real-time views. At this stage, the data can be persisted into a database to perform batch analysis when needed and leveraging the same technology stack.

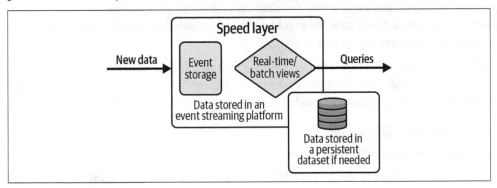

Figure 5-2. Kappa architecture

Data Catalog

Data is scattered across multiple sites, including databases, DWHs, filesystems, and blob storage. In addition, data could be stored in different areas of the data lake: raw, staging, production, or sensitive. This makes it difficult for data scientists to find the data they need and for business users to access the latest data. We need a solution to make all of these data sources discoverable and accessible.

A data catalog is a repository of all the metadata that describes the datasets of the organization, and it will help data scientists, data engineers, business analysts, and other users to find a path toward the desired dataset. In Figure 5-3, you can see a possible high-level architecture that describes how the data catalog can be connected to the data lakes and the other solutions of the data platform.

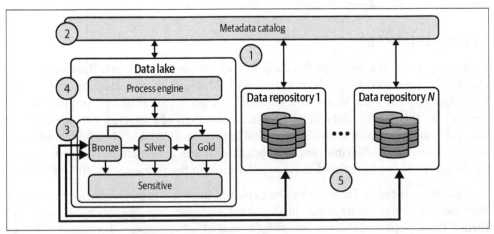

Figure 5-3. The data catalog supports data processing

If the data lives across several data repositories (one of them being the data lake) but the processing engine and the Gold repository for the analytical workloads are within the data lake, ensure that the data catalog is comprehensive and that the data is not duplicated. Make sure the metadata contains information about the level of the dataset (e.g., master or replica).

When bringing and transforming a master dataset within a data lake, there could be a need to sync after the computations. In Figure 5-3, you can see this high-level integration with data catalog of data processing:

1. Metadata catalog fulfillment.
2. Search for the desired data asset.
3. If the data asset is *not* already in the data lake, then make a copy of it into the Bronze storage area.
4. Execute your desired transformation on the copied data asset.
5. Update the original data asset if needed.

A data catalog can help with rationalizing the various datasets an organization may have because it can help find duplicated, unused, or similar datasets and delete, decommission, or merge them as appropriate. A data catalog can help organizations focus on the data that is most relevant to them and avoid using resources to store and process data that is not useful, all of which could lead to cost savings.

Whenever data is shared across an organization, it is beneficial to have associated data contracts. Data contracts tend to be JSON/YAML files that capture agreement between data producers and consumers on aspects such as the schema of the data, ingestion/publication frequency, ownership, and levels of data access, including anonymization and masking.

Hadoop Landscape

Hadoop remains the de facto standard for data lakes both on premises and in the cloud. The idea of the data lake started with MapReduce and Hadoop technology (see "Antipattern: Data Marts and Hadoop" on page 15). Hadoop's popularity has grown over the past 15 years, creating a rich ecosystem of projects for data ingestion, storage, processing, and visualization. This led companies like IBM and Cloudera to develop commercial distributions. Databricks provides a multicloud Hadoop capability. In Table 5-1, we have listed some popular tools in the framework split by use case.

The solutions listed in Table 5-1 can be deployed in an on-premises environment, but they can also be easily deployed in the cloud using an IaaS approach. Hyperscalers turned these popular products into fully managed solutions to reduce the burden of provisioning and infrastructure management on the user side, increase the inherent scalability and elasticity, and reduce costs. Table 5-1 also outlines the most popular solutions available in the cloud to facilitate the cloud migration and adoption of the most popular on-premises Hadoop technologies.

Table 5-1. Hadoop solutions by environment

Use case	On premises, Databricks	AWS	Azure	Google Cloud Platform
Workflows	Airflow, Oozie	Data Pipeline, Airflow on EC2, EMR	HDInsight, Data Factory	Cloud Composer, Cloud Dataproc
Streaming ingest	Apache Kafka, MapR Streams	Kinesis, Kinesis Data Streams, Managed Kafka	Event Hubs	Cloud Pub/Sub, Confluent Apache Kafka
Streaming computation	Beam, Storm	Beam on Flink, Kinesis Data Streams	Beam on HDInsight, Stream Analytics	Cloud Dataflow
SQL	Drill, Hive, Impala	Athena, Redshift	Synapse, HDInsight	BigQuery
NoSQL	HBase, Cassandra	DynamoDB	Cosmos DB	Cloud Bigtable
Filesystem	HDFS, Iceberg, Delta Lake	EMR	HDInsight, Data Lake Storage	Cloud Dataproc
Security	Sentry, Ranger, Knox	AWS IAM	Azure IAM	Cloud IAM, Dataplex
Batch computation	Spark	EMR	HDInsight, Databricks	Cloud Dataproc, Serverless Spark

Refer to the table as we review the data lake reference architectures for the three main cloud providers.

Cloud Data Lake Reference Architecture

In this section we are going to review some reference architectures for the implementation of a data lake in the public cloud leveraging services of the main three hyperscalers. As with any cloud architecture, there is no *one-size-fits-all* design. There will always be several different options available that could suit your specific needs.

Amazon Web Services

The managed Hadoop service on AWS is Amazon Elastic MapReduce (EMR). However, that provides only analytics data processing. AWS recommends that we think of data lakes more holistically and consider that analytics of structured data is better carried out using Amazon Athena or Amazon Redshift. Also, the raw data may not already exist in cloud storage (Amazon S3) and will need to be ingested. Therefore, the recommended way to implement a data lake on top of AWS is to leverage AWS Lake Formation. It is a fully managed service that enables the development and the automation of data collection, data cleansing/processing, and data movement to make the data available for analytics and ML workloads. It comes with a permissions service that extends the AWS IAM capabilities and allows for better data governance and security (i.e., fine-grade policies, column- and row-level access control, etc.). Looking at the architecture in Figure 5-4, we can identify the following main components:

- Data sources, which, in this case, are Amazon S3, relational, and NoSQL databases
- Storage zones on top of Amazon S3 buckets
- Data catalog, data governance, security, and process engine orchestrated by AWS Lake Formation
- Analytical services such as Amazon Athena, Amazon RedShift, and Amazon EMR to provide access to the data

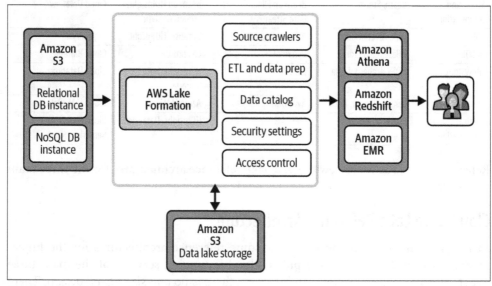

Figure 5-4. AWS data lake architecture

This architecture should work for any kind of use case managing structured, semi-structured, and unstructured data. Once the data has been prepared and transformed, it can easily be made available even to solutions (such as Databricks or Snowflake) outside of the data lake thanks to the pervasive nature of AWS S3 service, which can potentially be connected to any other service of the platform.

Microsoft Azure

On the Azure platform, there are several ways to implement a data lake because there are different solutions that can help with designing a possible target architecture. Typically, we'll see the architecture shown in Figure 5-5, in which we can identify the following main components:

Azure Data Lake Storage Gen2 (ADLSG2)
Object storage optimized for huge volumes of data, fully compatible with HDFS and where users typically implement all the data zones of the data lake

Azure Data Factory
Serverless solution to ingest, transform, and manipulate the data

Azure Purview
Solution that provides governance for finding, classifying, defining, and enforcing policies and standards across data

Azure Synapse Analytics
The analytics service used to issue SQL queries against the data stored in ADLSG2

Databricks
Complete analytics and ML solution based on the Spark processing engine

Power BI
Business intelligence (BI) reporting and visualization tool

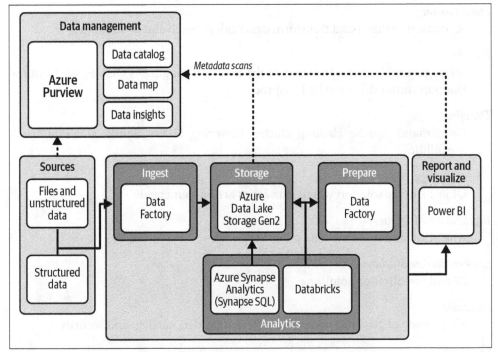

Figure 5-5. Azure data lake architecture

It has to be noted that Azure Databricks can be interchanged with Azure HDInsight. The main difference between the two is that Databricks is an Apache Spark–based analytics platform optimized for the Microsoft Azure cloud services platform while HDInsight is a managed full Apache Hadoop distribution (i.e., more than just Spark tools, but less tuned to Azure). If you want to work with the standard Hadoop ecosystem solutions, you should leverage HDInsight, while if you prefer to leverage a complete analytics and ML solution based on Spark, you should go for Databricks.

 While Databricks is available on all major cloud providers, its native and tight integration with Azure makes it unique in that it can be considered a first-party service rather than a third-party one.

Google Cloud Platform

On Google Cloud Platform (see Figure 5-6), the different serverless and fully managed components are communicating with one another via APIs. We can identify the following main components:

Data Fusion
A solution to ingest and transform data both in batch and in streaming

Pub/Sub
Messaging middleware to integrate the input arriving from Data Fusion and the Hadoop cluster delivered by Dataproc

Dataproc
On-demand Apache Hadoop cluster delivering HDFS, Spark, and non-Spark capabilities

Cloud Storage
Object storage solution where data zones are implemented

Bigtable and BigQuery
Analytical and real-time data processing engine

Looker/Looker Studio
BI and visualization solutions

Dataplex
Single pane of glass to handle data governance, data catalog, and security

Composer
Data workflow orchestration service based on Apache Airflow that empowers users to author, schedule, and monitor pipelines

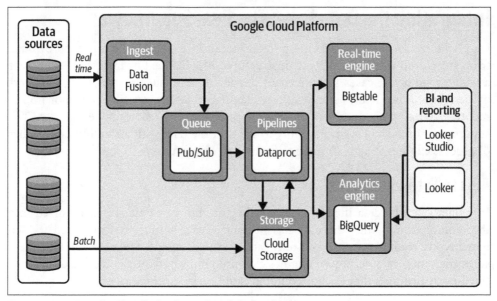

Figure 5-6. Google Cloud Platform data lake architecture

Depending on your use case, Hadoop or an HDFS cluster may not always be the best fit. Having the data in Cloud Storage gives you the freedom to start selecting the right tool for the job at hand, instead of being limited to the tools and compute resources available on the HDFS cluster. For instance, a lot of ad hoc Hive SQL queries can be easily migrated to BigQuery, which can employ either its native storage or read/query directly off Cloud Storage. Similarly, streaming applications may fit better into Apache Beam pipelines, and these can be run on Dataflow, a fully managed streaming analytics service that minimizes latency, processing time, and cost through autoscaling and batch processing.

> When choosing a cloud vendor, you should also consider the datasets that are natively available through their offerings. In the marketing or advertising space, for example, it can be very impactful to implement your business solutions using these datasets. Some examples of datasets include Open Data on AWS, the Google Cloud Public Datasets, and the Azure Open Datasets. If you advertise on Google or sell on Amazon, the ready-built integrations between the different divisions of these companies and their respective cloud platforms can be particularly helpful.

Now that you're familiar with the reference architecture of cloud data lakes, let's delve into how we can extend the data lake with third-party solutions.

Integrating the Data Lake: The Real Superpower

Data lake technology has become popular because it can handle any type of data, from structured tabular formats to unstructured files like text or images. This enables a wide range of use cases that were not possible before, such as analyzing suppliers by performing text analysis on invoices, identifying actors in a film scene, or implementing a real-time dashboard to monitor sales on an ecommerce website. The superpower of a data lake is its ability to connect the data with an unlimited number of process engines to activate potentially any use case you have in mind.

APIs to Extend the Lake

In a data lake, the data ingestion process begins with raw data being imported into the landing zone. After the data has been ingested, it must be processed (which may involve multiple passes) before it can be visualized and activated. Each of these steps may involve a variety of engines that are either part of the data lake itself or third-party products that are hosted in the cloud or, in some cases, on premises.

To make different systems, which may be located in hybrid environments, communicate and exchange data, you can use APIs. APIs are pieces of software that allow two or more systems to communicate via shared protocols such as HTTPS and gRPC. The majority of modern applications use APIs to integrate services and exchange data. Even when ad hoc connectors are available, they are usually built on top of APIs. You can think of APIs as highways where data can flow from one system to another. The security measures implemented to protect the data traffic are the toll booths, and the rate limits are the speed limits. Thanks to these highways, data can flow between multiple systems and be processed by any type of process engine, from a standard ETL to a modern ML framework like TensorFlow or PyTorch.

Organizations can evolve their data lakes using APIs to desired external services. APIs can also be used to monitor, configure, tweak, automate, and, of course, access and query the lake itself.

The Evolution of Data Lake with Apache Iceberg, Apache Hudi, and Delta Lake

The primary goal of integrating the data lake with other technologies is to expand its capability beyond the out-of-the-box features made available by the Hadoop framework. When we consider a standard Hadoop stack, there is one missing element that is typically handled with other technologies (for example, online transaction processing [OLTP] databases): ACID transactions management. Apache Iceberg, Apache Hudi, and Delta Lake are open source storage layers sitting on top of HDFS that have

---

been implemented to address this key aspect. While they each come with a set of different features (e.g., Apache Iceberg supports more file formats than Apache Hudi and Delta Lake), there are some elements in common:

- ACID compliance, giving users the certainty that the information they are querying is consistent
- Overcoming the inherent limitation of HDFS in terms of file size—with this approach, even a small file can work perfectly
- Logging of every single change made on data, guaranteeing a complete audit if ever necessary and enabling time travel queries
- No difference in handling batch and streaming ingestions and elaboration
- Full compatibility with the Spark engine
- Storage based on Parquet format that can achieve a high level of compression
- Stream processing enablement
- Ability to treat the object store as a database
- Applying governance at the row and column level

These storage solutions can enable several use cases that were usually handled by other technologies (such as the DWH, which we will investigate more in Chapter 6), mainly because of the ability to prevent data corruption, execute queries in a very fast mode, and frequently update the data. There are very specific scenarios where the transactional feature of this new enabled storage (i.e., update/delete) plays a crucial role—these are related to the GDPR and the California Consumer Privacy Act (CCPA). Organizations are forced by these regulations to have the ability to purge personal information related to a specific user in case of a specific request. Performing this operation in a standard HDFS environment could be time- and resource-consuming because all of the files that pertain to the personal data being requested must be identified, ingested, filtered, and written out as new files, and the original ones deleted. These new HDFS extensions simplify these operations, making them easy and fast to execute and, more importantly, reliable.

These open source projects have been widely adopted by the community, which is heavily investing in their development. For example, Apache Iceberg is widely used by Netflix, while Apache Hudi powers Uber's data platform. Even though Delta Lake is a Linux Foundation project, the main contributor is Databricks, the company behind the Spark engine that developed and commercialized an entire suite to handle big data workloads based on a vendor-proprietary version of Spark and Delta Lake.

In addition to ACID, there are two other features that are evolving the way users can handle data in a data lake:

Partition evolution

This is the ability to update the partition definition over a file (i.e., table). The partition is the information that allows a filesystem to split the content of a file into several chunks to avoid completing a full scan when retrieving information (e.g., extracting sales figures of Q1 2022—you should be able to query only data belonging to the first quarter of the year instead of querying the entire dataset and then filtering out the data you do not need). Considering the fact that the definition of a partition in a file can evolve because of a business need (e.g., working hours of a device for which we want to collect insights), it is critical to have a filesystem that is able to handle these changes in a transparent and fast way. HDFS (via Hive) can achieve this from a logical point of view, but the computational effort required makes it practically unachievable. Please note that, at the time of writing, this feature is offered only by Apache Iceberg.

Schema evolution

Just like the partition, the schema may need to be updated over time. You may want to add, remove, or update columns in a table, and the filesystem should be able to do that at scale without the need to retransform the data (i.e., without an ELT/ETL approach). Please note that while, at the time of writing, this is fully supported only by Apache Iceberg, all the solutions are able to handle schema evolution when leveraging Apache Spark as the engine.

Now that you have seen how you can expand the capabilities of a data lake and enrich the broad set of use cases that can be solved with them, let's have a look at how to actually interact with data lakes.

Interactive Analytics with Notebooks

One of the most important things when dealing with data is the ability to interactively get access to it and perform analysis in a very easy and fast manner. When leveraging a data lake, data engineers, data scientists, and business users can leverage a plethora of services like Spark, Pig, Hive, Presto, etc., to handle the data. A solution that has grown greatly in popularity in several communities, primarily with data scientists, is what we consider the best Swiss Army knife an organization may leverage for data analysis: Jupyter Notebook.

Jupyter Notebook is an open source application that can be used to write *live documents* containing a mix of text, code to be executed, plots, and charts. It can be considered a live book where, in addition to the text that you write using a markup language like Markdown, there is code that you execute that performs some activities on data (e.g., query, transformation, etc.) and eventually plots some results, generating charts or tables.

From an architectural perspective, you can think of the Jupyter Notebook running on top of a data lake as three different components, as presented on the lefthand side of

Figure 5-7. HDFS is the storage, the kernel the process engine, and Jupyter the server that leverages the process engine to access the data and, via the browser, provide users with the user interface to write and execute the content of the notebooks. There are several kernels that you can leverage (for ML, you'd often use PyTorch), but the most common choice for data engineering is Spark, which can be accessed using PySpark via code written in Python programming language (as shown on the righthand side of Figure 5-7).

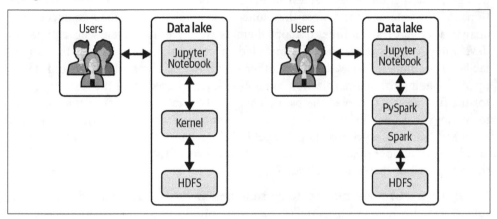

Figure 5-7. Jupyter general notebook architecture and Spark-based kernel

Once properly configured, you can start immediately writing text and code directly into the notebook and interact with datasets as you would while leveraging the Spark command-line interface. You can use notebooks to develop and share code with other people within the organization, perform quick tests and analysis, or quickly visualize data to get some extra insights. It is important to highlight that results are not *static* because they are *live* documents: this means that if the underlying dataset changes or if the piece of code changes, results will be different when the person with whom the notebook is shared reexecutes the notebook. Once you've finalized the analysis, usually there are two different paths that you can take:

- Share the source code of the notebook (Jupyter Notebook produces *.ipynb* files) with other data scientists, data engineers, developers, or anyone who wants to contribute. They can load the file in their environment and rerun the code (it is of course necessary to have the right access to the underlying storage system and to any other solution integrated via APIs).

- Make results static via the generation of an HTML page or a PDF document that can be shared to a broader set of users.

Notebooks have become the de facto standard solution for interactive data analysis, testing, and experimentation because of their extreme flexibility, both in terms of programming languages that you can leverage (thanks to the numerous available kernels) and in terms of activity that you can do (e.g., you can generate a chart starting from data in your data lake, or you can train a complex ML algorithm on a small subset of data before moving that to production).

What we have seen working with several organizations is that the *notebook approach* is a first step in putting in place a *journey to data democratization* (as we will discuss in the next section) because it allows the more technically savvy people to have an immediate and standardized access to the data, fostering an approach to collaborations. While data scientists were the pioneers of notebook use, data engineers and analytical engineers continue to adopt them as well. We have even seen companies developing custom libraries to be included in *notebook templates* with the aim to facilitate the integration with several other solutions (off the shelf or custom developed), bringing the standardization to another level and reducing the learning curve for the final users (and even the pain). This standardization, thanks to the container technology, has been brought even at the compute level: every time users within the company launch a notebook they are, behind the scenes, launching a container with an adequate number of computing resources and a set of tools that are immediately at their disposal for their data analysis.

Cloud hyperscalers are making some solutions available for managed versions of Jupyter Notebook—AWS SageMaker, Azure ML Studio, and Google Cloud Vertex AI Workbench, to name a few—that can help get rid of headaches related to the management of the underlying infrastructure thanks to the fact they are fully managed.

Now that you have a better understanding of how you can leverage Jupyter Notebook to expand the data lake, we'll turn our attention to helping you understand how people within organizations can handle data ingestion up to data visualization reporting, moving from a fully IT model to a more democratic approach.

Democratizing Data Processing and Reporting

The best value that data provides to an organization is that it enables decision makers and users in general to make informed decisions. To that end, data should be accessible and usable by any authorized individual without the need for ad hoc expertise and specialism. Even if it is possible to implement democratization of the data access within a company from a technical point of view, it is not sufficient to focus just on the technology. Organizations need to also implement data cataloging and governance operations. Having good metadata describing proper datasets will enable users to find the right information they need and to activate correct data processing and reporting. In this section we will explore the key technologies that can help an organization with switching from a fully IT-driven approach to a more *democratic* approach when building a cloud data lake.

Build Trust in the Data

When one of the authors of the book was working as a consultant for an important retail customer several years ago, he worked to develop solutions to automate the data extraction from the sales database to generate reports to be leveraged by the business users. He needed to be available every time decision makers had questions like the following:

- Where did you get this data from?
- How did you transform that data?
- What are the operations you made before generating the report?

Once he was assigned to another customer, the organization's IT team took over the entire end-to-end process. While they could fix bugs and monitor the report generation, they were unable to convince the decision makers that the data and reports were trustworthy because they did not have the right level of knowledge to answer these questions.

This trust was clearly a bottleneck that would have been removed by having final users be able to dig into their data in an autonomous way and audit it from ingest to the final reported value. This approach may have been unrealistic in the past, but the fact that people are now more *digitally experienced* helps a lot in shifting this method.

As illustrated in Figure 5-8, there is a clear transition in ownership and responsibility from the old world represented to the left to the new one represented to the right. While the majority of the work used to be carried out by the IT department, nowadays final users have in their hands tools that enable them to handle the majority of the activities from the data cataloging up to the data visualization with a great level of autonomy.

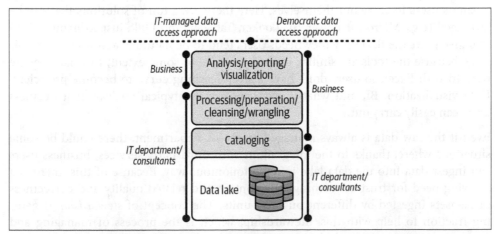

Figure 5-8. Data access approaches (centrally managed versus democratic data access)

Tools like Atlan, Collibra, Informatica, AWS Glue, Azure Purview, and Google Data-plex are making the process of metadata collection easier and faster. On one side, a lot of automation has been built to enable data crawling in an automated way, especially thanks to the integration with several database and storage engines (e.g., AWS Redshift and Athena, Azure Synapse, Google BigQuery, Snowflake, etc.), and on the other, facilitating data entry activities leveraging rich and easy-to-use user interfaces lets businesspeople carry out the majority of the work.

Moving up through the chain, we find that even the data processing, preparation, cleansing, and wrangling steps, which have always been for expert users (i.e., data engineers), can be handled directly by the final users. Of course, a subset of the data processing may still need to be fulfilled by data engineers/data scientists leveraging advanced process engines like Spark. For the activities that require subject matter experts (SMEs), tools like Talend Data Preparation or Trifacta Dataprep have been developed and made available with the clear goal to support non-data-engineering/data scientist users: exploration, transformation, and filtering are just a few of the activities that can be achieved, leveraging a very intuitive interface that delegates the processing to an underlying engine (e.g., Beam) that can apply all the mutations to vast datasets. This approach is even emphasized by the fact that the access to the underlying data, which sits on the HDFS cluster or directly on the object storage like AWS S3, Azure Data Lake, or Google Cloud Storage, can be achieved via several different tools offering a broad set of features and controls. This means that different kinds of users can leverage different kinds of tools to deal with the data. Data engineers, for example, can leverage Spark to develop their data transformation pipelines; data scientists can implement ML algorithms using scikit-learn, TensorFlow, or PyTorch; and business analysts can use Hive or PrestoSQL to execute what-if analysis using SQL queries.

The last step is the data visualization/reporting, which is typically the easiest for business users to carry out themselves. Here there are a ton of solutions that can be leveraged (e.g., Microsoft Power BI, Looker, Tableau, and Qlik, just to name a few) that give users the flexibility they need. Users tend to be naturally autonomous at this stage because the tools are similar in the approach, to some extent, to what they are used to with Excel, so users don't have a steep learning curve to become proficient. Data visualization, BI, and what-if scenarios are the typical analysis that business users can easily carry out.

Even if the raw data is always managed by the IT department, there could be some situations where, thanks to the integrations with third-party services, business users can ingest data into the data lake in an autonomous way. Because of this, there is a growing need for trust concerning data content and related quality and correctness of datasets ingested by different business units. The concept of *stewardship* is gaining traction to help with this. Stewardship, which is the process of managing and overseeing an organization's data assets to ensure that business users have access to high-quality, consistent, and easily accessible data, can be seen as a combination of three key factors:

- *Identify* the key stakeholders who have the right information on a timely basis.
- *Defend* the data from any kind of exfiltration, both internal and external, with a focus on personnel.
- *Cooperate* with other people inside or outside the company to unlock the value of data.

What we are seeing in many companies is that stewardship is not necessarily a role that people are assigned to, but it is more a title that they earn in the field thanks to their interactions with the tools and the quality of their information that they provide to the internal community. In fact, there are several tools (like Informatica Data Catalog, for example) that allow users to rate stewards in the same way purchasers can rate sellers on Amazon.

Now that you've seen the various options available to bring the organization toward a more modern and democratic approach, let's discuss the part of the process that is still mainly in the hands of the IT team: the data ingestion.

Data Ingestion Is Still an IT Matter

One of the most critical and important steps in a data lake is the data ingestion process. If poorly planned, the data lake may become a "data swamp" with a lot of unused data. This typically occurs because organizations tend to load every kind of raw data into the data lake, even without having a complete understanding of *why* they loaded the data or *how* they will leverage it. This approach will bring the creation of massive *heaps of data* that will be unused for the majority of the time. But even unused data remains in the lake and uses space that should be free for other activities. Stale data also tends to have gaps and inconsistencies and causes hard-to-troubleshoot errors when it is eventually used by someone. Because of that, it is important to follow the following best practices, which you can leverage during ingestion processes:

File format
There are several file formats that can be leveraged that come with pros and cons. If the primary goal is readability, CSV, JSON, and XML are the most common ones. If instead performance is the most relevant goal, then Avro, Parquet, or Optimized Row Columnar (ORC) are the ones that suit better:

- Avro (row-based format) works better when intense I/O and low-latency operations are required (e.g., event-based source, streaming dashboards).
- Parquet and ORC (columnar-based format) are more suitable for query use case.

File size

Typically, in the Hadoop world, *larger is better*. Files usually have a size of dozens of gigabytes, and when working with very small files (e.g., IoT use case scenario), it is a good idea to leverage a streaming engine (such as Apache Beam or Spark Streaming) to consolidate the data into a few large files.

Data compression

Data compression is incredibly important to save space, especially in data lakes that are potentially ingesting petabytes of data every single day. Additionally, to guarantee performance it is crucial to select a compression algorithm that is fast enough to compress/decompress the data on the fly, saving a decent amount of space. The standard ZIP compression algorithm is not generally suitable for such applications, and what we are seeing is that organizations tend to leverage Snappy, an open source algorithm developed by Google that provides performance aligned with data lakes' needs.

Directory structure

This is a very important topic because, based on the use case and on the process engine to be leveraged, your directory structure can vary a lot. Let's take as an example an IoT use case handled via HBase: imagine you are collecting data from devices globally distributed and you want to extract information of a specific day from messages generated by devices in a specific location. One good example of directory structure might be */country/city/device_id/year/month/day/ hours/minute/second*. If instead the use case is a batch operation, it may be useful to put the input data in a folder called IN and the output data in a folder called OUT (of course, it has to be identified with the best possible prefix to avoid misunderstanding and data duplication).

Depending on the nature of the data (batch versus streaming) and the target of the data (e.g., AWS S3, Azure Data Lake Storage, Google Cloud Storage), it will be possible to leverage several solutions: users can load the data leveraging scripts (running in PowerShell or bash, for example), or they can ingest the data directly using APIs or native connectors. Users can stream the data directly into the platform (e.g., AWS Kinesis, Azure Event Hub, or Google Pub/Sub), or they can upload it as a raw file into HDFS for future processing. IT departments usually manage these activities because they can involve a lot of automation and at the same time a lot of integration/data processing that require ad hoc skills. However, there are solutions like Fivetran that are simplifying the way users can configure data ingestion into the cloud. For such a solution, even less-skilled people (e.g., business users) could potentially load data in the lake, extending the democratization concept we discussed earlier.

Now that you have seen how to democratize access to the data, let's see from a high-level view how data lakes can facilitate the training and prediction of ML algorithms. You will learn more about that in Chapter 11.

ML in the Data Lake

As we discussed before, it is possible to store any type of data in its raw format in a data lake—this is unlike a DWH, where data needs to be structured or semi-structured. In particular, it is possible to store unstructured data (images, videos, natural language, etc.) in their typical formats (JPEG, MPEG, PDF, etc.). This makes it extremely convenient to ingest data of all types into the data lake, which can then be used to develop, train, and predict ML algorithms, especially the ones based on deep learning (refer to "Applying AI" on page 29).

Training on Raw Data

The typical ML framework you would use varies based on the type of data. For structured data, you can leverage libraries like Spark, XGBoost, and LightGBM. These frameworks can directly read and process data in CSV files, which can be stored as-is in a data lake. For unstructured data, the most commonly used ML frameworks are TensorFlow and PyTorch. These frameworks can read most image and video formats in their native form, which is the form that the raw data will be stored in. Thus, in Figure 5-9, where we walk through the steps in training ML models, the prepared data can be identical to the collected and stored data, and the labels can be part of the data itself—either a column in the CSV files or based on how images/videos are organized (for example, all images of screws can be stored in a folder named *screws*). This makes training ML models on a data lake extremely straightforward.

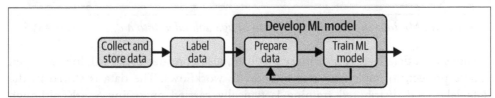

Figure 5-9. Steps of training ML models

There are some efficiency considerations, however—directly reading JPEG or MPEG files will lead to the ML training programs being I/O bound. Therefore, the data is often extracted and stored in formats such as TensorFlow Records in the data lake. Because these formats optimize for throughput when reading from cloud storage, they help maximize GPU utilization. GPU manufacturers also provide capabilities to read common formats, such as Apache Arrow, directly from cloud storage into GPU memory, thus speeding up the ML process.

Predicting in the Data Lake

Because the ML frameworks support directly reading data in the raw formats, invoking models on the raw data is also very straightforward. For example, in Figure 5-10, we show you an image classification workflow on AWS. Note how the image is ingested as-is to the cloud storage bucket and the ML model is invoked on the uploaded image. Similar capabilities are available in GCP and Azure as well, which we'll cover more extensively in Chapter 11.

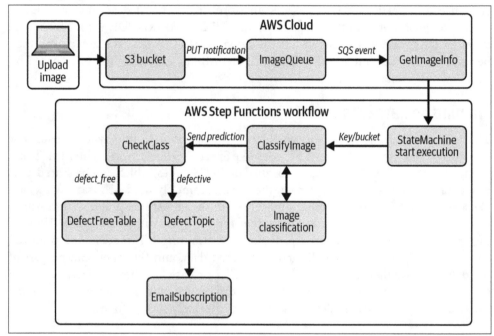

Figure 5-10. ML inference carried out on an image uploaded into a data lake on AWS

If choosing a data lake as a primary platform, also consider using MLflow, an open source project, to implement end-to-end ML workflows. The data is stored in the data lake, and distributed training is typically carried out using Spark, although integrations with TensorFlow and PyTorch also exist. Besides training and deployment, MLflow also supports advanced features such as model registries and feature stores. This capability to directly process raw data in ML frameworks is one of the compelling advantages of data lakes.

Summary

In this chapter you have seen a little more in detail what a real data lake is, what the challenges are, and the patterns that you can adopt to make it the core pillar of the data platform of an organization. The key takeaways are as follows:

- Data plays a key role in every organization to help make robust decisions within a short time frame and possibly in real time.

- A data lake provides more flexibility than a DWH because it allows users to play with any kind of data (i.e., structured, semistructured, and even unstructured) and to leverage a wide variety of solutions and tools coming from the open source ecosystems.

- Organizations struggled in managing data lakes in old on-premises environments. Cloud environments are a great solution for organizations to store data, reduce TCO, and focus on business value instead of hardware management.

- The main advantages to cloud adoption are: (1) reduce the TCO by saving money on storage and compute; (2) obtain scalability by leveraging the reach of hyperscalers; (3) adopt a fail-fast approach to speed up experimentations by leveraging the elasticity of the underlying platform; and (4) benefit from a consistent data governance approach in the platform across several products to comply with security and control requirements.

- In data lakes there is a repository of all the metadata that describes the datasets of the organization, which will help data scientists, data engineers, business analysts, and any users who may need to leverage data to find a path toward the desired dataset.

- Data lakes enable batch and streaming operations and facilitate the implementation of Lambda/Kappa patterns.

- The market is strongly investing in data lakes, particularly in those that are cloud based. So a data lake can be extended by leveraging APIs or integration with third-party solutions.

- One common integration is the adoption of Iceberg or Delta Lake on top of HDFS to make the storage ACID compliant and enable other kinds of use cases (mainly those that request a strong consistency in data).

- Jupyter Notebook is the most common approach used to implement a data analysis, experimentation, and test-based approach within organizations.

- Data lakes facilitate data democratization access within the organization because the majority of the activity can be carried out on a self-service basis.

- Because data is stored in native formats in a data lake, and because ML frameworks support reading these formats, data lakes facilitate ML without any special hooks.

In the following chapter, we will look at the alternative to a data lake, a data warehouse.

CHAPTER 6

Innovating with an Enterprise Data Warehouse

In Chapter 3, you learned that the choice between a data lake and a data warehouse as the central component of your cloud data platform comes down to whether your organization is engineering/science-first (choose a data lake) or analytics-first (choose a DWH). In Chapter 5, we focused on the concept of data lake as a central element in the design of a data platform. In this chapter, you will learn how to address the same problems of cost, democratization, flexibility, and governance using a modern data warehouse as the central element instead.

We will start with a quick recap of the problems being addressed by building a data platform and discuss the technology trends that make a cloud DWH an appealing solution. Then we will do a deep dive into what a modern DWH architecture looks like and how you can effectively enable data analysts and data scientists with it.

A Modern Data Platform

Whenever you undertake a large technology project, you should first ask yourself what business goals are you trying to accomplish, what are your current technology challenges, and what technology trends do you want to leverage. In this section we will focus on helping you understand how to address these questions when building a modern data platform and how an enterprise DWH approach can steer the focus in your data platform design. Many of these concepts have already been touched on in the previous chapters, but it is useful to reframe them here as it will help you connect the design of a modern DWH with the problems the architecture is solving.

Organizational Goals

In our customer interviews, CTOs repeatedly raised these organization goals as being important:

No silos
> Data has to be activated across the entire enterprise because users in one part of the business need access to data that other departments create. For example, a product manager determining how to design next year's product might need access to transaction data created and managed by the retail operations team.

Democratization
> The data platform has to support domain experts and other nontechnical users who can access the data without going through technical intermediaries but who should be able to rely on the quality and consistency of the data.

Discoverability
> The data platform has to support data engineers and other technical users who need access to data at different stages of processing. For example, if we have a dataset in which raw, incoming transactions have been reconciled, a data scientist needs to be able to get the reconciled dataset. If they can't discover it, they will rebuild a reconciliation routine. Therefore, it should be possible to discover all these "intermediate" datasets so that processing steps are not duplicated across the organization.

Stewardship
> Datasets should be under the control of teams that understand what they are. For example, financial data should be under the control of the finance department, not of IT.

Single source
> Data should be read in place. Minimize the copying and extracting of data.

Security and compliance
> IT should serve as a broker for data, ensuring that only people with the right permissions can access it. It is imperative to implement all compliance checks required by regulations (e.g., GDPR, CCPA, Gramm-Leach-Bliley Act). Make sure to implement solutions for classifying data into sensitive/restricted data versus open or industry-specific data.

Ease of use
> Make reporting easier since there are hundreds of analysts building reports to support a variety of functions.

Data science
> Make data science teams more productive since these roles tend to be expensive and difficult to hire.

Agility
> Make insights available to decision makers faster.

While the relative order of these goals varies between organizations, all of these goals figure in one way or another in every organization we spoke to. Therefore, a modern data platform should enable CTOs to achieve these goals.

Technological Challenges

What prevents CTOs from accomplishing these goals with the technologies that they have already deployed within the organization? CTOs tend to mention these technological challenges:

Size and scale
> The quantity of data their organization is collecting has dramatically increased over time and is expected to continue to increase. Their current systems are unable to scale and remain within the speed and cost constraints of their business, leading to compromises such as sampling the incoming data or heavily prioritizing new data projects.

Complex data and use cases
> Increasingly, the data being collected is unstructured data—images, videos, and natural language text. Their current systems for managing structured and unstructured data do not intersect. However, there is increasingly a need to use structured data (e.g., product catalog details) and unstructured data (e.g., catalog images, user reviews) together in use cases such as recommendations.

Integration
> Over time, we have seen the availability of many new sources and sinks of data to the technology landscape that organizations should and want to leverage. For example, they would love to manage sales information in Salesforce, ads campaigns in Adobe, and web traffic in Google Analytics. There is a need to analyze and make decisions on all this data in tandem.

Real time
> Much of the new data is collected in real time, and there is a competitive advantage to being able to process and make decisions on the data as it arrives. However, organizations do not have a data platform that seamlessly supports streaming.

These are, of course, just a more nuanced version of the traditional big data challenges: volume, variety (of data and systems), and velocity.

Technology Trends and Tools

To enable their organization to achieve these business and technological goals, a cloud architect can leverage the trends and tools described in the previous chapters. For convenience, we've summarized them here:

Separation of compute and storage
> Public cloud providers allow you to store data on blob storage and access it from ephemeral computational resources. These computational resources consist of software such as Google BigQuery, AWS Redshift, Snowflake, Amazon EMR, Google Dataproc, Cloud Dataflow, or Databricks that were custom-built or adapted to take advantage of this separation of computing and distribute data processing over multiple workers. They span both structured and unstructured data.

Multitenancy
> Cloud computing resources are built to allow multiple tenants. Therefore, there is no need to create distinct clusters or storage arrays for each department in an organization. Thus, two separate departments can store their data in a single DWH and access each other's data from compute resources that they each pay for—each team can spin up their own analytics on the common, shared dataset. Similarly, an organization can use its computing resources to access data from multiple organizations and do analytics on the joined datasets. Unlike traditional Hadoop clusters, it is not necessary to run the compute workload collocated with the data.

Separation of authentication and authorization
> Cloud IAM solutions can ensure that a central IT team can secure identities while the owners of the data control access. In fact, by providing access to groups, it is possible to allow the accessing organization to manage the membership while the data owners manage only business logic of which teams are provided what access.

Analytics hubs
> Serverless DWHs (and data lakes, as we have seen in the previous chapter) allow the architect to break down data silos even outside the boundaries of the organization. While the data owner pays for storage, the data consumer pays for querying. Also, while the data owner decides which groups have access, membership of the group can be managed by the data consumer. Thus, partners and suppliers can share data without having to worry about querying costs or group memberships.

Multicloud semantic layer

Tools such as Informatica or Looker make it possible to create a semantic layer that stretches across hyperscalers (such as AWS, GCP, or Azure), multicloud data platforms (such as Snowflake or Databricks), and on-premises environments. The semantic layer can rewrite queries on the fly to provide a consistent and coherent data dictionary. (Please note that semantic layers are covered in more detail later in the chapter.)

Consistent admin interface

Data fabric solutions provide a consistent administration experience on the public cloud no matter where the data is stored, whether in a DWH or in data lake formats such as Parquet files on blob storage.

Cross-cloud control pane

Tools such as BigQuery Omni provide a consistent control pane and query layer regardless of which hyperscaler (AWS, GCP, or Azure) your organization uses to store the data. These are useful if the concern is to ensure that the same tooling can be used regardless of which hyperscaler's storage a particular dataset lives in. The trade-off is an increased dependency on the GCP control pane.

Multicloud platforms

Snowflake, Confluent, and Databricks provide for the ability to run the same software on any hyperscaler. However, unlike in the previous bullet point, the runtimes on different clouds remain distinct. These are useful if the concern is to ensure that it is possible to move from one hyperscaler to another. The trade-off is an increased dependency on the single-source software vendor.

Converging of data lakes and DWHs

Federated and external queries make it possible to run Spark jobs on data in the DWH and SQL queries on data in the data lake. We will expand on this topic in the next chapter.

Built-in ML

Enterprise DWHs like AWS Redshift and Google BigQuery provide the ability to train and run ML without having to move data out of the DWH. Spark has an ML library (Spark MLlib), and ML frameworks such as TensorFlow are supported in Hadoop systems. Thus, ML can be carried out on the data platform without having to extract data to take to a separate ML platform.

Streaming ingest

Tools such as Kafka, AWS Kinesis, Azure Event Hub, and Google Cloud Pub/Sub support the ability to land data into hyperscalers' data platforms in real time. Tools such as AWS Lambda, Azure Functions, Google Cloud Run, and Google Cloud Dataflow also support transforming the data as it arrives so as to quality control, aggregate, or semantically correct data before it is written out.

Streaming analytics

DWHs support streaming SQL, so that as long as data is landed in the DWH in real time, queries reflect the latest data.

Change data capture

Tools such as Qlik, AWS Database Migration Service, and Google Datastream provide the ability to capture changes to an operational relational database (such as Postgres running on AWS Relational Database Service [RDS] or MySQL running on Google Cloud SQL) and stream them in real time to a DWH.

Embedded analytics

It is possible to use modern visualization tools such as Power BI to embed analytics into the tools (mobile phones or websites) that end users use—it is not necessary to make end users operate dashboards.

The *hub-and-spoke architecture* provides a proven way to achieve the CTOs' desired goals and take advantage of the above technological capabilities.

Hub-and-Spoke Architecture

When designing a modern cloud data platform centered around a DWH, the hub and spoke is the ideal architecture. In this architecture, the DWH acts as a *hub* that collects all the data needed for business analysis. *Spokes*, which are custom applications, dashboards, ML models, recommendation systems, and so on, interact with the DWH via standard interfaces (i.e., APIs). Tools such as Sigma Computing, SourceTable, and Connected Sheets even provide a spreadsheet interface that simulates Excel running on top of the DWH. All of these spokes can access data directly from the DWH without having to make a copy.

We suggest this approach to startups with no legacy technologies to accommodate, organizations that want a complete do-over to achieve a full-scale transformation, and even large enterprises because it is scalable, flexible, and resilient.

It is scalable because new (modern) DWHs can easily integrate new data sources and use cases to the existing infrastructure without having to reconfigure the entire system. It is flexible because you can customize the overall architecture to meet the specific needs of an enterprise (e.g., enabling streaming). And it is resilient because it can withstand more failures than other architectures.

A modern cloud native enterprise DWH forms the hub of the hub-and-spoke architecture, and the spokes are data providers and data consumers, as depicted in Figure 6-1. Please refer to components of the diagram as you read the following paragraphs.

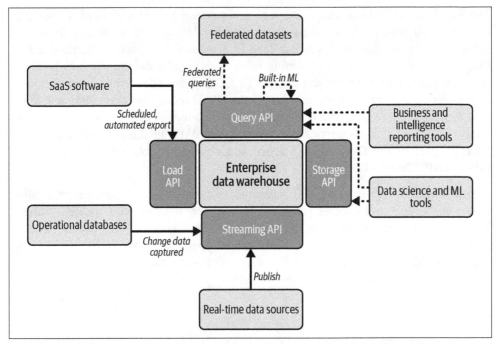

Figure 6-1. Hub-and-spoke architecture; a modern enterprise DWH forms the hub

An analytics-first data and ML capability involves loading raw data into a DWH (*enterprise DWH*) and then carrying out transformations as needed to support various needs. Because of the separation of compute and storage, there is only one unique copy of the data. Different compute workloads such as querying (*Query API*), reporting/interactive dashboards (*business and intelligence reporting tools*), and ML (*data science and ML tools*) work on top of this data that sits in the DWH. Because you can leverage SQL for all the transformations, you can use views and materialized views to carry out elaborations, making ETL pipelines unnecessary. These views can invoke external functions, thus allowing for the enrichment of data in the DWH using ML APIs and models. In some cases, you can even train ML models using just SQL syntax and you can schedule complex batch pipelines via simple SQL commands. Modern DWHs support directly ingesting (*Load API*) even streaming data (*Streaming API*), and so you have to leverage streaming pipelines only when you need to perform low-latency, windowed aggregations analysis on data as it comes in. Always remember to assess the final cost of your solution and compare it with the benefits you will receive. Sometimes one strategy (batch) may be better than the other (streaming), and vice versa.

The key idea behind the hub-and-spoke architecture is that you land all the data into the enterprise DWH as efficiently as possible. When data is coming from SaaS software (such as Salesforce), you can load it through a scheduled, automated export mechanism. When instead it is coming from *operational databases* such as Postgres, you can land it in near real time through CDC tools. Meanwhile, *real-time data sources* are expected to publish new data to the DWH when new events happen. Some data sources are federated (*federated datasets*), which means that you will dynamically query and treat them as part of the DWH itself. With all the enterprise data now logically part of the DWH, data science and reporting tools can act on the data (*Storage API/Query API*).

If you don't have preexisting ETL pipelines that you need to port or preexisting end users whose tool choices you have to support, the hub and spoke is simple, powerful, fast, and cost-effective. An example manifestation of this architecture on Google Cloud is shown in Figure 6-2. The other hyperscalers offer more options (e.g., Athena, Redshift, Snowflake on AWS); we'll cover the variations in Chapter 7.

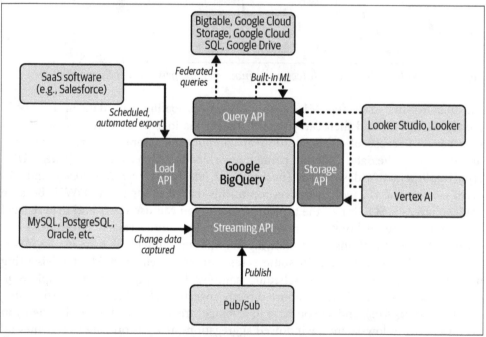

Figure 6-2. Hub-and-spoke architecture as manifested on Google Cloud

In its fully automated form, the hub and spoke is a great choice for enterprises without strong engineering skills and for small departments doing shadow IT, because there is very little code to maintain when it comes to data ingestion. Also, you can complete data science and reporting activities with only a knowledge of SQL.

It is worth noting that the capabilities that enable an analytics-first DWH are all recent developments. Separation of compute and storage came about with the public cloud: previously, the big data paradigm was dominated by MapReduce, which required sharding data to local storage. Analytics workloads required the building of data marts that were business specific. Due to performance constraints, it was necessary to carry out transformations before loading the data into these data marts (i.e., ETL). Stored procedures were DWHs, not external functions, which themselves relied on developments in autoscaling, stateless microservices. ML deployments required bundling and distributing libraries, not stateless ML APIs. ML workflows were based on self-contained training code, not ML pipelines consisting of containerized components. Streaming involved separate codebases, not unified batch and stream processing.

Now that you have seen the basic concepts of the hub-and-spoke architecture, let's deep dive into its main components: ingest, business intelligence, transformations, and ML.

Data Ingest

One set of spokes in the hub-and-spoke architecture (the boxes gravitating around the enterprise DWH in Figure 6-1) corresponds to various ways to land (or ingest) data into the DWH. There are three ingest mechanisms: prebuilt connectors, real-time data capture, and federated querying. We will look at each of these respectively in this section.

Prebuilt connectors

Landing data into the DWH can be extremely easy when leveraging popular SaaS platforms because they make available connectors that automatically ingest data with a few clicks. Every cloud native DWH (Google BigQuery, AWS Redshift, Snowflake, Azure Synapse, etc.) typically supports SaaS software such as Salesforce, Google Marketing Platform, and Marketo. If you happen to be using software that your choice of DWH doesn't support, look at whether the software vendor provides a connector to your desired DWH—for example, Firebase (a mobile applications platform) can directly export crash reports from mobile applications into BigQuery for analytics ("crashlytics").

You can set up these SaaS services to push data into common DWHs (e.g., Salesforce will automatically push data into Snowflake) or set up the import of these datasets into the DWH using services like the BigQuery Data Transfer Service. This is often termed *Zero ETL*—just as serverless doesn't mean that there are no servers, only that the servers are managed by someone else, Zero ETL means that the ETL process is managed by your SaaS vendor or your DWH vendor.

A third option is to use a third-party provider of connectors such as Fivetran. Their prebuilt connectors provide a turnkey ability to integrate data from marketing, product, sales, finance, and other applications (see Figure 6-3).

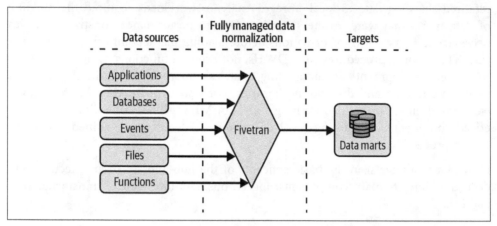

Figure 6-3. Third-party vendors such as Fivetran can automatically handle landing data from a wide range of sources into a cloud DWH such as BigQuery, Redshift, or Snowflake

Between the transfer services of the cloud provider, software vendors that support cloud connectors, and third-party connector providers, you can buy (rather than build) the ability to export data routinely from your SaaS systems and load them to the enterprise DWH.

Real-time data

What if you want your DWH to reflect changes as they happen? You need to leverage a smaller set of tools called CDC tools. Operational databases (Oracle, MySQL, Postgres) are typically part of the support, as are enterprise resource planning (ERP) tools like SAP. Make sure that these tools use the Streaming API of the DWH to load data in near real time. On Google Cloud, Datastream is the recommended CDC tool, and on AWS, it is Database Migration Service (DMS).

If you have real-time data sources, such as clickstream data or data from IoT devices, look for a capability to publish the events as they happen using the Streaming API of the DWH. Because the Streaming API can be accessed through HTTPS, all you need is a way to invoke an HTTPS service every time an event happens.

If the provider of your IoT devices doesn't support push notifications, then look for a way to publish events into a message queue (for example, using Message Queuing Telemetry Transport or MQTT) and use a stream processor (Dataflow on GCP, Kinesis on AWS) to write those events into the DWH (see Figure 6-4).

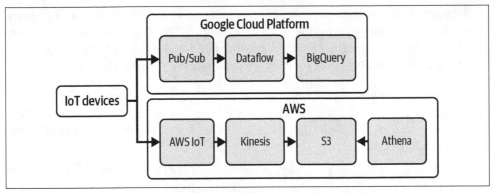

Figure 6-4. Landing real-time data from an IoT device into a DWH

Federated data

You may not even need to land the data into the DWH to use it. Modern cloud DWHs are able to run queries on datasets in standard formats such as Avro, CSV, Parquet, and JSONL (line-oriented JavaScript Object Notation) without moving the data into the DWH. These are called *federated* queries and often require either that the data format be self-describing or that the schema be prespecified. For example, getting Google BigQuery to perform federated queries on Avro files, a self-describing format, involves three steps:

1. Create a table definition file using `bq mkdef --source_format=AVRO gs://file name` and edit the defaults if necessary. For example, you might change a field that, in Avro, is an integer to be treated as a real number.

2. Use the resulting table definition file to create a BigQuery dataset using `bq mk --external_table_definition mydataset.mytablename`.

3. Query the dataset with SQL as normal.

Note that the data remains on Cloud Storage in Avro format. This is what makes this a federated query. If the data format is not self-describing, the `mkdef` command allows you to specify a schema.

It is possible even to combine these steps and apply a *schema on read* so that the schema definition is only for the duration of the query. For example, to have Azure Synapse query Parquet files in an Azure data lake, you can query as follows:

```
SELECT ... FROM
  OPENROWSET(
    BULK 'https://....dfs.core.windows.net/mydata/*.parquet',
    FORMAT='PARQUET'
  ) AS Tbl
```

In the case of federated queries, the querying engine is the DWH. It is also possible to use an external querying engine (such as a PostgreSQL relational database) to carry out the queries. Such queries are called *external* queries (see Figure 6-5). For example, to get Amazon Redshift to query a Postgres database, follow these three steps:

1. Make sure that your RDS PostgreSQL instance can accept connections from your Amazon Redshift cluster. To do this, you need to set up physical networking and ensure that the Redshift cluster is assigned an IAM role authorized in the PostgreSQL instance.

2. In Redshift, create an external schema using CREATE EXTERNAL SCHEMA FROM POSTGRES passing in the database, schema, host, IAM, and secret.

3. Query the schema as normal.

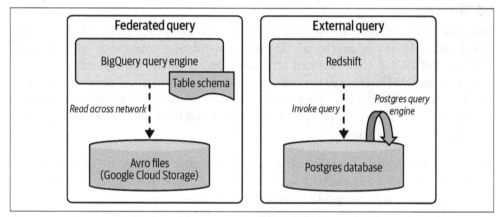

Figure 6-5. Example of federated versus external query approach, both of which are available in AWS and GCP

In all these instances, the key thing to note is that data remains in place and is queried from there—it is not loaded into the DWH. Because the opportunities for optimization are more limited when data remains in place (and cannot be partitioned, clustered, etc.), federated and external queries tend to be slower than native queries.

Given that federated and external queries are slower, why use them? Why not simply load the data into the DWH and treat the DWH as the source of truth? There are a few situations where it can be advantageous to avoid moving the data:

- In some cases, storage within the DWH is more expensive than storage outside of it. It may be more cost-effective to keep the data in a federated data source for very rarely queried data. When you need the best possible performance, use the native storage system offered by the DWH solution. If instead flexibility is more important, try to leverage federated data sources.

- If the data is frequently updated in a relational database, it may be advantageous to treat the relational database as the golden source. Doing CDC from the operational database to the DWH may introduce unacceptable latency.

- The data may be created or needed by workloads (such as Spark). Because of this, it may be necessary to maintain Parquet files. Using federated/external queries limits the movement of data. This is the most common use case when you already have a data lake.

- The data may belong to an organization that is different from the one that is querying it. Federation neatly solves the problem. However, suppose you are using a fully serverless DWH such as Google BigQuery that is not cluster based. In that case, it is possible to provide direct access to partners and suppliers even to native storage.

The last situation is one of the reasons that we recommend a fully serverless DWH that does not expect you to move data to a cluster, create data extracts, or provide specific applications (rather than specific users) access to the data.

Now that you have a better knowledge of the available options for data ingestion, let's deep dive into how to make the data speak by having a look at the various capabilities we can develop on the BI side.

Business Intelligence

Data analysts need to be able to rapidly obtain insights from data. The tool they use for this purpose needs to be self-service, support ad hoc analysis, and provide a degree of trust in the data being used (*business and intelligence reporting tools* in the hub-and-spoke architecture). It needs to provide several capabilities: SQL analytics, data visualization, embedded analytics, and a semantic layer, all of which we will cover throughout this section.

SQL analytics

As highlighted in the previous sections, SQL is the main language when querying the DWH. SQL is the *lingua franca* of data analysts and business analysts within an organization. These analysts will often carry out ad hoc queries on the DWH to help answer questions that come up (such as, "How many liters of ice cream were sold in Romania during the last heatwave?"). But in many cases, the questions become routine, and users operationalize them in the form of reports leveraging ad hoc tools like Power BI or Looker.

These reporting tools, commonly known as BI tools, aim to provide a view of the entire data estate of the organization by connecting to a DWH (*business and intelligence reporting tools* in the hub-and-spoke architecture in Figure 6-1) so that analysts can make data-driven decisions.

Considering that it is not practical to expect an analyst to collect, clean, and load some piece of data at the time that they need it, the data needs to already be there. That's the reason why the hub-and-spoke model with a central enterprise DWH is so popular.

However, you should make sure that the BI tool is cloud ready and capable of dealing with large volumes of fast-arriving data. Early-generation BI tools would require that the data be extracted into online analytical processing (OLAP) cubes for performance reasons (see Figure 6-6). This simply won't do—it leads to a proliferation of stale, exported data or huge maintenance burdens to support separate OLAP cubes for every possible use case. You want the BI tool to transparently delegate queries onto the DWH and retrieve the results. This is the best way to take advantage of the scale of the DWH and the timeliness of its streaming interfaces. SQL engines in the enterprise DWH have been upgraded to a level that they are able to handle multiple parallel queries or maintain in memory a huge amount of data, which allows organizations to get rid of the OLAP approach.

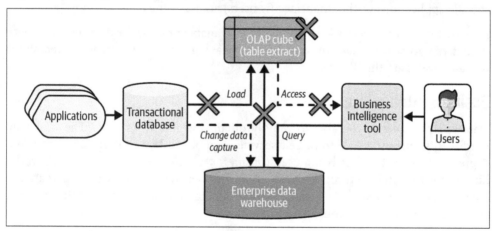

Figure 6-6. Make sure that the BI tool pushes all queries to the enterprise DWH and doesn't do them on OLAP cubes (extracts of the database/DWH)

Visualization

Your SQL queries will produce tables. However, it can be difficult to gain understanding and insights from raw tables alone. Instead, you will often plot your results as graphs, charts, or maps. Visualizing the results of SQL queries is often what leads to insight.

In exploratory data analysis, visualization is ad hoc. However, the visualization has to help frame answers to common questions using common charting elements. This is the remit of dashboarding tools like Tableau, Looker, Power BI, and Looker Studio.

Good dashboards keep the audience in mind and tell stories. They work both as a high-level overview of the current state but also as a launching point for further interactive analysis. They display contextually relevant, important metrics using the appropriate form of a chart.

Embedded analytics

Visualization through traditional dashboard tools is sufficient if you wish to share the analytics results with a handful of internal people. Such users will appreciate the rich controls and interactivity that a dashboard provides. What if you are a crafts marketplace or telecom operator, and you want each artist or each kiosk to have access to near-real-time graphs of the performance of their own store?

When you are providing customized reports to thousands of users, you don't want to provide end users with a feature-rich dashboard interface that can be hard to support and maintain. Instead, what you need is a lightweight graphics visual layer that can be embedded within the tool that the user is already using. It is common to embed the analytics within the website or mobile app that artists visit to list items for sale or that kiosk operations visit to order new items.

Providing consistent, live metrics of their store performance can significantly enhance the ability of artists and operators to make money in your marketplace. It is also possible to better connect workflows—for example, using analytics, sellers might be able to change the price of frequently back-ordered goods easily. Providing ML capabilities such as forecasting the demand of products might also provide the marketplace with new revenue streams.

Semantic layer

There is a tension between self-service analytics and consistency. It is important to give every business analyst in your company the ability to rapidly create dashboards without waiting on a central IT team. At the same time, it is imperative to maintain consistency in the way dashboards perform calculations (e.g., shipping costs have to be calculated in the same way across dashboards). While it is important that business analysts can build complex dashboards themselves, it is also important that analysts reuse existing visualizations as much as possible. The traditional approach to providing consistency and reuse has been to centralize calculations and foundational capabilities within IT. However, such centralized, IT-centric solutions are typically too brittle and too slow to satisfy business users in a data-driven environment.

Modern BI tools like Looker or MicroStrategy offer a *semantic layer* (see Chapter 2) to help address this tension. A semantic layer is an additional layer that allows you to facilitate an end user's access to data autonomously using common business terms; it works via a decoupling between the nomenclature adopted by the table creator and the names adopted by the business users. LookML, which Looker calls its semantic model layer, is a data language based on SQL (see Example 6-1). It provides data stewards the ability to create reusable dimensions or measures that business analysts can reuse and extend. These definitions are made available in a data dictionary for easy discovery and management.

Example 6-1. The semantic layer consists of centralized definitions of metrics and dimensions; this example from Looker shows a metric (overall health score)

```
dimension: overall_health_score {
    view_label: "Daily Account Health Scores"
    description: "Weighted average of Usage, User, Support and CSAT Scores"
    Type: number
    Sql: (${usage_score}*2+${user_score}*2+${support_score}+${csat_score})/6 ;;
    Value_format_name: decimal_1
}
```

These semantic layers function as a BI data source in and of themselves. Tableau, for example, can connect to Looker's semantic layer instead of directly to the DWH.

Although business users will typically not see or interact with LookML-like tools directly, they get to build dashboards that use the defined dimensions and metrics. This helps foster reuse so that each analyst doesn't have to define from base table columns every dimension or metric that they employ. Centralizing the definition of a metric also decreases the likelihood of human error and provides a single point at which definitions can be updated. Having such a centralized definition exist in a text file permits easy version control as well.

You have seen how you can dive into the data with the help of the BI tools and, via a semantic layer, facilitate business users managing the data by themselves. Sometimes this approach is not enough, and you need to prepare the data before starting with the ingestion into the DWH. In the next section we will focus on this topic.

Transformations

Suppose you land raw data from ERP systems into a DWH. If the ERP is SAP, it's likely that the column names are in German and reflect the application state, not what we would consider data that is useful to persist. We don't want to force all our users to have to transform the data into a usable form every time they need it. So where should the transformation take place?

One option is to define the way columns have to be transformed in a semantic layer that is part of your BI tool as discussed in the previous section. However, this limits the definitions to dimensions and metrics, and accessing these definitions will be difficult from non-BI tools.

A better approach is to define transformations in SQL and create views, tables, or materialized views. In this section we will have a look at the common options available to handle transformations within a DWH. This is another advantage of the hub-and-spoke architecture: when data transformations are implemented in the DWH, the results are immediately available to all use cases that require them.

A third approach is to take advantage of the application development platform available on the hyperscaler. Use the event mechanism (Eventarc, EventBridge, Event Grid) to launch a serverless function (Lambda, Cloud Functions) whenever a new table partition gets created. The function can then transform and "push" the modified data into backend systems by invoking their APIs, thus initiating business actions (such as shipping notifications). This is called *reverse ETL* because the direction of data flow is away from the DWH.

ELT with views

Instead of ETL, it is possible to load data into the DWH as-is and transform it on the fly when reading it through views (see Example 6-2). Because the views carry out the transformation on the fly after the data is loaded into the DWH (no transformation is carried out before loading), this is commonly called extract-load-transform (ELT) in contrast to the typical ETL workflow.

Example 6-2. In this example from Azure Synapse Analytics, the SQL code creates a view by joining two tables

```
CREATE VIEW view1
AS
SELECT fis.CustomerKey, fis.ProductKey, fis.OrderDateKey,
    fis.SalesTerritoryKey, dst.SalesTerritoryRegion
FROM FactInternetSales AS fis
LEFT OUTER JOIN DimSalesTerritory AS dst
ON (fis.SalesTerritoryKey=dst.SalesTerritoryKey);
```

Instead of querying the raw tables, users query the view. The SQL that creates the view can select specific columns, apply operations such as masking to the columns, and join multiple tables. Thus, ELT provides a consistent, governed view of the raw data to business users. Because the final query runs the *view query* before it further aggregates or selects, all queries reflect up-to-date information based on whatever data is present in the DWH.

Views, however, can become quite expensive in terms of computational resources, time, and/or money. Consider, for example, the view shown in Example 6-2 that joins the sales orders tables with the sales territory. All sales orders from all the territories over the entire lifetime of the business are being queried in this view. This is the case even if the analyst querying the view is interested in only a specific year or region (and in that case, it makes a lot of sense to filter out the data that is not relevant before performing the join).

Scheduled queries

If the tables are updated infrequently, it can be far more efficient to extract the data into tables periodically. For example, in Google BigQuery, as reported in Example 6-3, we specify the destination table, how often to run the query, and the query itself.

Example 6-3. In this Google BigQuery example, raw data from the Orders table is extracted and aggregated, and aggregated results stored in a destination table, every 24 hours

```
bq query ...
    --destination_table=Orders_elt.lifetime_value \
    --schedule='every 24 hours' \
    --replace=true \
    'SELECT
        customer_id,
        COUNT(*) AS num_purchases,
        SUM(total_amount) AS lifetime_value
    FROM Orders.all_orders
    GROUP BY customer_id'
```

The raw table is queried only once every 24 hours in the example shown. While there is an increase in storage cost associated with the destination table, storage costs are typically orders of magnitude cheaper than computational costs. Therefore, the cost of creating the destination table is quite manageable.

The key advantage of scheduled queries is that analysts query the destination table and not the raw data. Therefore, analyst queries are relatively inexpensive.

The drawback of scheduled queries is the results returned to analysts can be up to 24 hours out of date. The degree to which queries are out of date can be reduced by running the scheduled query more frequently. Of course, the more often the extraction query is scheduled, the more the cost advantages start to dissipate. Another drawback of scheduled queries is that they can be wasteful if the resulting destination table is never queried.

Materialized views

It is clear that the most efficient way to balance obsolete data and cost is to extract raw data into a destination table when you request a view for the first time. Subsequent queries can be fast because they can retrieve data from the destination table without doing any extraction. Meanwhile, the system needs to monitor the underlying tables and reextract the data when the original tables change. You can make the system even more efficient by updating the destination table with new rows of raw data rather than requerying the entire table.

While you can build a data engineering pipeline to all this, modern cloud DWHs support fully managed materialized views out of the box. Creating a materialized view in these systems is analogous to creating a live view (see Example 6-4), and you can query it just like any other view. The DWH takes care of ensuring that queries return up-to-date data. The DWH vendor charges a few costs for managing the materialized view.

Example 6-4. Creating a materialized view in Snowflake with automatic data update

```
create materialized view vulnerable_pipes
(segment_id, installation_year, rated_pressure)
as
select segment_id, installation_year, rated_pressure
from pipeline_segments
where material = "cast iron" and installation_year < "1980"::date;
```

Be careful, though—some DWHs (like Amazon Redshift, at the time of writing) do not automatically manage the materialized view for you; you are expected to set up a schedule or trigger to REFRESH the materialized view. In that sense, what they term a materialized view is actually just a table extract.

Google BigQuery, Snowflake, Databricks, and Azure Synapse do transparently maintain the materialized view content. The view content is automatically updated as data is added to the underlying tables.

Security and lineage

Data governance best practice is to ensure that an organization keeps track of all data transformations from its ingestion up to its usage.

An important aspect to consider is related to the identification of the resources (e.g., entire datasets or some fields within a table) that have to be considered sensitive and need to be protected by design. It is pivotal not only to prevent access to information that should be considered secret within a company but even to be ready to correctly manage the data in light of compliance with government regulations that in some cases are becoming more and more stringent (e.g., GDPR in Europe,

Health Insurance Portability and Accountability Act or HIPAA in the United States, etc.). It is important to note that, when talking about security and compliance, your focus should not be limited to who is accessing what (that can be generally addressed via a fine-grained access control lists [ACLs] policy management approach and data encryption/masquerading techniques); it should also be on:

- The origin of the data
- The different transformations that have been applied before its consumption
- The current physical data location (e.g., data lake in Germany or DWH in the United Kingdom)

The tracking of this sort of metadata is called *data lineage*, and it helps ensure that accurate, complete, and trustworthy data is being used to drive business decisions. Looking at data lineage is also helpful in situations where you need to guarantee data locality because of some local legislation (e.g., telecommunication metadata in Germany): if you can track *where* the data is during its lifecycle, then you can put in place automations to prevent the access, usage, and movement of that information by people who do not meet the minimum requirements.

As you have seen, metadata plays a central role in helping companies organize their data and govern its access. It is also crucial for evaluating the *quality* of the collected data in terms of accuracy, completeness, consistency, and freshness: poor-quality data might lead to wrong business decisions and potential security issues. There are several techniques, and related tools, that can support data quality activities, but the most common ones are:

Standardization
> The process of putting data coming from different sources into a consistent format (e.g., fix inconsistencies in capitalizations, characters, updating values in the wrong fields, data formats, etc.)

Deduplication
> The process of identifying duplicate records (leveraging a similarity score) and then proceeding with the deletion of the duplicated values

Matching
> The process of finding similarities or links between datasets to discover potential dependencies

Profiling and monitoring
> The process of identifying a range of data values (e.g., min, max, mean), revealing outliers and anomalies that could imply, for example, the need for a data fix or a schema evolution

If you use the native managed services of a cloud vendor, when you perform data transformations the tools will typically manage and carry along metadata. Thus, if you use, for example, Data Fusion, views, materialized views, etc., on Google Cloud, the Data Catalog is updated and lineage maintained. If you build your transformation pipeline using Dataflow, you should update the Data Catalog. Similarly, the crawlers will automatically update the Data Catalog on AWS, but you need to invoke the Glue API to add to the catalog if you implement your own transformations.

You have seen how the DWH (the *hub* in our architecture) can drive data transformation to make it available to all use cases you want to implement, keeping track at the same time of all the metadata you need to maintain a robust lineage of all the elaborations. Now let's have a look at how you can craft the structure of the organization to match the hub-and-spoke architecture.

Organizational Structure

In many organizations, there are many more business analysts than engineers. Often, this ratio is 100:1. A hub-and-spoke architecture is ideal for organizations that wish to build a data and ML platform that primarily serves business analysts. Because the hub-and-spoke architecture assumes that business analysts are capable of writing ad hoc SQL queries and building dashboards, some training may be necessary.

In an analyst-first system, the central data engineering team is responsible for (see the filled shapes in Figure 6-7):

- Landing the raw data from a variety of sources into the DWH. Many sources can be configured to directly publish to modern DWHs.
- Ensuring data governance, including a semantic layer and the protection of PII.
- Workloads that cross business units (e.g., activation), involve data across business units (e.g., identity resolution), or require specialized engineering skills (e.g., ML).
- Common artifact repositories such as data catalog, source code repository, secret store, feature store, and model registries.

The business unit is responsible for (see the unfilled shapes in Figure 6-7):

- Landing data from business-specific sources into the DWH
- Transforming the raw data into a form usable for downstream analysis
- Populating the governance catalogs and artifact registries with business-specific artifacts
- Reports, ad hoc analytics, and dashboards for business decision making

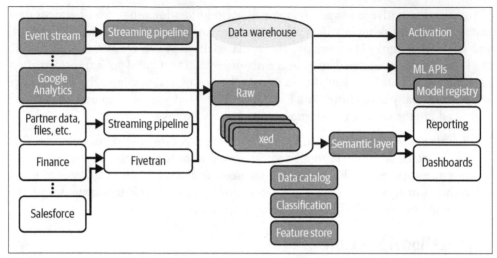

Figure 6-7. The central data engineering team is responsible for the filled shapes, while the business unit is responsible for the unfilled shapes

Figure 6-7 shows Google Analytics, Finance, and Salesforce as illustrative of data sources. In our example, Google Analytics data may be needed across multiple business units and is therefore ingested by the central data engineering team. Finance and Salesforce data is needed only by specific business units and is therefore ingested by that business unit.

Each business unit manages its own deployment. It is the responsibility of the central team to land data into the DWH that the business team uses. This often means that the software that the central team uses needs to be portable across different clouds and the data format that is produced by the pipelines is a portable format. For this reason, Apache Spark and Parquet are common choices for building the ETL pipelines.

If two business units choose to use the same DWH technology, data sharing across those two business units becomes simpler, so, where possible, we recommend using the same DWH technology (BigQuery, Snowflake, Redshift, etc.) across the organization. However, in businesses that grow via acquisitions, this is not always possible. Based on our experience, it is better to use a single cloud technology for your DWH to get the most out of its capabilities across all departments, even if you have a multicloud strategy. We have worked with organizations that were leveraging two or even more technologies, and the effort they put into maintaining alignment among all the systems was not worth the benefits.

In this section you have seen how you can modernize your data platform via the implementation of a hub-and-spoke architecture, putting at the center your DWH. You have understood how multiple spokes can gravitate around the central hub, your modern DWH, to enable whatever use case you want to implement both batch and streaming, leveraging pure SQL language, and to be compliant with data governance requirements. In the next section we discuss how the DWH can enable data scientists to carry out their activities.

DWH to Enable Data Scientists

Data analysts support data-driven decision making by carrying out ad hoc analysis of data to create reports and then operationalize the reports through BI. Data scientists aim to automate and scale data-driven decisions using statistics, ML, and AI. What do data scientists and data science tools need from a modern cloud DWH? As you saw in Figure 6-1, they need to interact with the DWH in various ways to execute queries or to simply get access to the low-level data. In this section we will have a look at the most common tools they can leverage to achieve this goal.

As you saw in the previous chapter, data scientists need to carry out experiments to try out different forms of automation and learn how the automation will work on various slices of historical data. The primary development tools that data scientists use for their experimentation, as we have seen earlier, are *notebooks*. Therefore, they need to have ways to access data in the DWH efficiently. This has to be for both exploratory data analysis through the query interface of the DWH and operationalization through the storage interface of the DWH (please refer to Figure 6-1). It is important to ensure that your cloud DWH supports both these mechanisms. Let's have a look at how these mechanisms work.

Query Interface

Before automating decision making, data scientists need to carry out copious amounts of exploratory data analysis and experimentation. This needs to be done interactively. Therefore, there needs to be a fast way to invoke SQL queries from the notebook.

A Jupyter magic (such as the %%bigquery line in the cell in Figure 6-8) provides a way to invoke SQL queries from the notebook without boilerplate code. The result comes back as a native Python object, called a DataFrame, that can be acted upon using pandas, a library of data analysis functions.

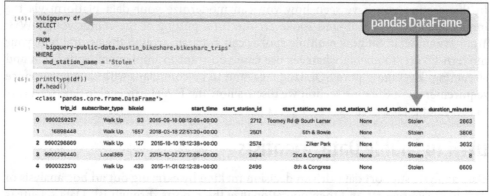

Figure 6-8. From a notebook, you can invoke SQL queries on the DWH without boiler-plate code and get the result back as an object that is easy to work with; in this example we are invoking BigQuery

It is important to note that this is done without creating in-memory extracts of the data. The cloud DWH carries out the SQL queries in a distributed way. The notebook server doesn't need to run on the same computational infrastructure as the DWH.

This combination of using the DWH backend for large-scale data processing and the programmatic and visualization capabilities of the notebook frontend is potent and necessary for data scientists to be productive.

Storage API

While the interactive capabilities of the notebook-DWH connection are important for exploration and experimentation, they are not what you need for automation. For automation, the speed of data access is paramount. It should be possible for ML frameworks to bypass the query API and directly access the storage layer of the DWH. The storage access should support parallel reading from multiple background threads because the common scenario is for the reading of one batch of data to happen while the ML accelerator (GPU or TPU) is carrying out heavy computations on the previous batch.

Instead of using the Query API, therefore, use the Storage API that ML frameworks support to read data efficiently and in parallel out of the DWH. Reading data from Google BigQuery using the Storage API from Spark and TensorFlow is shown in Example 6-5.

Example 6-5. Reading data directly from Google BigQuery using Spark (top) or TensorFlow (bottom) without going through the query layer

```
df = spark.read \
  .format("bigquery") \
```

```
        .load("bigquery-public-data.samples.shakespeare")
def read_bigquery():
    tensorflow_io_bigquery_client = BigQueryClient()
    read_session = tensorflow_io_bigquery_client.read_session(
        "projects/" + PROJECT_ID,
        "bigquery-public-data", "samples", "shakespeare",
        ...,
        requested_streams=2)

    dataset = read_session.parallel_read_rows()
    transformed_ds = dataset.map(transform_row)
    return transformed_ds
```

Query interface and Storage API are the two methods that data scientists use to access the data in the DWH to carry out their analysis. Now there is a new trend to consider—the ability to implement, train, and use an ML algorithm directly in the DWH without having to pull out the data. In the next section we will have a look at how it works.

ML Without Moving Your Data

Some modern cloud DWHs (BigQuery and Redshift, at the time of writing) also support the ability to train ML models on data in the DWH without having to first extract data out. They do this by training simple models in SQL and more complex models by delegating the job to Vertex AI and SageMaker, respectively. Let's have a look at how you can leverage both training and serving (known as *activation*) of your ML algorithm directly from your DWH.

Training ML models

Let's imagine you want to train an ML model to predict whether or not a user will churn given the characteristics of an account and charges on the account: it is possible to do everything leveraging the historical data, as shown in Example 6-6. The types of models trained can be quite sophisticated.

Example 6-6. Develop and train a classification ML model in AWS RedShift, leveraging historical data you already have in the DWH

```
CREATE MODEL customer_churn_auto_model FROM (SELECT state,
            account_length,
            area_code,
            total_charge/account_length AS average_daily_spend,
            cust_serv_calls/account_length AS average_daily_cases,
            churn
    FROM customer_activity
    WHERE  record_date < '2020-01-01'
    )
TARGET churn FUNCTION ml_fn_customer_churn_auto
```

```
IAM_ROLE 'arn:aws:iam::XXXXXXXXXXX:role/Redshift-ML'SETTINGS (
  S3_BUCKET 'your-bucket'
);
```

You can train a recommender system using historical data on what visitors actually purchased, as shown in Example 6-7.

Example 6-7. Develop and train a recommendation ML model in Google BigQuery, leveraging historical data you already have in the DWH

```
CREATE OR REPLACE MODEL bqml_tutorial.my_implicit_mf_model
OPTIONS
 (model_type='matrix_factorization',
  feedback_type='implicit',
  user_col='visitorId',
  item_col='contentId',
  rating_col='rating',
  l2_reg=30,
  num_factors=15) AS
SELECT
 visitorId,
 contentId,
 0.3 * (1 + (session_duration - 57937) / 57937) AS rating
FROM bqml_tutorial.analytics_session_data
```

Example 6-8 shows an anomaly detection system written using just two SQL statements.

Example 6-8. Anomaly detection model developed in SQL in BigQuery

```
CREATE OR REPLACE MODEL ch09eu.bicycle_daily_trips
OPTIONS(
    model_type='arima_plus',
    TIME_SERIES_DATA_COL='num_trips',
    TIME_SERIES_TIMESTAMP_COL='start_date',
    DECOMPOSE_TIME_SERIES=TRUE
)
AS (
    SELECT
        EXTRACT(date from start_date) AS start_date,
        COUNT(*) AS num_trips
    FROM `bigquery-public-data.london_bicycles.cycle_hire`
    GROUP BY start_date
);

SELECT *
FROM ML.DETECT_ANOMALIES(
    MODEL ch09eu.bicycle_daily_trips,
    STRUCT (0.95 AS anomaly_prob_threshold))
ORDER BY anomaly_probability DESC
```

Being able to do ML using just SQL without having to set up data movement opens up predictive analytics to the larger organization. It democratizes ML because data analysts leveraging typical BI tools can now implement predictions. It also dramatically improves productivity—it is more likely that the organization will be able to identify anomalous activity if it requires only two lines of SQL than if it requires a six-month project by data scientists proficient in TensorFlow or PyTorch.

ML training and serving

Training an ML model is not the only ML activity that modern DWHs support. They also support the ability to:

- Export trained ML models in standard ML formats for deployment elsewhere
- Incorporate ML training within the DWH as part of a larger ML workflow
- Invoke ML models as external functions
- Load ML models directly into the DWH to invoke ML predictions efficiently in a distributed way

Let's look at all four of these activities, why they are important, and how a modern DWH supports them.

Exporting trained ML models

ML models trained on data in the DWH can be invoked directly on historical data using ML.PREDICT in a *batch* mode. However, such a capability is not enough for modern applications that require real-time results (e.g., an ecommerce application that, based on the connected user, has to decide which ads to display in the page). It is necessary to be able to invoke the model *online*—that is, as part of a synchronous request for single input or a small set of inputs.

You can accomplish this in Redshift by allowing the model to be deployed to a SageMaker endpoint and in Google Cloud by exporting the model in SavedModel format. From there, you can deploy it to any environment that supports this standard ML format. Vertex AI endpoints are supported, of course, but so are SageMaker, Kubeflow Pipelines, iOS and Android phones, and Coral Edge TPUs. Vertex AI and SageMaker support deployment as microservices and are often used in server-based applications, including websites. Deployment to pipelines supports use cases such as stream data processing, automated trading, and monitoring. Deployment to iOS and Android supports mobile phones, and deployment to Edge TPUs supports custom devices such as the dashboards of cars and kiosks.

Using your trained model in ML pipelines

It is rare that a data scientist's experiment consists of just training an ML model. Typically, an experiment will consist of some data preparation, training multiple ML models, doing testing and evaluation, choosing the best model, creating a new version of the model, setting up an A/B test on a small fraction of the traffic, and monitoring the results. Only a few of these operations are done in the DWH. Therefore, the steps that are done in the DWH have to be part of a larger ML workflow.

ML experiments and their workflows are captured in ML pipelines. These pipelines consist of a number of containerized steps, a few of which will involve the DWH. Therefore, data preparation, model training, model evaluation, etc., have to be invocable as containers when they are part of an ML pipeline.

Pipeline frameworks offer convenience functions to invoke operations on a cloud DWH. For example, to invoke BigQuery as a containerized operation from Kubeflow Pipelines, you can use a BigQuery operator.

Invoking external ML models

ML is the common way nowadays to make sense of unstructured data such as images, video, and natural language text. In many cases, pretrained ML models already exist for many kinds of unstructured content and use cases—for example, pretrained ML models are available to detect whether some review text contains toxic speech. You don't need to train your own toxic speech detection model. Consequently, if your dataset includes unstructured data, it is important to be able to invoke an ML model on it.

In Snowflake, for example, it is possible to invoke Google Cloud's Translate API using an EXTERNAL FUNCTION. You can do this by creating an API integration through a gateway and then configuring Snowflake as demonstrated in Example 6-9.

Example 6-9. Snowflake third-party APIs integration example

```
create or replace api integration external_api_integration
    api_provider = google_api_gateway
    google_audience = '<google_audience_claim>'
    api_allowed_prefixes = ('<your-google-cloud-api-gateway-base-url>')
    enabled = true;
create or replace external function translate_en_french(input string)
    returns variant
    api_integration = external_api_integration
as 'https://<your-google-cloud-api-gateway-base-url>/<path-suffix>';
```

Given this, it is possible to invoke the Translate API on a column from within a SELECT statement:

```
SELECT msg, translate_en_french(msg) FROM ...
```

Loading pretrained ML models

Invoking ML models using external functions can be inefficient because the computation does not take advantage of the distributed nature of the DWH. A better approach is to load the trained ML model and have the DWH invoke the model within its own computing environment.

In BigQuery, you can do this by first loading the TensorFlow model and then invoking it by using `ML.PREDICT` from within a `SELECT` statement as presented in Example 6-10.

Example 6-10. BigQuery loading TensorFlow model stored in Google Cloud Storage and predicting results

```
CREATE OR REPLACE MODEL
  example_dataset.imported_tf_model
OPTIONS
  (MODEL_TYPE='TENSORFLOW',
    MODEL_PATH='gs://cloud-training-demos/txtclass/export/exporter/1549825580/*')
SELECT *
FROM ML.PREDICT(
  MODEL tensorflow_sample.imported_tf_model,
  (SELECT title AS input FROM `bigquery-public-data.hacker_news.stories`))
```

Because `ML.PREDICT` does not require an external call from the DWH to a deployed model service, it is usually much faster. It is also much more secure since the model is already loaded and cannot be tampered with.

Summary

In this chapter we focused on describing how a DWH can be the central core of a modern data platform, analyzing how to leverage a hub-and-spoke architecture to enable data analysis and ML training and activation. The key takeaways are as follows:

- A modern data platform needs to support making insights available to decision makers faster.
- The hub-and-spoke architecture is the ideal architecture for organizations with no legacy technologies to accommodate. All data is landed into the enterprise DWH in as automated a manner as possible.
- Data from a large number of SaaS software can be ingested using prebuilt connectors.
- A DWH can be made to reflect changes made in an OLTP database or ERP system using a CDC tool.

- It is possible to federate data sources such as blob storage, ensuring that some data does not need to be moved into the DWH.

- It is possible to run external queries on SQL-capable relational databases.

- To assist business analysis, invest in a SQL tool that pushes operations to a database instead of relying on extracting OLAP cubes.

- When you have thousands to millions of customers, it's more scalable to provide a lightweight graphics visual layer that can be embedded within the tool that the user is already using.

- Build a semantic layer to capture KPIs, metrics, and dimensions to foster consistency and reuse.

- Views provide a way to make the raw data landed in the DWH more usable. Scheduled queries to extract view content to tables can be more cost-effective. Materialized views provide the best of both worlds.

- Data governance and security are becoming more crucial because data is exploding, architectures are becoming more complex, the number of users accessing and leveraging the data is increasing, and legislators are introducing more stringent rules to handle the data.

- Data scientists need to be able to interactively access the DWH from notebooks, run queries without boilerplate code, and access data in bulk directly from the warehouse's storage.

- Being able to do ML without any data movement and have the resulting ML model be usable in many environments helps foster the use of AI in many parts of the business.

- Organizationally, some data engineering and governance functions are centralized, but different business units transform the data in different ways, and only as and when it is needed.

In the next chapter we will discuss the convergence of the data lake and DWH worlds and see how modern platforms can leverage the best of the both paradigms, giving end users maximum flexibility and performance.

CHAPTER 7

Converging to a Lakehouse

As you know by this point, there are two main approaches that organizations can take when designing their data platform: following a data lake or a DWH paradigm. Both approaches come with pros and cons, but the question is: is it possible to make both technologies coexist to have a convergent architecture? In this chapter we will explore this topic, starting with a brief motivation for this idea, and then we will analyze two broad variants of the convergent architecture—known as the *lakehouse architecture*—and help you decide how to choose between them.

The lakehouse concept is becoming increasingly popular because it allows for a more flexible and scalable way to store and analyze structured, semistructured, and unstructured data at scale. A lakehouse can handle the entire lifecycle of structured and unstructured data, combining the best of the data lake and DWH approaches you learned in the previous two chapters in a governed manner. At the end of this chapter we will describe how to evolve toward the lakehouse architecture.

The Need for a Unique Architecture

Data lakes and DWHs emerged to meet the needs of different users. An organization with both types of users is faced with an unappealing choice.

User Personas

As you have learned in the previous chapters, some key differences between a data lake and a DWH are related to the type of data that can be ingested and the ability to land unprocessed (raw) data into a common location. Therefore, the typical user of these two paradigms is different.

Traditional DWH users are BI analysts who are closer to the business, focusing on deriving insights from data. Data is traditionally prepared by the ETL tools based on the requirements of the data analysts. These users are typically using the data to answer questions. They tend to be proficient in SQL.

Data lake users, in addition to analysts, include data engineers and data scientists. They are closer to the raw data, with the tools and capabilities to explore and mine the data. They not only transform the data to make it accessible by the business (i.e., data that can be transferred to the DWHs) but also experiment with it and use it to train their ML models and for AI processing. These users not only find answers in the data, but they also find the questions that are relevant for the business and prepare the data to make it useful to other users. They tend to be proficient in a coding language such as Python, Java, or Scala.

Antipattern: Disconnected Systems

As a result of these different needs, we often see different IT departments or teams managing the DWH and the data lake. However, this split approach has an opportunity cost: organizations spend their resources on operational aspects rather than focusing on business insights. As such, they cannot allocate resources to focus on the key business drivers or on challenges that would allow them to gain a competitive edge.

Additionally, maintaining two separate systems, both of which have the same end goal of providing actionable insights from data, can cause data quality and consistency problems. The extra effort required to transform data from one system to use it alongside data from the other may put off end users completely. This can also lead to *data puddles* across the enterprise, which are datasets stored on individual's machines, causing both a security risk and inefficient use of data.

Antipattern: Duplicated Data

Why not simply connect the two systems with data being synced by the platform team? You may end up with the architecture represented in Figure 7-1, where the data lake and the DWH coexist to enable self-service analytics and ML environments.

Note that in this architecture the data, which is *centrally managed* by the platform, is the one that resides within the data lake. All the other data (e.g., DWH, BI/reporting tools, notebooks, etc.) can be considered a duplicated/transformed version of the original data that from one side helps with getting better performance and facilitating analysis (e.g., materialized views), but, as you have already seen in the previous chapters, it generates a lot of drawbacks because it leads to the generation of data silos.

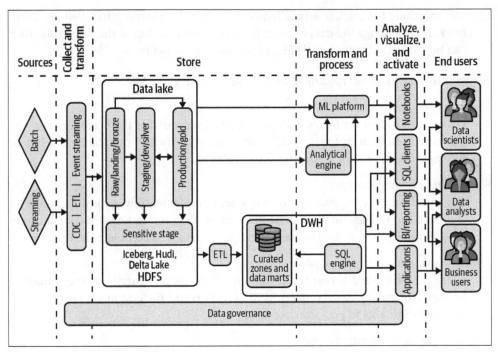

Figure 7-1. Data lake and DWH coexistence

Let's have a look at the main building blocks of the data journey:

1. Data from various sources (batch and/or streaming) is *collected* and *transformed/ wrangled/prepared* (even on the fly) to be *stored* in the data lake, where it will pass by all the different stages (bronze, silver, and gold). Since the beginning, the data is subject to security, data quality, and data governance checks.

2. Data can now be *processed* via the *analytical engine* solutions (e.g., Spark) that interact with SQL clients, batch reporting, and notebooks.

3. The data in parallel can be transformed and ingested into business-specific segments in the DWH, the data marts, to handle BI workloads. Maintaining data marts is a complex and costly activity because it requires a lot of ETL engineering and it is challenging to keep all the needed data up to date. And this has to be done in a perpetual manner. Furthermore, all the data governance activities have to be repeated in the DWH.

4. The DWH powers the BI tools and SQL clients, but sometimes it is not able to give the adequate level of performance requested by the final users, so people tend to download the data, create local copies, and work with that.

5. ML solutions (e.g., scikit-learn, TensorFlow, Keras), generally handled via notebooks, can leverage the data coming from the data lake, but at the same time they can be connected with the DWH and the analytical engine.

An architecture like this typically includes a series of drawbacks:

Proliferation of the data
Data exists in various forms and, potentially, even outside the boundaries of the platform (i.e., local laptops), which may cause *security and compliance risks, data freshness issues,* or *data versioning issues.*

Slowdown in time to market
Organizations may spend up to two weeks implementing a minor change to a report for management because they must first request that data engineers modify the ETLs in order to access the data necessary to complete the task.

Limitation in data size
Users may not have access to all the data they need to carry out their analysis because, for example, data marts in the DWH could include just a subset of the necessary info due to performance needs.

Infrastructure and operational cost
These could increase due to the complexity of ETLs that need to be put in place.

It's bad practice to have duplicated/transformed data like this, and you should minimize it as much as possible. Ideally, you will get rid of duplicates and self-managed data with the goal of having all the data in a platform-managed mode that is available to all of the actors for analysis (i.e., on the right side of the architecture diagram depicted in Figure 7-1).

At this point you may ask yourself why organizations are leveraging this kind of architecture. The reason for this is pretty straightforward: because, as recently as 2018, this was the only way to give to the many different users all the solutions needed to meet their needs.

Technology evolves and, especially thanks to the advent of the cloud, new solutions have been developed to bring better possibilities in terms of data handling. Let's have a look at how we can improve on this combined architecture.

Converged Architecture

By this point, it's clear that a full convergence between data lake and DWH can help final users get the most from their platform and hence from their data. But what is the architecture for such an end state, and what is the path to get there?

Two Forms

The key factor in the converged lakehouse architecture is that the DWH and data lake share a common storage. Two different compute engines—a SQL engine (for DWH use cases) and a distributed programming engine (for data lake use cases)—read and process the data without moving it around.

This common storage can take one of two forms:

- The data is stored in an open source format (Parquet, Avro, etc.) on cloud storage, and you can leverage Spark to process it. At the same time, you can use Spark SQL to provide interactive querying capability (the Databricks solution). In addition, DWH technologies (e.g., BigQuery, Athena, DuckDB, Snowflake, etc.) can support you in running SQL directly on the datasets without any data copying or movement. You can use open source formats combined with a technology such as Delta Lake or Apache Iceberg that improves the underlying performance.

- Alternatively, the common storage can be a highly optimized DWH format (e.g., the native format within BigQuery, Snowflake, etc.) where you can of course natively leverage SQL. In addition, these DWHs support the use of compute engines such as Spark directly on the native data.

Both of these are compromises. Just because the other type of workload is supported does not mean that it is of equal performance. A data lake is slower/costlier on SQL workloads than a data warehouse. And a data warehouse is slower/costlier on Spark and ML workloads than a data lake.

Choose based on user skills

We recommend making the choice between the two forms based on who your primary users are. A SQL engine operating on cloud storage (the first option) loses many of the optimizations that make DWHs interactive and suitable for ad hoc querying. A data lake running SQL (the second option) loses the schema-free data processing capability that makes data lakes so flexible. So choose the form of hybrid architecture based on which type of user and workload you want to support very well and which one you want to support in a compromised way.

At a very high level, the first option is best for users who are proficient programmers. Build a lakehouse with the data lake (i.e., cloud storage) as your storage if the majority of your users are programmers who do a lot of data wrangling in code, such as to write ETL pipelines and to train ML models. The main advantage of data lakes is that they permit flexible data processing by programmers. The second option is best for users who want to interact with the data to gain insights from it. Build a lakehouse with the DWH as your storage if the majority of your users are analysts rather than programmers, by which we mean that they can either write SQL or use a dashboard tool (like Tableau, Power BI, or Looker) that will generate SQL. The main advantage of DWHs is that they permit self-service, ad hoc querying by business users.

Complete evaluation criteria

What we have discussed so far is just a preliminary attempt to identify the right approach for your organization. Other factors include the volume of data to be ingested, whether you need streaming, how much of your data is structured or semi-structured, and whether you work in a regulated industry with heavy data governance needs.

You should list all the features of both data lake and DWH approaches discussed in Chapters 5 and 6 and produce an evaluation matrix, assigning a score from 0 to 5 (0 being less important, 5 being mandatory) to each element. This will help you to have a more cohesive understanding of your needs and make the right choice for your lakehouse approach.

Now that you have a better understanding of the different alternatives you can use to implement your lakehouse, let's take a closer look at both options to better understand how they work behind the scenes.

Lakehouse on Cloud Storage

Separation of compute and storage provides the perfect habitat for a convergence of the data lake and DWH. The cloud provider is able to enable distributed applications for interactive queries by bringing compute to the storage. This allows the cloud provider to allocate storage and compute independently to an organization's jobs, something that is hard to do on premises where machines have to be procured months in advance. The amount of data and the compute required to analyze it can scale dynamically from warm pools of compute clusters. When storage is decoupled from the compute, you can utilize it for many different use cases. The same storage that was once file-based data lakes for structured data can serve as storage and data for the DWH. This key convergence enables you to store data once, utilizing views to prepare the data for each specific use case.

Let's have a look at the foundational elements of such architecture, how to get there, and why it is something that can prepare you for future needs.

Reference architecture

We are utilizing cloud storage (AWS S3, Google Cloud Storage, or Azure Blob Storage) for both the data used by a Spark cluster and the DWH that serves BI reporting.

This enables Spark code that data lake teams spent years perfecting to be run on ephemeral compute clusters that connect to always-available storage. It allows the compute to move to the data, rather than the data to have to be shuffled among local disks (as it would with HDFS). The high throughput of cloud storage unlocks better speed and performance. Both Databricks and the hyperscalers offer Spark clusters as a managed service, further abstracting the required management of the infrastructure.

Convergence of the data lake and DWH (see Figure 7-2) is about simplifying and unifying the ingestion and storage of the data, and leveraging the correct computing framework for a given problem. For structured and semistructured data, writing all of the data as it is streamed into tables using a CDC tool enables users to use simple SQL to transform the data and build logical views to query the information in a way that aligns with business use cases. Because views are heavily leveraged in this pattern, there can be column elimination, partitioning, and logic to optimize the speed of the queries while maintaining a historical ledger of the data streamed into the tables.

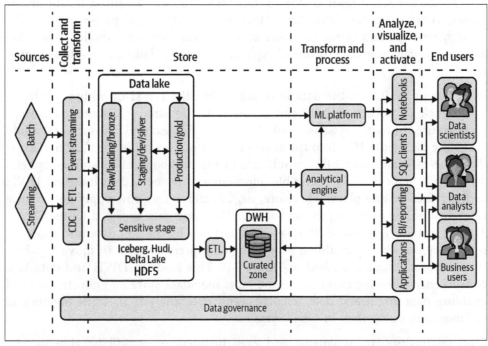

Figure 7-2. Data lakehouse reference architecture—cloud storage approach

Conversely, data that is ingested via a batch pipeline can use a similar approach by which all of the data is written to a table and SQL is used to create views with the most recent version of each record. Like the streaming data, a historical ledger is maintained in the raw tables, allowing data scientists to use all of the data for building and testing ML models. In this architecture, users can leverage scheduled queries or an event-based Lambda architecture for data ingestion.

In contrast to the architecture in Figure 7-1, which has two different engines (i.e., the analytical engine and the inner DWH SQL engine), the reference architecture in Figure 7-2 has a single analytical engine that can access both data lake and DWH data. This is important to note because it allows for a more streamlined and efficient data analysis process.

The main goal of data lakehouse solutions like Dremio and Databricks is to enable high-performance data processing while also supporting analytics and BI directly on the data lake storage. They usually provide a semantic layer that allows you to abstract the underlying data and provide to the analytical engine a view on the data that enables fast query processing without the need to implement data marts.

The *Production/Gold* layer of the project (see Chapter 5) can be the business-driven views or materialized tables that are governed and purpose-built. The underlying logic and storage provide access to end users and applications alike, allowing you to use the converged data platform for Hadoop, Spark, analytics, and ML.

It no longer matters if the data is stored within the DWH or within the freely floating cloud bucket. Behind the scenes it is the similar distributed storage architecture, but data is structured differently. For example, data lakes would move the data from HDFS to the same object storage outside the cluster. This is the same as what cloud EDW would use as the backbone of its storage system. As a result, data is easily accessible and managed by both data lake and DWH architectures in one place. Therefore, organizations can now apply governance rules around data residing in the lake and the same data accessed by the DWH. Thanks to that, you can break down silos not just by putting data into a central repository but also by enabling processing and query engines to move to wherever that data is, as described in Figure 7-3. This leads to DWH and data lake convergence, allowing them to use the same metadata store and governance and enabling data engineers, data scientists, and data analysts to work together in collaboration rather than in siloed systems.

Data engineers, data scientists, and even business users will be able to perform self-serving queries on any kind of data they may have, leveraging one single point of access. And even in terms of development, the work will be easier because there is only one system to interact with instead of a plethora of different tools. Another point in favor of this approach is the centralization of security and governance that is made stronger via the elimination of self-managed copies of the data.

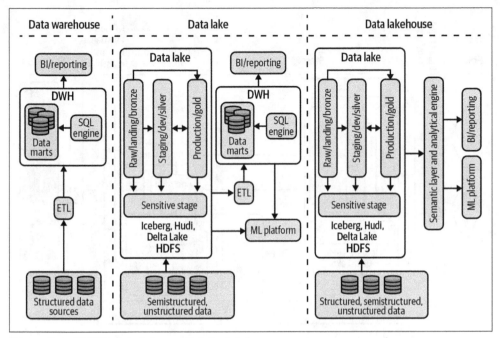

Figure 7-3. DWH, data lake, and data-lakehouse-on-storage approaches

Migration

Moving from the architecture in Figure 7-1 to the one in Figure 7-2 is an iterative process that keeps the data lake but migrates the data warehouse. Start by introducing a single analytical engine that is connected to the data lake storage, to take care of all the data processing, as represented in Figure 7-4. Then, migrate away from the DWH SQL engine through various substeps, following the process described in Chapter 4.

Since this process can take several repetitions, it is important to start by identifying a quick win use case (as covered in Chapter 4) that could demonstrate the benefits of the new solution to create consensus within the organization. From there it will be possible to continue expanding the footprint of the new solution until it becomes the "de facto" analytical engine of the entire platform. A very good place to start is generally the world of interactive queries for data exploration: users can interact with the new engine performing data analysis on a variety of data that spans across the data lake and DWH. They can carry out queries directly with the new tool or via the integration with BI and reporting solutions. Once the benefits of the change become tangible, the old DWH engine can be slowly decommissioned to save costs, reduce complexity, and limit the need to download the data for offline elaboration, as the users will now have access, based on the organizations' data governance rules, to all the data of the company. Of course, brand-new workloads should only be implemented leveraging the new analytical engine.

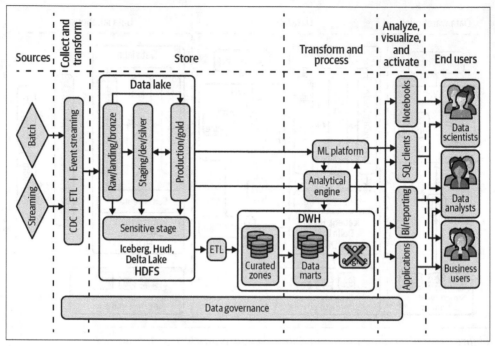

Figure 7-4. Journey to data lakehouse—central analytical engine

Future proofing

Once fully deployed, the interaction with datasets sitting mainly in the data lake and in the DWH (*only the curated ones*) will be bidirectional: that means that the analytical engine will be able to read and write directly on the underlying storage systems that are usually storing the data in an open format like Apache Parquet or Apache Avro. This is a great benefit because the underlying technology can be seen as a consistent and common medium across different types of storage systems. The analytical engine will be flexible enough to use either a schema-on-read approach (that is typical of the data lake pattern) or a more structured approach like the SQL-based data system. Another important benefit that becomes out of the box when adopting a lakehouse architecture is the ease of streaming adoption.

As you will see in the next chapter, real-time access to the data is becoming increasingly important for every kind of business, and the fact that you can treat streaming data in the same way as standard stored data is surely something that can bring additional value. In fact, in this architecture, streaming data pipelines can read and write data in real time, knowing that the underlying technology (e.g., Apache Iceberg, Apache Hudi, or Delta Lake—please refer to "The Evolution of Data Lake with

Apache Iceberg, Apache Hudi, and Delta Lake" on page 136) can ensure full ACID transactions, bringing consistency within the system and always handling the most recent and up-to-date data. You can use these technologies in either a proprietary (e.g., Databricks) or an open source manner on EMR, Dataproc, etc. The final decision of which is the right choice for your organization is up to you. The key factors to consider are flexibility, maintenance, and support.

SQL-First Lakehouse

The main goal of SQL-first lakehouse solutions is to enable high-performance analytics and BI while also supporting flexible data processing with Spark directly on the DWH storage. An advantage of this architecture is that business users can carry out orchestration and ML.

Let us examine the fundamental elements of such architecture, how to achieve it, and why it can be beneficial to you in the future.

Reference architecture

Using a DWH as a data lake of course requires that the DWH solutions are able to handle not only standard SQL queries on tables but also native integration with Spark-based environments, ML capabilities, and streaming features. Modern DWHs like BigQuery, Athena, Synapse, and Snowflake support these capabilities to varying extents that will, no doubt, have improved by the time you are reading this. In Figure 7-5 you can see a reference architecture where the DWH acts as a central analytical engine point for the platform. As you can see from the diagram, the data flows from the original sources (in various forms and velocity) through both the data lake and the native DWH storage. From here you can identify four main storage areas:

- The data lake storage that is equal to what we have seen in the previous section
- The DWH storage split in three dimensions:

  Raw
  The data coming as-is from the various sources (batch or streaming)

  Enriched
  Raw data with a first layer of transformation

  Curated
  Enriched data ready for final transformations

Spark (ETL) or SQL (ELT) can carry out all the transformations.

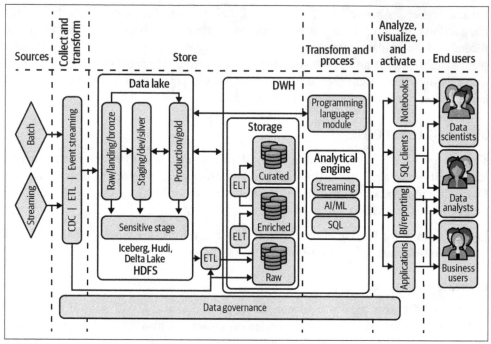

Figure 7-5. Data lakehouse—SQL-first approach

In this approach to building a lakehouse, using SQL is the preferred approach to handling and transforming your data. A SQL-first approach leverages the highly optimized, interactive querying capabilities of the DWH to keep costs down and opens data-driven decision making to business users.

When you need to tackle more advanced data processing, you may be able to leverage a structured programming language like Spark. This is especially true when working with ML algorithms, be it structured data (e.g., boosted tree regression/classification) or unstructured data (e.g., NLP). This is due to the fact that these kinds of operations are not flexible to implement in SQL (inflexible, but not impossible: BigQuery and Redshift SQL have some ML functions today at the time of writing, and other DWHs will no doubt support them shortly). Utilizing Spark also allows you to avoid having to rewrite legacy data processing jobs that may have been written in Spark in SQL.

Modern DWH solutions come with the ability to execute Python, Spark, and even serverless functions directly from their engines and, most importantly, without moving or copying data outside the data store where it resides. BigQuery, for example, achieves this by providing the ability to write stored procedures in Spark, executed in an ad hoc Serverless Spark environment, that can be called in a SQL statement. Snowflake provides Snowpark, a built-in Python engine that is capable of running Spark (and other programming languages). Athena achieves this by operating off standard-format files in formats such as Parquet so that the same data can be read from managed Hadoop environments like EMR. Also, data lake technologies such as Databricks support directly reading and writing to the native warehouse storage through optimized bulk APIs such as the BigQuery Storage API.

One of the key advantages of the data lakehouse paradigm is that it has urged vendors (and the industry in general) to develop increasingly powerful DWHs to make several complex solutions very easy to use for a broad set of users. This is particularly true for ML. Business users can train and deploy ML models leveraging standard SQL code, and they can leverage open source solutions, like dbt, to easily automate and productionize data preparation. It is pretty common nowadays to see business analysts who are, for example, able to autonomously forecast, with a high level of accuracy, customer demand to put in place efficient inventory management or to predict the best price based on historical data.

While the SQL support for ML is great, the majority of the tasks related to ML technology are in the hands of data engineers and data scientists who tend to be more keen to leverage Python frameworks they are more familiar with. Especially when dealing with the development of deep learning models on unstructured data, you need to manipulate massive datasets leveraging open source languages to train models that have to be served to final users. This is why the native integration among the various data sources is playing a pivotal role: the ability to leverage the Spark support is a key feature of the paradigm that gives a high level of freedom to users.

With the proliferation of the development of ML models, another category of operations that the platform has to handle arose: ML operations (MLOps). In MLOps, users want to keep track of the data versioning, data lineage (especially important for audit purposes), and model updates leveraging the same approach adopted in the development of software (i.e., DevOps). Solutions like Databricks MLflow, Google Vertex AI, or Amazon SageMaker are natively connected with modern DWH, giving final users a unified experience when dealing with the ML model lifecycle.

Migration

As with the lakehouse-on-cloud-storage approach, the transition to a SQL-first lakehouse is an iterative process that requires several steps to be fully operational, as represented in Figure 7-6. The first step is to enable data ingestion directly into the DWH: the data sources have to be directly connected not only with the data lake but especially with the three types of DWH storage (i.e., raw, enriched, and curated). Once the data is fully ingested into the central data repository, both in batch and in streaming mode, it is time to cut out external analytical engines, elevating the SQL engine of the DWH as the main one. Here it is pivotal to pay attention to how you're going to move data lake workloads into the DWH, leveraging the built-in programming language module (i.e., Python or Spark engines/connectors) to operate directly on the native storage format. The ML workloads, which initially are still handled outside the DWH, will be insourced as the last iteration of the process.

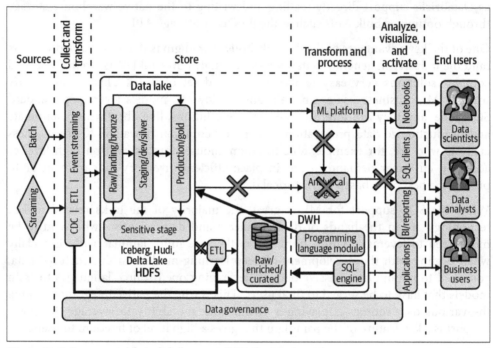

Figure 7-6. Journey to data lakehouse—SQL-first approach

During the phases of the migration, following the SQL-first approach, organizations will discover that a huge number of pipelines will have to be written in SQL.

In this architecture, it is more performant to implement data processing in SQL (although ETL in Spark remains a possibility). This often requires a new type of skill within your organization, termed *analytics engineering*. You may be able to easily find workers skilled in analytics engineering within your organization (refer to "Data Analysis–Driven Organization" on page 76) since SQL is a widespread language (more so than Spark or other programming languages) and can be learned rapidly. In fact, this is a point in favor of democratization because adopting this paradigm will make data access easier for a huge number of employees.

Analytics engineers will be responsible for much of the data enrichment and curation, and they will be able to bring in their domain knowledge and require only SQL skills. The different types of datasets (raw, enriched, and curated) will likely each be utilized by different types of users. In general, most end users, analytical teams, and applications will utilize the curated data, while data engineers and data scientists will probably prefer to access the raw/data lake and enriched data.

In this scenario it is important to note that streaming and ML capabilities are included in the analytical engine: this means that they are natively available to everyone, even to people who are not advanced in writing code in TensorFlow, PyTorch, Keras, or scikit-learn. This is a great achievement in enabling democratization of data and tool access to employees within the organization, and it will enable more and more users to achieve more with their data. Finally, it is important to note that data governance is handled in a federated and transversal way, creating a unified and centralized place to manage, monitor, and govern the data, making it accessible to a variety of users and tools.

Future proofing

Once the migration has been completed and the organization has developed an architecture as outlined in Figure 7-6, the majority of interactions will be SQL based. It is possible to leverage other programming languages for use cases where SQL is difficult or off-the-shelf libraries are available, making the non-SQL option more attractive.

The benefit of a SQL-first lakehouse architecture is huge because it provides a single place for data storage and democratizes access to it via a standard and widely known programming language (SQL) that is supported by a large number of tools used by business users. The major benefit, compared with the cloud storage–based data lakehouse, is exactly this ability to bring a broader set of users closer to the data and allow them to create innovative solutions (i.e., ML)—the more people who have the ability to employ the data (in a governed way), the more innovation your organization will see.

The Benefits of Convergence

If you are a startup or in the fortunate situation of doing greenfield development, start with a pure data lake or a pure DWH, depending on your use case and skill set (see Chapter 3). For everyone else, we recommend the lakehouse architecture. Regardless of whether you choose a lakehouse-on-storage or a SQL-first lakehouse, choosing a lakehouse architecture provides the following benefits:

Time to market
> You can ingest and use data straightaway, whether from batch or real-time data sources. Rather than employing complex ETL pipelines to process data, data is "staged" either in a messaging bus or through object storage. Then it is transformed within the converged DWH/data lakes, enabling users to act as the data is received.

Reduced risk
> You can continue leveraging existing tools and applications without rewriting them. This reduces the risk and costs associated with change.

Predictive analytics

Moving away from the traditional view of data marts and data mining to real-time decision making using fresh data increases business value. This is only possible because the governance and strictness around DWHs have come down, reducing barriers to entry.

Data sharing

The converged environment is now the one-stop shop for all the types of users (i.e., data analyst, data engineer, and data scientist) you may have. They can all access the same managed environment, getting access to different stages of data when they need it. At the same time, different roles can have access to the same data through different layers, and this is governed by platform-wide access rights. This not only increases the data governance but also allows simpler access management and auditing throughout the data ecosystem.

ACID transactions

In a typical DWH, the data integrity is maintained, and multiple users reading and writing the data see a consistent copy of the data. Although ACID is a key feature in the majority of the databases, traditionally it has been rather difficult to provide the same guarantees when it comes to traditional HDFS-based data lakes. There are schemes such as Delta Lake and Apache Iceberg that try to maintain ACID semantics (refer to "The Evolution of Data Lake with Apache Iceberg, Apache Hudi, and Delta Lake" on page 136); they store a transaction log with the aim of keeping track of all the commits made to a data source.

Multimodal data support

Semistructured and structured data are key differentiators with the DWHs and data lakes. Semistructured data has some organizational properties such as semantic tags or metadata to make it easier to organize, but data still does not conform to a strict schema. In the converged world, this is accommodated with extended semistructured data support. On the other hand, for unstructured use cases, data lakes are still required apart from edge cases.

Unified environment

Traditionally, different tools and environments, usually orchestrated by ETLs, manage data capture, ingest, storage, processing, and serving. In addition, processing frameworks such as Spark, Storm, Beam, etc., provide built-in ETL templates to enable organizations to build ETL pipelines. However, with capable cloud EDWs and integrated cloud tools, this pipeline is now all handled by a single environment. ELT does most of the traditional ETL tasks such as cleanse, dedupe, join, and enrich. This is made possible at different stages of the data lake implementation within the DWH. Furthermore, with the support of core DWHs, you can have access through a united environment to concepts such as stored procedures, scripting, and materialized views.

Schema and governance

In reality, business requirements and challenges evolve over time. As a result, the associated data changes and accumulates, either by adapting to new data or by introducing new dimensions. As the data changes, applying data quality rules becomes more challenging and requires schema enforcement and evolution. Furthermore, PII data governance becomes more important as new data sources are added. There needs to be a data governance solution allowing organizations to have a holistic view of their data environment. In addition, it is paramount to have the ability to identify and mask PII data for different purposes and personas.

Streaming analytics

Real-time analytics enables immediate responses, and there would be specific use cases where an extremely low-latency anomaly detection application is required to run. In other words, business requirements would be such that it has to be acted upon as the data arrives on the fly. Processing this type of data or application requires transformation done outside of the warehouse.

Having a single system to manage simplifies the enterprise data infrastructure and allows users to work more efficiently.

Summary

In this chapter we focused on describing how you can mix data lake and DWH technology in a brand-new mixed architecture called a lakehouse. We presented the two most common architectures and how to get there. The key takeaways are as follows:

- There are two main approaches that organizations have followed in designing their data platform: a data lake or a DWH paradigm.

- Both approaches come with pros and cons, but there's a new option: convergence in the form of a lakehouse that allows you to have the best of both worlds.

- There are two possible approaches to take when opting for a lakehouse. Choose between them based on the primary skill set of your developers.

- One approach to a lakehouse is to converge the data lake and DWH to use the same data in cloud storage. The Spark jobs will be changed from using HDFS to read from the cloud. A Spark-based SQL engine is used. Over time, this will lead to the decommission of the DWH engine.

- The second lakehouse option is to move data lake workloads into the DWH and use built-in Python engines or Spark connectors to operate directly on the native storage format.

- There are several benefits of the lakehouse approach: decreased time to market, ability to easily implement predictive analytics and to break down silos and ETL pipelines, schema and governance, and streaming analytics are just a few.

At this point, we have covered the backbone data platform architectures (data lake, data warehouse, and data lakehouse). In the next two chapters, you will learn how to incorporate streaming and edge/hybrid requirements into this architecture.

CHAPTER 8

Architectures for Streaming

In this chapter, you will learn why the industry trend is inexorably away from batch and into streaming. We will discuss different streaming architectures and how to choose between them. We will also do a deeper dive into two of these architectures—micro-batching and streaming pipelines—and discuss how to support real-time, ad hoc querying in both these architectures. Finally, sometimes the reason to do streaming is to autonomously take some action when certain events happen, and we will discuss how to architect such automated systems.

The Value of Streaming

Businesses along the entire technology maturity spectrum, from digital natives to more traditional companies, across many industries are recognizing the increasing value of making faster decisions. For example, consider business A, which takes three days to approve a vehicle loan. Business B, on the other hand, will approve or deny a loan in minutes. That increased convenience will lead business B to have a competitive advantage.

Even better than faster decisions is being able to make decisions *in context*. Being able to make decisions while the event is proceeding (see Figure 8-1) is significantly more valuable than making the decision even a few minutes later. For example, if you can detect a fraudulent credit card when it is presented for payment and reject the transaction, you can avoid a costly process of getting reimbursed.

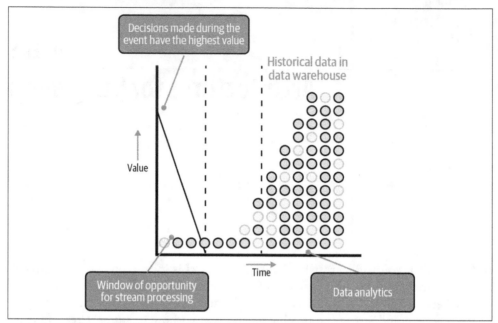

Figure 8-1. The value of a decision typically drops with time; stream processing allows an organization to make decisions in near real time

Industry Use Cases

Whether it is fraud detection, transaction settlement, smart devices, or online gaming, industry after industry has started to adopt streaming.

In healthcare, we see streaming being used for real-time patient monitoring, alerting on falls or self-harm, providing personalized care with IoT medical devices, and optimizing drugs and supply and inventory in hospitals.

In financial services, we see streaming being used to detect and prevent fraud, predict and analyze risk, identify transactions that run afoul of compliance regulations, and deliver personalized offers to customers.

In retail, we see streaming being used for personalized marketing in websites, providing real-time inventory across multiple channels (website, mobile, physical stores), alerting on fulfillment issues, dynamic pricing, product recommendations, and omni-channel customer visibility.

In media and entertainment, we see streaming being used to generate personalized content, deliver targeted ads, minimize customer churn, and prevent subscriber fraud. In telecommunications, we see similar use cases around customer churn and subscriber fraud. In addition, streaming is used to improve network reliability and optimize network capacity planning.

Streaming Use Cases

Think of streaming as data processing on unbounded datasets. Technologically, the challenge with streaming is twofold. One is that the dataset is infinite and never complete. Because of this, all aggregates (such as maxima) can be defined only within time windows. The other is that the data is in motion and held in temporary storage. This makes it difficult to apply conventional programming techniques and concepts such as file handles to read and process the data. Because of this complexity, there is a huge benefit to dividing streaming use cases into four categories in increasing order of complexity and value:

1. *Streaming ingest*
   When you care only about keeping up with the stream of data and landing it in a persistent store.

2. *Real-time dashboards*
   Useful when you wish to visualize data as it comes in. You may also be interested in statistics and charts of time-windowed aggregates of the data.

3. *Stream analytics*
   When you wish to carry out computations on the data as it arrives. Usually, this is to alert human operators about threshold exceedance or abnormal patterns.

4. *Continuous intelligence*
   The automation of stream analytics so that actions can be taken without any human intervention.

In the sections that follow, we will look at the architecture for each of these. You will see that the architecture is quite modular, and you can get away with architecting simple systems and adding complexity as and when additional needs arise. It is not necessary to build the final, most complex, autonomous system to get value from streaming. However, this does assume that you carry out your data processing in frameworks like Apache Beam that will allow you to seamlessly move from batch to stream. While Beam was created by Google as the API for its managed Cloud Dataflow service, Apache Flink and Apache Spark both support Beam. Therefore, you can use managed Flink and Spark implementations on other hyperscalers to run Beam pipelines.

These categories build on one another, so the first one is fundamental to all four types of use cases. To make faster decisions, you need to ingest data in near real time, as the event happens. This is called *streaming ingest*, which we will cover next.

Streaming Ingest

Streaming ingest can be done in two ways:

- You could aggregate events and write only the aggregates (such as hourly averages) to the persistent store. This is called *streaming ETL* because the aggregation is a transformation (the *T* in ETL) and comes between extraction and loading into the persistent store.
- Alternatively, you could ingest (load) the data directly into a data lake or DWH and expect clients to transform the data at the time of analysis. This is called *streaming ELT*.

Let's take a more detailed look at these two approaches in the following subsections.

Streaming ETL

Streaming ingest is sufficient if your goal is to provide the business with more timely data. First of all, you need to focus on *where* the data is ingested in the cloud, because it matters a lot. You need to store the data in a location where you can access it for processing or querying. For queries, it is important to ensure that the results reflect the latest data.

To achieve the goal of real-time insights, therefore, the ingest has to happen into a system that allows real-time ingest and querying. Modern DWHs such as Google BigQuery, AWS Redshift, and Snowflake have this capability. Therefore, commonly, you will carry out streaming ETL into such a DWH, as described in Figure 8-2.

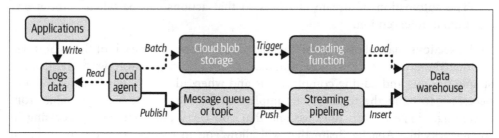

Figure 8-2. Two options for streaming ETL of logs data: micro-batching (shown with dashed lines) or streaming pipeline (shown with solid lines)

The goal of streaming ETL, therefore, is usually to land the data into a DWH. Log data written from multiple applications is read by a local agent that is responsible for making the log's data available for real-time monitoring and querying. You can adapt this same architecture for other types of real-time data, whether from IoT devices or from online games, by recasting what the data is and by using an appropriate local agent.

The local agent can make the data available for real-time querying in one of two ways (see Figure 8-2):

Micro-batching

Data corresponding to, say, the last five minutes is written to a file on cloud blob storage. The arrival of a new file in the cloud blob storage triggers a loading function (such as Google Cloud Functions, Google Cloud Run, AWS Lambda, Azure Functions, etc.). The function can process the data and then load the file into the final destination. Micro-batching involves some latency.

Streaming pipeline

The local agent can publish an event corresponding to each log event to a message queue (such as Kafka) or a topic (such as Cloud Pub/Sub). These events are pushed to a streaming pipeline (such as AWS Glue or Google Cloud Dataflow) that processes the events and inserts them into the final destination. This makes the event immediately available for querying.

The role of the loading function or streaming pipeline is to process the data to make it much more usable by downstream users and applications. Typically, you would leverage data processing to:

- Convert event data into the schema required by the DWH table
- Filter event records to keep only the data specific to the business unit that operates the DWH
- Interpolate or otherwise fill in missing values in events (e.g., you would use the most recently valid value)
- Connect events across time (e.g., you would leverage identity resolution methods to connect events into user sessions, and even across sessions)
- Aggregate events into more consumable chunks—for example, writing out time averages (e.g., total page visits over the past minute rather than every page visit) or per session values (e.g., one record noting which buttons were clicked in a session rather than separate events for every button click)
- Enrich the data with additional sources (e.g., currency conversion)
- Mask, encrypt, or otherwise protect sensitive fields

If you do not need to perform any of the aforementioned activities and the loading function is simply a pass-through, consider whether you can use the streaming ELT approach in the next section.

When leveraging the micro-batching approach, it is helpful to understand where the latency comes from. The obvious culprit is that data loaded into the DWH could be five minutes old in our example. But that is usually not the big problem. If a 5-minute latency is unacceptable, you can go down to 30 seconds. The real problem is that the

DWH load jobs are queued, so they may not happen immediately. Check the SLA of your DWH for what this delay could be. Usually, this loading delay is what makes micro-batching in stream ingest unacceptable for many use cases. It is, however, a valid architecture if the batches consist of, say, daily data and an hour's latency in loading is acceptable.

The micro-batching approach is usually less expensive than the streaming pipelines one. Some DWHs (notably Google BigQuery) have a pricing tier where loading data is free. Even in DWHs like Snowflake that charge for both loading and inserts, inserts are more expensive and require a higher tier. Additionally, you only pay the computational cost of loading while the function is running. Especially if you are loading data once a day, the computational cost of micro-batching can be quite minimal. Autoscaling in AWS Glue and Cloud Dataflow do close the gap as the frequency of micro-batching increases.

We've covered the first of the two approaches mentioned earlier. Now let's move on to the second: streaming ELT.

Streaming ELT

The streaming ETL approach you have learned before assumes that you can anticipate the kind of cleanup, aggregation, or enrichment that the consumer of the data will need. After all, you are transforming the raw data before writing it to the DWH. This could be a lossy operation. As the number of consumers of the data grows and it becomes impossible to anticipate the kinds of transformation different consumers need, many organizations switch their data pipelines from streaming ETL to streaming ELT. Streaming ELT is also a better fit than streaming ETL if the transformations require business-specific knowledge and are better carried out by business users rather than programmers.

In streaming ELT (see Figure 8-3), the local agent directly loads or inserts the raw data into the DWH. Consumers of the data can apply whatever transformations they require. In some cases, you can provide logical or materialized views of the data to make it convenient to data consumers.

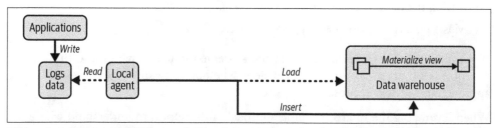

Figure 8-3. Streaming ELT can also be done in micro-batches (dashed lines) or as events happen (solid lines)

The big drawback of streaming ELT is that the amount of data being written to the DWH can be large—the transformation step in many ELT pipelines significantly thins the data and writes only aggregate data to the DWH. Therefore, streaming ETL versus ELT is very much a decision that you make based on business value and cloud costs.

Counterintuitively, the more data you have, the more cost-competitive streaming ELT becomes. As the data volume gets larger, it makes more sense to process the data *more* frequently. To see why, imagine that a business is creating a daily report based on its website traffic and this report takes two hours to create. Now suppose that the website traffic grows by 4x. The report will now take eight hours to create. How do you get back to two hours? Well, fortunately, these are embarrassingly parallel problems. So autoscale the job to 4x the number of machines. What if, instead, we consider an approach that makes the reports more timely?

- Compute statistics on six hours of data four times a day.
- Aggregate these six hourly reports to create daily reports.
- You can now update your "daily" report four times a day.
- The data in the report is now only six hours old.

This is, of course, the micro-batching idea. The computational cost of both these approaches is nearly the same. Yet the second approach reduces latency, increases frequency, spreads out the load, and handles spikes better. Plus, the organization gets more timely, less stale reports, which can provide huge business benefits for almost no extra cost. The more data you have, the more sense it makes to go from six-hour reports to hourly updates, to minute-by-minute updates, to real-time updates. Once you need near-real-time updates to multiple consumers, streaming ELT becomes a very attractive option.

Streaming Insert

In Figures 8-2 and 8-3, we assumed that we needed a local agent that would look at available data and load or insert the data into the persistent store. It is not necessary to have this intermediary—if the DWH provides a streaming API, a cloud native application may disintermediate the local agent and use a cloud client library to do the insert itself (see Figure 8-4).

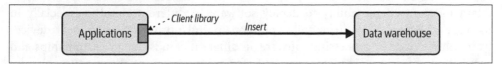

Figure 8-4. Streaming ELT in a cloud native application can take advantage of client libraries to directly insert the data

For example, in BigQuery, a streaming insert involves a REST API call and can be accomplished in Python. Snowpipe Streaming provides this capability in Snowflake, but in Redshift, you have to use a pass-through transformation step in Kinesis.

Some messaging systems (e.g., Google Pub/Sub) also offer specific subscription types that load events into the DWH as they happen, so applications can simply publish events to the messaging topic or queue and have the events show up in the DWH in real time.

Streaming from Edge Devices (IoT)

In Figure 8-2, we assumed that events in streaming ETL would be published to a general-purpose message queue such as Kafka from a custom local agent.

In the case of Internet of Things (IoT), cloud providers usually have a more targeted solution (see Figure 8-5). Azure provides IoT Devkit for edge software and IoT Hub for the remote cloud component. On AWS, the local agent will use software that has prebuilt AWS IoT Greengrass components, and the remote queues will be managed by AWS IoT Core. On Google Cloud Platform, the edge components might consist of Coral devices and TensorFlow Lite software, while the remote cloud component might be Clearblade IoT Core.

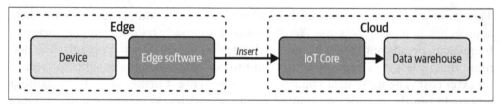

Figure 8-5. For streaming data from IoT devices on the edge, make use of IoT-specific functionality

You can use the provided edge software development kit (SDK) and devices to do local processing, data management, ML inference, etc. Leveraging the provided remote cloud component, you can activate bespoke functionalities such as device management, and you can transparently handle situations such as unreliable networks, device restarts, etc.

Regardless of the cloud provider, the edge SDKs will support standard protocols such as MQTT in addition to proprietary ones. Choose a standard protocol to retain for yourself the ability to deploy software to different clouds—especially in the case of edge devices, it is quite common to end up having to support devices from other clouds or processing software on different clouds due to partnerships and acquisitions. If using Greengrass on AWS, for example, you might want to consider using the MQTT broker Moquette to ensure portability.

Streaming Sinks

In Figures 8-2 and 8-3, we assumed that we needed to land the streaming data into a DWH to support interactive querying. This is not necessarily the case. There are two exceptions: unstructured data and high-throughput streams.

If you are streaming video, then disregard all the above and use a framework meant for video. On the edge, your video camera will support a live streaming protocol such as Real-Time Streaming Protocol or WebRTC. Use this to send the live video feed to the cloud. On Google Cloud, Cloud Video Intelligence will convert from the live streaming protocol to a decodable video stream and write the stream to files on cloud storage. On AWS, Kinesis Video Streams provides a similar integration with AWS SageMaker and publishes ML inference results to Kinesis Data Streams. Similarly, Azure Video Indexer allows you to extract insights from video.

DWHs are a general-purpose answer for persistent storage and interactive, ad hoc querying. However, DWHs are not a good solution for high-throughput and/or low-latency situations. Typical throughput supported by DWH streaming inserts is on the order of a gigabyte per second, and typical latencies are on the order of seconds. If you want to stream terabytes of data per second or want millisecond latencies, then DWHs are not a good choice. Use Cloud Bigtable on Google Cloud or DynamoDB on AWS instead. Of course, these are NoSQL databases, so you are trading off the convenience of SQL for the real-time ingest and querying. Conversely, do not choose Bigtable or DynamoDB if your scale or performance needs do not reach these levels: a SQL solution will be less expensive in terms of both infrastructure and required skills.

It is also possible to stream to files on cloud blob storage if immediate querying is not a concern or if your architecture consists purely of a data lake rather than being a data lakehouse (see Chapter 7). Apache Beam, for example, can be used to store unstructured or semistructured data on Google Cloud Storage. When doing so, it is important to decide how to shard the files—stream processing frameworks will automatically shard the files once the files reach a certain size, but these will be essentially based on timestamp (since records are getting streamed out), and this may not be suitable for your needs.

Real-Time Dashboards

Regardless of whether you are storing aggregate data or landing real-time data into the DWH, you may want to provide decision makers with the ability to visualize the data as it is coming in. You can do this through *real-time dashboards*.

Live Querying

The dashboard tools periodically query the DWH as to which events are landed and update their graphics. This architecture requires that the dashboard push down the query to the cloud DWH (see Figure 8-6). In other words, all queries are "live" and reflect the latest data in the DWH.

Figure 8-6. Dashboards periodically query the DWH using SQL

Earlier approaches such as data cubes and data marts—which involve materializing the subset or aggregate of DWH data used by the graphics—are no longer necessary. Even though dashboard tools like Tableau have the capability to create and maintain extracts, it is preferable to query the DWH live—modern cloud DWHs can handle it.

If your DWH offers convenience or performance features tailored for dashboards (such as caching of datasets in memory, time-bound caching of queries, optimizations to return previous query results if the data has not changed, etc.), you should turn them on. For example, in Google BigQuery, turn on BI Engine. In AWS Redshift, use dense compute nodes because these are tailored for the heavier compute that dashboards will impose.

Materialize Some Views

It is preferable that you do not have complex SQL querying code in the dashboard tool. Create views that retrieve the required data and have the dashboard tool query the view. Reuse query logic among views through user-defined SQL functions.

If you discover that some views are accessed very often, convert the view to be a materialized view (see Figure 8-7). This provides the performance benefit of dashboard-maintained database extracts without the extra governance burden posed by datasets floating around the organization.

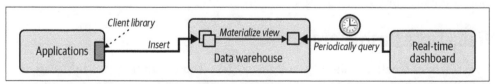

Figure 8-7. Use materialized views for frequently requested extracts

Do not go overboard, however: paraphrasing Knuth, premature optimization remains the cause of much evil. Minimize the use of materialized views and allow most queries to happen live. Materialized views add storage costs, and they add a lot of unnecessary expense if the particular extract is rarely displayed.

Stream Analytics

When implementing a dashboard, you may need to go beyond just displaying data. You may need to display alerts, useful to the decision makers, that are based on automatically extracted insights and predictions. This is called *stream analytics*. You can determine if an alert is warranted via the computation of analytics on an event-by-event basis or on a time-based schedule. Doing it as the event arrives is better, and to do this, you will need a streaming pipeline. If you choose to do it on a time-based schedule, micro-batching is sufficient.

Streaming analytics is useful in these situations:

Time-series analytics
> To track assets, predict impact of events, and do predictive maintenance

Clickstream analysis
> To make real-time offers, create dynamic websites, and optimize a customer journey

Anomaly detection
> To predict equipment failure, prevent fraud, and monitor system health

We'll look at each of these respectively as we progress through this section. The architecture for these situations can serve as a template for other streaming analytics use cases that you may have—you will end up writing to both topics and dashboards as in time-series analytics, using a backfill pipeline as in clickstream analytics, or using multiple time windows as in anomaly detection.

Time-Series Analytics

The most common application of stream analytics is to validate data values periodically or to compute time-based averages.

For example, suppose a physical asset (such as a delivery vehicle) streams its location to the cloud and we would like to analyze the location of the asset and alert if:

- The asset moves out of some predetermined geographic area
- The asset's speed is above some predetermined limit for the location that it is in

The architecture of this use case is shown in Figure 8-8.

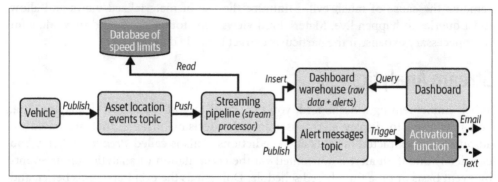

Figure 8-8. Architecture for time-series analytics

You can land the location data in real time into the DWH through an ETL pipeline that is pushed new location information from an event stream (Kafka, Pub/Sub, etc.). The streaming pipeline (implemented in technology such as AWS Glue, Google Cloud Dataflow, Apache Flink, etc.) processes the real-time stream, validates the location, and writes alerts to a special topic. An activation function then is triggered on new events to this topic and takes care of sending the alerts via email, text, etc., to interested parties.

The stream processor is capable of applying time windows to the incoming event stream to compute statistics like the average speed. It is also capable of obtaining static values from a database (such as the speed limit in any specific location). Therefore, it is also capable of carrying out the second computation and alerting on it as well.

It is a best practice to write alert messages not only to the alert topic but also to the EDW. In order to provide users control over what alerts they receive, it is better to not have the streaming pipeline directly send emails or text messages. This separation of responsibility also allows you to build dashboards that can show the frequency of such alerts and permit users to explore the alerts and hopefully recognize a pattern.

Clickstream Analytics

A clickstream consists of the sequence of events (such as button clicks, page views, etc.) carried out by visitors within an application or website. To collect this data, organizations instrument their websites so that user activities invoke a web action that, in turn, ends up in a DWH. As a lot of business has moved online, it has become possible for organizations to gain insights into customer behavior based on the clickstream.

While it is possible to write custom JavaScript code for such instrumentation and collect and process the data in a custom streaming pipeline, it is much more common to use prebuilt tooling such as Google Marketing Platform or Salesforce Marketing Cloud. Google Marketing Platform consists of Google Tag Manager, which is how you instrument your website, and Google Analytics, which collects this information and provides a way to export clickstream data into Google BigQuery, from where you can transfer it to any other DWH. You can use connectors from companies such as Fivetran to similarly export data from Salesforce Marketing Cloud to the desired DWH. Also check whether your SaaS software provides the capability to synchronize its internal data with a DWH. Salesforce, for example, offers this capability for Snowflake and BigQuery.

Once the data is in a DWH, you can analyze it using SQL. Clickstream data is used for A/B testing, tracking changes in item popularity, and identifying sales friction. You can do all these through appropriately crafted SQL. However, the processing code will handle situations such as:

- Customers who start on one device and finish the transaction on another. The automatic session tracking may not capture this unless the customer is logged in on both devices. In general, user identification is a challenge, since only a small subset of users will be logged in. Every other mechanism (cookies, device IDs, IP addresses, etc.) fails quite frequently and can be improved upon if you have more data. The combined use of all the data available across all channels to tie together what is likely the same user is called *identity stitching*. The lakehouse where the resulting set of unique user IDs and corresponding attributes is stored is called a *Customer Data Platform* (CDP).

- Privacy compliance, which will often require that collected data is appropriately anonymized and user data aggregated in such a way that individual actions cannot be identified. It is quite common that you will have to redact information from text fields filled out by users.

- Activity by automated agents such as spiders (search bots) and bad actors looking for security vulnerabilities.

This kind of processing is hard to do in SQL. Because of these situations, even when prebuilt CDPs such as Segment or Bloomreach are used, it is common to build a postprocessing "backfill" pipeline to handle cases that are unique to your organization (see Figure 8-9). This streaming pipeline might be able to do a better job of identity stitching, privacy aggregation, and bot detection than the more general-purpose code provided by the prebuilt tools. At the same time, the pipeline might be able to enrich the clickstream feed based on other data sources within the organization (such as information about customers, products, prices, inventory levels, etc.). It is this backfilled, postprocessed data that you can use for further analysis.

If you use the clickstream data to build personalization or recommendation systems, it is necessary to also take actions while the customer is on the website. This will fall under the continuous intelligence use case, which we cover later in this chapter.

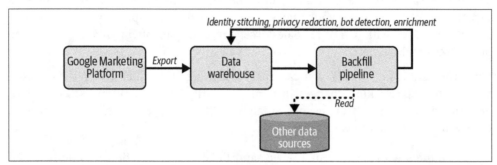

Figure 8-9. Use a backfill pipeline to enrich clickstream data and improve identity stitching, privacy redaction, and bot detection

Anomaly Detection

Anomaly detection involves identifying unusual patterns as the data is arriving. In any situation where you have a lot of data on what "usual" behavior looks like, but it is hard to write specific rules on what abnormal activity looks like (because bad actors keep changing their attack mechanism or because the environment is subject to change), anomaly detection can be very useful. Anomaly detection is used to detect mispriced items (all of a sudden, the popularity of an item shoots up), overloaded equipment, bot activity in online games, security threats, etc.

A signature-based pattern is the primary technique used by many organizations to identify viruses and other cybersecurity threats. In a signature-based pattern, the system leverages repositories of viruses detected in the past against new menaces. However, it is difficult to detect new attacks using this technique because no pattern or signature is available. When using anomaly detection, you usually cluster incoming data over, say, the past three days (see Figure 8-10). Any events that are far from existing clusters are assumed to be suspect. This allows for the environment to adapt (since clustering is done only on the most recent three days of data), and it allows you to identify abnormal patterns as long as they are not already too widespread.

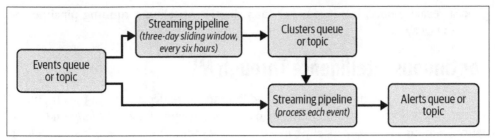

Figure 8-10. Anomaly detection involves two streaming pipelines: one to compute clusters within a sliding window and a second to compare incoming events against the clusters

Resilient Streaming

When ingesting and processing streaming data, there will be malformed data that you receive or unexpected data values that you do not know how to process.

In batch processing, it is common to simply throw an exception and expect the programmer to find the logic error, fix it, and rerun the batch job. However, in stream processing, the pipeline needs to continue running. You also don't want to just ignore errors.

Therefore, it is crucial that every streaming analytics job sets up a dead-letter queue to store any events that were unable to be processed. You can periodically inspect these dead-letter queues and (as with batch jobs) fix the logic errors.

Once you have fixed the logic error, you have to update the currently running streaming pipeline without any data drops. Tools like Cloud Dataflow provide the ability to *update* a running pipeline in place or to *drain* the event queue and seamlessly transfer processing to a new pipeline.

Updating a running pipeline keeps in-flight data and resumes processing within the new pipeline. To do this, it reuses the persistent store from the old pipeline for the updated pipeline. As a result, the two streaming pipelines must meet certain compatibility requirements. If you are in a situation where compatibility is maintained, you should follow this approach because you can achieve exactly-once semantics. Events will be processed exactly once (i.e., either the old one or the new one), and aggregates will be accurate.

If the pipelines are not compatible (perhaps because the bug fix changed the data transmitted between steps), the next best approach is to drain the existing pipeline before starting the new pipeline. The existing job stops pulling from its input sources and completes processing of all in-flight and buffered data, causes triggers to emit the contents of open windows, and sends new events to the new pipeline. Draining pipelines is essential to ensure at-least-once processing semantics—this is not as good as exactly-once, but it is better than simply canceling a running pipeline and throwing away data.

Continuous Intelligence Through ML

It is not necessary to have a human in the loop to make decisions. As the amount of data grows, it is very common to move to a system of *human over the loop*. In this situation, actions are automatically carried out in response to real-time insights, alerts, and predictions. A human supervisor can override an action that would otherwise be automatically applied, but a system is designed to operate autonomously without any human intervention. This is known as *continuous intelligence*.

To enable the system to operate autonomously, you will need to automate the following:

- Train an ML model on historical data, and retrain the model on subsequent data if necessary.
- Invoke the trained ML model as events come in. This is called *inference*.
- Take actions based on the prediction of the ML model.

Let's look at some considerations for each of these steps.

Training Model on Streaming Data

ML models are trained on historical data. How much data should you train the model on? This depends on the problem at hand. The general guidance is that you should only train the model on data that is similar to what it will encounter once it is put into production. Moreover, data from several years ago is often from a completely different context and may capture trends and relationships that are not relevant today.

Therefore, when training an ML model on streaming data, you are unlikely to train the model on the entire historical archive. Instead, you are interested in training on recent data, where "recent" refers to data that has the same characteristics as data that you are about to receive. "Recent" in this context could be the past three days (as in our anomaly detection example, shown in Figure 8-10) or the past three years in unchanging environments.

Windowed training

If you are training very frequently and the training data consists of relatively small time periods, you can use a sliding window streaming pipeline as in Figure 8-11. This is extremely common when you are extrapolating time series (such as doing demand prediction solely on the historical demand cycle).

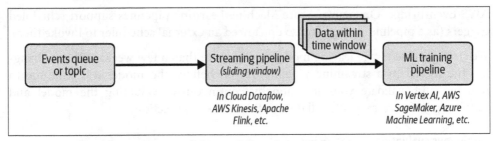

Figure 8-11. Training on events within a sliding time window

What you need for this is:

- A streaming pipeline to create a dataset consisting of data within the time window.
- An automated training pipeline in Google Cloud Vertex AI, AWS SageMaker, Azure Machine Learning, etc., that is parameterized in terms of where it obtains the training data. (The training pipeline also deploys the model to an endpoint, as we will discuss in "Streaming ML Inference" on page 215.)

Note that the word "pipeline" here refers to different things. The streaming pipeline involves processing of data in motion, whereas the training pipeline consists of ML operations (preprocessing data, training model, evaluating model, deploying model, etc.). We will discuss ML pipelines in greater detail in Chapter 11.

Scheduled training

For situations where a trained model will be valid for a moderately long time period (on the order of days to weeks), you can use a scheduled job to initiate training, as described in Figure 8-12. The training job will retrieve data from the DWH or other persistent store corresponding to the past month, for example.

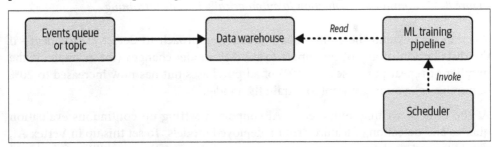

Figure 8-12. Scheduled training

You can schedule a Vertex AI ML training pipeline on Google Cloud using Google Cloud Scheduler. On AWS, scheduling a SageMaker pipeline is a supported target in

AWS EventBridge. On Azure, Azure Machine Learning pipelines support scheduled triggers (as a pipeline setting) and so don't need an external scheduler to invoke them.

We strongly discourage leaving models going more than a few weeks without changing the model in a streaming pipeline. If you believe the model will continue to remain valid, validate your intuition by continuously evaluating the model and retraining it if necessary. We will discuss this in the next section.

Continuous evaluation and retraining

The most complex situation is using a model until you determine it is no longer fit for purpose. To determine that the model has *drifted* in performance, you will need to employ *continuous evaluation*. For example, if you have a model to predict whether a user will buy an item, you could verify a few days later if the user has bought the item in question. You can then carry out a weekly evaluation of the model based on predictions made two weeks ago and for which the true answer is now available. When the evaluation metric drops below some preset threshold, the model can be retrained (see Figure 8-13).

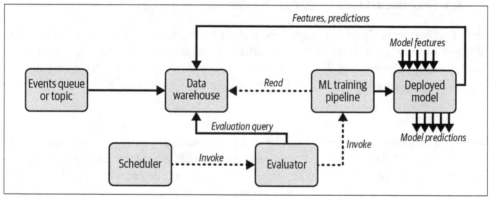

Figure 8-13. Continuous evaluation to automatically initiate retraining

You can also extend the continuous evaluation approach to detect *feature drift*—if the distribution of any of the inputs to the ML model changes (for example, if the number of repeat purchases was 10% of all purchases but has now increased to 20% of purchases), you might want to retrain the model.

At the time of writing, only Vertex AI supported setting up continuous evaluation queries and detection of feature drift on deployed models. To set this up in Vertex AI, you will need to define an evaluation query and turn on the capability of deployed models to write out a sample of features and corresponding predictions to the DWH. Periodically run the evaluation query and use the resulting metric to determine whether the pipeline needs to be invoked.

Consult your cloud provider documentation on whether this scenario is now supported. If it is, the mechanism is likely to be somewhat similar. If not, you will have to build the corresponding pipelines and capabilities in a bespoke way.

Streaming ML Inference

Normally, you invoke the trained ML model as events come in and obtain ML predictions for those events.

It is possible to load the model object into the streaming pipeline and call the prediction signature of the model. This is usually the most efficient way to invoke ML predictions. However, it doesn't scale beyond small models and projects.

For example, the ML prediction may be required by non-Python code and by programs that are running on hardware that doesn't have GPUs (e.g., think about an industrial machine that has to automatically identify whether the item in the assembly line has defects or a web server that needs to reject toxic reviews). To handle these situations, the model is usually deployed to an endpoint so that it can be invoked as a microservice. The model will then be invoked by sending an HTTP request to it, with the input to the ML model being the payload.

ML inference is not efficient if it is invoked one event at a time. Because modern ML frameworks are based on matrix operations, they are much more efficient if you pass in a small batch of events for inference. This is what is shown in Figure 8-14.

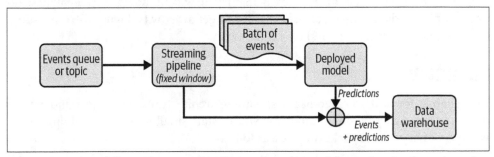

Figure 8-14. Streaming inference typically involves accumulating a batch of events and sending them to a deployed model for inference

Automated Actions

If all that is required is that human users be able to view the predictions of the ML model and make decisions, it is sufficient to land the predictions in a DWH, as shown in Figure 8-15. However, what if you need the system to autonomously take some action based on the prediction of the ML model? You could use an ML model for a task that requires automation, such as to automatically issue a coupon to the person who's likely to abandon the shopping cart or to create a ticket to change an about-to-fail part on a machine. You can invoke these actions in a serverless way through cloud functions like Lambda, Fargate, Google Cloud Functions, Google Cloud Run, or Azure Functions. To support this, you will need to write out a subset of the enriched events meeting alerting criteria to a place from which you can trigger the cloud function (see Figure 8-15).

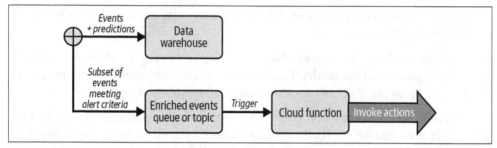

Figure 8-15. Supporting automated actions—this diagram is a continuation of Figure 8-14

We have looked at a number of streaming use cases and scenarios and how they can be architected and implemented using cloud native technologies. Compose the architecture for your own streaming solution based on what your needs are. For example, if you will be doing ML on streaming data, you will choose one of the training architectures in Figures 8-11, 8-12, and 8-13 and combine it with the inference architecture of either Figure 8-14 or 8-15. If you will be doing only analytics, do not complicate the architecture—see if you can get away with Figure 8-8, and add a backfill architecture (Figure 8-9) only if necessary.

Summary

This chapter focused on cloud native streaming architectures, where you understood that they are highly modular and allow you to start small and add capabilities only when necessary. The key takeaways are as follows:

- In many industries, being able to make decisions while the event is proceeding is significantly more valuable than making the decision even a few minutes later.
- Streaming architectures are quite modular, and you can get away with architecting simple systems and adding complexity as and when additional needs arise.
- Streaming ingest is sufficient if the goal is to provide the business with more timely data.
- Micro-batching is usually less expensive than streaming pipelines, but streaming pipelines make the event immediately available for querying whereas there is latency (greater than the chunking frequency) involved in micro-batching.

- As the number of consumers of the data grows and it becomes impossible to anticipate the kinds of transformation different consumers need, many organizations switch their data pipelines from streaming ETL to streaming ELT.

- If the DWH provides a streaming API, a cloud native application may disintermediate the local agent and use a cloud client library to do the insert itself.

- For streaming data from IoT devices on the edge, make use of IoT-specific functionality such as edge SDKs and edge hardware devices.

- DWHs are not a good solution for high-throughput and/or low-latency situations. In such situations, use NoSQL analytics stores such as Cloud Bigtable or DynamoDB.

- Have your dashboard tool push down the query to the cloud DWH, create views for reuse, and materialize some views to optimize performance/cost.

- In time-series analytics, write alerts to an alert topic and to the DWH to support both autonomous actions and human exploration.

- Use a prebuilt tool for clickstream analytics, but supplement it with a backfill pipeline to enrich clickstream data and improve identify stitching, privacy redaction, and bot detection.

- Anomaly detection involves two streaming pipelines: one to compute clusters over long time periods and the other to compare incoming events to the most recent clusters and raise an alert.

- For resilient streaming, make sure that you update running pipelines. If updating is not possible, drain them. Do not simply cancel a running production pipeline.

- If you are training very frequently and the training data consists of relatively small time periods, use a sliding window streaming pipeline to supply training data to the ML training pipeline.

- For situations where a trained model will be valid for days to weeks, a scheduled job can be used to initiate training.

- To determine whether a deployed model has drifted in performance, you will need to employ continuous evaluation.

- Because modern ML frameworks are based on matrix operations, they are much more efficient if you pass in a small batch of events for inference.

- To support autonomous actions, you will need to write out a subset of the enriched events (events + predictions) meeting alerting criteria to a topic on which a cloud function is triggered.

In the following chapter, you will see an overview of approaches and techniques for distributed architectures focusing on edge computing, a pattern that can reduce latency, increase security, and lower costs.

CHAPTER 9

Extending a Data Platform Using Hybrid and Edge

So far in this book, we have discussed how to plan, design, and implement a data platform using the capabilities of a public cloud. However, there are many situations where a single public cloud will not be enough because it is inherent to the use case for data to originate at, be processed at, or be stored in some other location—this could be on premises, in multiple hyperscalers, or in connected intelligent devices such as smartphones or sensors. In situations like these, there is a new challenge that needs to be addressed: how do you provide a holistic view of the platform so that users can effectively mix and join the data spread across different places? In this chapter you will learn the approaches, techniques, and architectural patterns that your organization can take when dealing with such distributed architectures.

Furthermore, there are other situations where you need to make your data work in a partially connected or disconnected mode environment. You will learn in this chapter how to deal with such a situation leveraging a new approach, called *edge computing*, that can bring a portion of storage and compute resources out of the cloud and closer to the subject that is generating or using data itself.

Why Multicloud?

As a data leader, your organization wants you to continuously look for ways to boost business outcomes while minimizing the technology costs you incur. When it comes to data platforms, you are expected to manage the entire data lifecycle by adopting the best solution available in the market, or at least the one best suited to the business's needs.

A Single Cloud Is Simpler and Cost-Effective

Consolidating your entire software architecture on a single cloud provider is very appealing for several reasons:

Simplicity
> When using a single cloud provider, the resulting technology stack is much simpler and more streamlined. It is often the case that services within a cloud are natively integrated. For example, on Google Cloud, the DWH tool (BigQuery) can natively read data from the managed relational database (Cloud SQL) with no data movement. There is similar zero-ETL integration between Redshift and Aurora on AWS and between Azure SQL Data Warehouse and Azure SQL Database (via Azure Synapse Link).

Learning curve
> When you have only one cloud, it is easier for employees to move around within the organization. Onboarding new employees becomes easier, and it is easier for staff to use tools built in other parts of the organization.

Cost
> Using a single cloud provider makes everything from security to contracting simpler. The cost savings on IT and legal services alone can make a single cloud the best choice. Because cloud providers provide discounts based on usage, it is possible to extract larger discounts by consolidating all technology expenditure in one provider.

For these reasons, we recommend that small and medium-sized businesses choose a single cloud provider and design their architecture using fully managed services available on that hyperscaler.

Multicloud Is Inevitable

We find lots of organizations that may want to be on a single cloud but end up with a hybrid or multicloud environment. Why?

Acquisitions
> Even if your organization started out with a single cloud, you may acquire a company that runs its entire technology stack on another cloud. Now, you are a multicloud shop. This is the most common scenario, as the cost of replatforming can be very high and not be worth the drag on the business.

Best cloud
> There *are* differences in the capabilities available on different hyperscalers. If you really like BigQuery or DynamoDB or Azure OpenAI, believe they are best of breed, and have architected your application around those capabilities, you will want that application to run on Google Cloud, AWS, or Azure, respectively, even

if the rest of your technology infrastructure is elsewhere. The differences in productivity available with the best/most familiar tools, the ability to start shadow IT initiatives with just a credit card, and the disinclination to rewrite what's working mean that many organizations slowly evolve into a de facto multicloud system.

Support customers

If you are building software that runs within your customers' environments, you will need to support all the major clouds because you will have customers on all three clouds. This is why, for example, SAP or Teradata is available on AWS, Azure, and Google Cloud.

When faced with these inevitabilities, it is important to recognize that there is no reason to become a roadblock. It is no longer necessary to be tied to a single vendor and build your entire data stack around a single technology. Cloud technologies are far more open than traditional on-premises technologies, and businesses can now create complex architectures that rely on multiple interconnected environments running various solutions from several vendors or fully open source software (e.g., there are companies that are implementing their main site in one cloud provider and the disaster-recovery site in another one to reduce the risk of dependencies on a single hyperscaler). Of course, this level of freedom comes at a cost (in terms of technology and personnel) that is different and requires additional governance and management. For example, if you are working with multiple hypervisors, you will need to deal with different platforms that may require different skills, and you will also have more contracts to manage, which will increase the management burden. However, as you will see later, this approach is becoming increasingly popular due to the advantages it can offer.

Multicloud Could Be Strategic

In talking with IT executives of large enterprises, it is pretty common for us to hear that they are working on a digital transformation journey that includes a multicloud strategy. There are several examples of large organizations that are already adopting a multicloud approach: for example, Apple, which for its iCloud services is leveraging all three main public hyperscalers (*https://oreil.ly/ZLo-B*); or Twitter, which (before a recent buyout) used Google Cloud Platform (*https://oreil.ly/IEtIt*) for its data platform but powered its news feed using AWS (*https://oreil.ly/uNvmL*); or HSBC, which splits workloads between Google Cloud and AWS and migrates some legacy services to Azure (*https://oreil.ly/SSjc2*).

When done right, multicloud allows you to add value for the business by combining the best-of-breed solutions deployed on different environments. It is, in practice, the development of a brand-new ecosystem of interconnected services that becomes the landing zone for all the company's solutions.

What are the main drivers for the adoption of a multicloud environment? The most relevant are:

Fear of lock-in
This is one of the biggest concerns organizations have because they do not want to fall under the "tyranny" of a single provider. This is not a technology concern (as there is no way to escape lock-in, either to a cloud or to a multicloud software vendor) but more of a business strategy one.

Exit strategy
The ability to leave a provider in case of a failure (that can be even a contractual breach).

Leverage
Your management may want to preserve negotiating leverage with the hyperscalers by maintaining two or more cloud providers.

Commercial
It may be that your organization uses Microsoft's enterprise software, sells on Amazon, and advertises on Google. There may be a larger commercial imperative to have a footprint on more than one public cloud.

Regulatory requirements
Maybe one provider does not offer proper services in selected regions or with an adequate set of services in that region (e.g., disaster recovery).

Sustainability
Companies want to choose the best sustainable cloud because it is critical to meet future trends in environmental, social, and corporate governance strategy.

Innovation
Adoption of solutions without barriers of cost, commercial aspect, or functionality.

Knowledge
It is critical to provide an environment for employees to succeed without barriers and where people can leverage the skills they have already gained during their career or can gain new ones.

Portability
Hyperscaler proprietary solutions tend to be limited in terms of where you can run them, whereas open source solutions that run on multiple clouds are often also usable on premises and on the edge.

Now that you have a better understanding of why you should consider a multicloud strategy for your business, let's look at some architectural patterns you can use to make it a reality.

Multicloud Architectural Patterns

Multicloud architectures can use different patterns to connect data and allow users to interact with all the solutions required for analysis. In this section, you will learn about the most common patterns you will encounter when working with these paradigms.

Single Pane of Glass

One of the biggest challenges is to develop a solution to enable data analysis across several data silos that might be seated in various locations managed by different vendors. To achieve that, it is essential to leverage open solutions that are *cloud agnostic* by definition and that are capable of being connected with several and different data sources, with the ability to blend the data when needed. There are mainly two different approaches that can be leveraged here:

- BI tool–based approach, as depicted in Figure 9-1
- Processing engine–based approach, as depicted in Figure 9-2

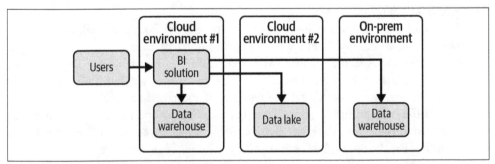

Figure 9-1. Single pane of glass leveraging a BI solution

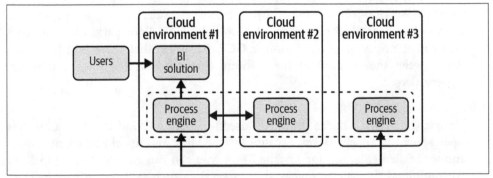

Figure 9-2. Single pane of glass leveraging a distributed process engine solution

In the first one, you are delegating to the BI tool (e.g., Looker or Power BI) the task of connecting multiple sparse data sources, retrieving related information, executing queries remotely, and eventually aggregating results. In the second approach, you are instead giving the process engine (e.g., PrestoSQL, BigQuery Omni) the ability to be connected with various data sources sitting in different environments. There could be in this case two different approaches:

- Leverage a distributed environment spanning multiple hyperscalers (e.g., Big-Query Omni), providing the final users with a single pane of glass to interact with the solution
- Leverage connectors (e.g., Java Database Connectivity [JDBC]) to query and blend data across multiple systems

Write Once, Run Anywhere

A common approach to gain cloud optionality is to use software that can be run as-is on different hyperscale platforms. There are several potential ways to achieve this pattern:

Managed open source software
> You could use Apache Airflow (an open source tool) for your workflow orchestration but avoid the overhead of managing it by using Amazon Managed Workflows for Apache Airflow (MWAA), Cloud Composer on Google Cloud, or Azure Data Factory on Azure. This way, developer-written code is portable across clouds, but you still get the benefits of managed services, other than for small differences in initial setup. This pattern of using open source with different managed services on different hyperscalers works in several other situations, including Presto, Spark, PyTorch, and TensorFlow.

Multicloud products
> Tools such as Snowflake, Confluent Kafka, and Databricks are available as fully managed services on the major hyperscalers. As such, it is possible to take a Snowflake workload consisting of Snowflake SQL, Snowpark, etc., on AWS and run it nearly as-is on Azure or GCP. Be aware that there is often some lag between the versions of the software that are available on the different hyperscalers.

Multiple runners
> Google Cloud made the software API used for writing Cloud Dataflow pipelines open source as Apache Beam. Because Apache Flink and Apache Spark now offer runner implementations for Apache Beam, you can run Apache Beam pipelines with minimal changes on managed Flink services such as Amazon Kinesis Data Analytics.

OSS abstraction layer

Instead of invoking an LLM through the prompting APIs offered by Azure OpenAI or Google Cloud Vertex AI, you could choose to access the models through LangChain, which provides a consistent interface. This allows you to keep the software workload portable between different LLM providers (although you will have to verify that the prompts in question do work interchangeably).

OSS on IaaS

Open source software such as Dask, Modin, RAPIDS, etc., can be run on virtual machines or clusters rented from the hyperscalers. Try to avoid this unless you have the scale of usage where managing the software on IaaS is cost-effective.

Bursting from On Premises to Cloud

This is a pattern aimed to support organizations who have a large data lake on prem and want to expand their footprint into the cloud but are not ready to complete a full migration yet. Hybrid workloads can help address their immediate pain points, and as an added bonus, they can actually pave the way for future migration by showing how easy it is to adopt and use cloud technologies.

The easiest way to get started with a cloud approach is to burst on-prem Hadoop workloads. Bursting is great for organizations with significant investments in both the hardware and Hadoop-related stack that are capacity constrained. Prime candidates for bursting are large one-off jobs—for example, monthly reports that require a large cluster to process the data. Bursting works really well for the cases where multiple jobs can run against the data uploaded to a blob storage service (e.g., AWS S3, Google Cloud Storage, Azure Blob Storage) and where the data used for processing can be incrementally updated. One of the main advantages of this solution is that the same Spark or Hive job that runs on prem can run on a PaaS cluster (e.g., Amazon EMR, Google Cloud Dataproc, Azure HDInsight). It resonates with the organizations that value open source solutions and prefer no vendor lock-in. What is important here is that all the upstream processes of ingesting the data into the data lake remain unchanged. All of this significantly minimizes the risk of redoing and retesting existing processes and shortens the time to the first deployment.

How does it actually work? This approach uses Hadoop's distributed copy tool, also known as *DistCp*, to move data from your on-premises HDFS to the target cloud blob storage. Once the data is transferred, a PaaS cluster gets created and Spark jobs can be run on this cluster. Once the job is completed, the cluster gets destroyed, the job results are saved, and, if you are not planning to run additional jobs, the blob storage bucket can be destroyed too. Orchestration of the burst workloads can be done leveraging open source solutions like Airflow that can work both on premises and in the cloud (available even in a PaaS mode, via Google Cloud Composer, for example), as you can see in Figure 9-3.

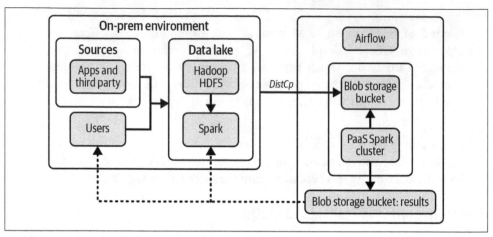

Figure 9-3. Bursting Hadoop on-premises workload

Additional use cases that this pattern covers are:

- The ability for organizations to test version upgrades. It is often less risky and less costly to start a PaaS cluster in the cloud with a particular Spark version and verify that the job works on a subset of on-prem data.

- Experimentation and testing new technologies (e.g., integration of third-party services directly in Spark jobs).

Bursting is a common pattern that we have seen so many times in several organizations; let's have a look at how we can expand it.

Pass-Through from On Premises to Cloud

This pattern can be viewed as complementary to the previous one. In the previous scenario, we showed how to move a portion of the on-prem data lake to a cloud blob storage bucket using a Hadoop native tool, DistCp. Once the data is there, then—in addition to Hadoop native tools—the organization can leverage other process engines' (e.g., AWS Redshift, Google BigQuery, Azure Synapse) tools to process the data, as described in Figure 9-4.

Several workloads can be enabled by leveraging a cloud process engine:

- Process ORC, Parquet, or Avro files, including Hive-partitioned data, leveraging federated queries.

- Join on-prem originated data with data in the cloud: a great example is joining an organization's transactional data located on prem with data loaded from marketing tools like Adobe or Google Analytics.

- Build models based on on-prem data leveraging AI/ML tools.
- Run batch predictions at scale on the on-prem data.

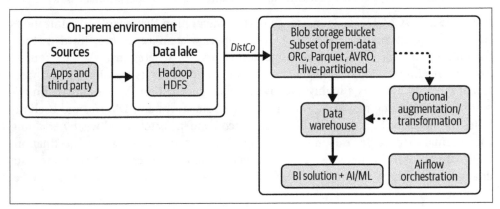

Figure 9-4. Hadoop pass-through to enable process data in the cloud

With this approach, it is important to note some key points:

- In contrast to the full migration, there is no need to change any of the systems that feed or use the on-prem data lake.
- Data analysis can be done through a cloud process engine in addition to the Hadoop tools.
- Once the data is transferred to the cloud storage bucket, there is no additional delay or processing needed to access federated data via the selected process engine.
- The same data transferred to the cloud bucket can be processed by the same Spark jobs that run on prem.
- Integration platform as a service (iPaaS) solutions like Informatica, Talend, TIBCO, or MuleSoft can be handled to facilitate the integration of data sources and maintain synchronization.

Data Integration Through Streaming

Organizations have barriers between databases and applications, on premises and in the cloud. Processes are batch, so they don't support the fast operational decision making that businesses demand. Services are often self-managed, legacy and not built for the cloud, and expensive to run and maintain. This results in expensive, slow, and fragmented system architectures.

Change streaming is the movement of data changes as they happen from a (typically database) source to a destination. Powered by CDCs, change streaming has become a critical data architecture building block. Global companies are demanding CDC to provide replication capabilities across different data sources and provide a real-time source of streaming data for real-time analytics and business operations.

But what is CDC? CDC is an approach to data integration that enables organizations to integrate and analyze data faster, using fewer system resources. It's a method for pulling only the latest changes (updates, inserts, or deletes) from a data source, often by reading the log of changes that the source keeps for its own internal transactional integrity. CDC is a highly effective mechanism for limiting the impact on the source when loading new data into operational data stores and DWHs, and it eliminates the need for bulk-load updating and inconvenient batch windows by enabling incremental loading or real-time streaming of data changes into a data destination. CDC can be used in many use cases that derive value from constant access to data changes as they happen; the most common use cases, in order of commonality, are as follows:

Analytics

By integrating CDC for loading data into a DWH, organizations can, for example, get up-to-date materialized views of source data. Organizations can use this continuously updated data to build up-to-date dashboards for the data. These can be used, for example, for monitoring your systems and for deriving up-to-date insights about the state of your business, as described in the Figure 9-5. There is always a trade-off you have to consider between the business impact of data freshness and the cost to collect and process it.

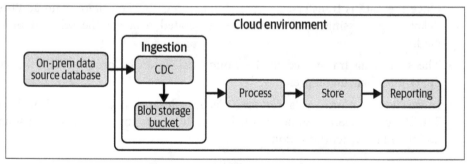

Figure 9-5. CDC architecture to enable analytics

Database replication and synchronization scenarios

By integrating CDC for loading data into SQL databases, organizations can get up-to-date materialized views of their source data in these databases. Organizations can use this continuously updated data in the destination databases for a low-downtime database migration from the source to the destination or for multi/hybrid-cloud configurations, where the source and destination reside in different hosting environments, as you can see in Figure 9-6.

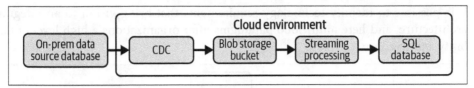

Figure 9-6. CDC architecture to enable database replication and synchronization

Event-driven architectures

Modern microservices-based architectures rely on central hubs of data that are updated with events continuously from across your organization to be event driven. By continuously writing into destinations such as a cloud blob storage, organizations can build event-driven architectures that are based on consumption of event data from these destinations, as described in Figure 9-7.

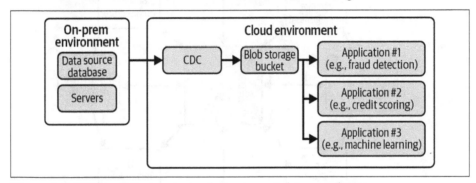

Figure 9-7. CDC architecture to implement event-driven architecture

Now that you have a better understanding of the possible patterns that allow you to build multicloud data capabilities, let's have a look at how to adopt an overall multicloud strategy.

Adopting Multicloud

Adoption of a multicloud paradigm is a part of a strategy that should be then translated into an IT architecture.

Framework

To translate a multicloud strategy into a multicloud IT architecture, enterprise architects leverage some common framework like TOGAF (The Open Group Architecture Framework) to identify business needs, define what data is needed to support the process, and define how this data is processed by the applications (Architecture Development Model [ADM] process), as represented in Figure 9-8. Once completed, it is possible to identify technology requirements that bring vision to an integrated architecture, and here multicloud paradigms offer organizations a high level of flexibility and freedom.

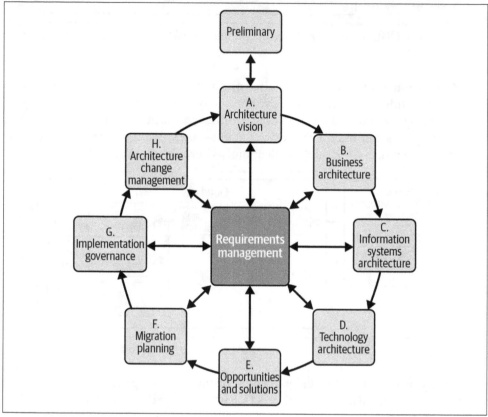

Figure 9-8. ADM cycle as per the TOGAF framework (https://oreil.ly/nWTYa)

Having access to a wide range of services is certainly an opportunity, but it is important to manage it carefully to avoid losing focus. It is crucial to identify the services that can help you achieve your business goals in accordance with your strategy and organizational rules, particularly on the compliance side. This is especially important today, as organizations are increasingly (re)insourcing IT functions to take ownership and control of their software and solutions.

Let's take the financial services industry as an example. We can see that a lot of investment has been made in transforming legacy environments (mainly based on mainframe solutions) into something modern, especially on the data side. Fraud detection systems are based on real-time analytics, know-your-customer processes work thanks to advanced ML algorithms, and anti-money laundering requires the ability to process huge amounts of data. Obtaining access to such a specific solution/workload can be difficult if relying on a single provider; hence, organizations are looking at a multicloud approach to get the best of breed to meet their needs.

Time Scale

It is important to identify the time scale at which multicloud is to be adopted. Specifically:

- Some organizations *may never fully migrate to the public cloud*, perhaps because they are in finance or healthcare and need to obey strict industry regulations on how data is stored. For them, "data residency" is very important. Some enterprises may want to protect their legacy on-prem workloads like SAP, Oracle, or Informatica but at the same time want to take advantage of public cloud innovations like fully managed DWHs.

- Other large enterprises instead are committed to their multiyear journey to *modernize with native public cloud*: they will have to adopt multicloud architectures as an end state for years.

- Finally, there are organizations who are *not ready to migrate yet* but *have challenges of meeting business SLAs due to ad hoc large batch jobs*: they want to take advantage of the scalable capacity of public clouds and avoid the cost to scale up the on-premises infrastructure.

With the preceding concepts in mind, how do you end up with a multicloud architecture? Let's dig into that.

Define a Target Multicloud Architecture

You can follow the same approach (covered in the previous chapters) as when you worked with one single (public or private) cloud provider, but you need to (1) repeat the approach for every vendor involved and (2) do so in the context of an overarching target architecture.

The following steps will help you define and adopt your target cloud architecture:

1. *Define your strategy.*
    You need to have a clear understanding of your goals before adopting a multicloud strategy. These goals could be related to business, strategy, or technology. Once you know your goals, you need to identify the drivers that are pushing you toward a multicloud strategy. These drivers could be cost, lack of features, openness, or regulatory compliance. For example, if you are adopting a multicloud strategy for leverage, you would want to put your most easily transferable workloads (e.g., Hadoop or Kafka) on the secondary cloud. Once you have a clear understanding of your goals and drivers, you can proceed to the next steps in your multicloud journey.

2. *Develop the team.*

When talking about cloud in general, the number of skills that are needed can be incredibly high. Identity, security, networking, coding, etc., are just a few of the topics that cloud engineers should be able to master. When dealing with multicloud architectures, this set of skills becomes numerous because even if the topics are interchangeable from a high-level point of view, there is the need to bring deep and specific knowledge related to the platform that engineers have to operate. It's usually imperative that you set up a Cloud Center of Excellence as described in "Step 1: Strategy and Planning" on page 42 so that all the needed skills are brought together under a "single hat," becoming the reference for the entire project.

3. *Assess.*

To identify a candidate target solution, it is necessary to have a better understanding of what is currently operational. This part is crucial because it can completely change the approach in the following steps. Are you going to perform a lift and shift to maintain solutions your organization has, or is it better to adopt an approach based on replatforming/redeveloping to get the most from the cloud provider? Usually, in this step there are tools that simplify the discovery and that collect several pieces of data that can be used to define a migration plan. Moving to a fully serverless architecture with cloud native tools tends to be the best solution, but it may not be feasible in the short term with the resources you have at your disposal.

4. *Design the architecture.*

Once the business goals are clear and you have the sufficient knowledge to make everything real, start to translate requirements into a technology architecture. Define how components will talk to one another, how they will exchange information, and how they can work together to execute defined tasks. The architect's goal is to identify the best possible solution to give more flexibility to the final users, guaranteeing the maximum level of security and performance while keeping an eye on the overall cost.

5. *Prepare a migration plan.*

Once you have collected all the information about where to start and where you want to go, you must identify how to get there: modality, timelines, effort required, and milestones. It is even important to understand what the relationships between different activities/environments are and what are possible dependencies, if any.

6. *Build the landing zone.*

Everything starts with the landing zone's definition (as you have read in Chapter 4), the foundational environments where workloads will be deployed: identity and access management, network connectivity, security, monitoring, and cost management are just a few of the elements that need to be taken into consideration at this stage. This stage is fundamental to prepare the target environment receiving data as per the model defined in the previous step.

7. Migrate and transform.
Based on all the things defined in the previous steps, it is time to migrate solutions into the new architecture. In this final step, we will shift our applications to the new environments, apply new services, or entirely rebuild applications leveraging native services.

Now that you have a better understanding of how to deal with multicloud architecture, let's deep dive into another hybrid paradigm: edge computing.

Why Edge Computing?

Edge computing in a nutshell is the architectural pattern that promotes the execution of the data processing right where the data is generated, even though it's at the periphery of the architecture.

Edge computing is a complement of the cloud computing paradigm. While cloud enables organizations to get access to infinitely scalable computing and storage resources with a centralized approach, edge computing is meant to address different challenges. Edge computing helps organizations handle workloads that require data to be processed in place (or with a very low latency) or when activities need to be running even in case of a disconnection from the network. While cloud computing is more oriented toward bringing the business to planet scale, edge computing is more focused on bringing capabilities closer to the decision point (i.e., factories, points of sale, etc.).

Bandwidth, Latency, and Patchy Connectivity

Data coming from machinery deployed in factories has permitted manufacturing companies to analyze how their instruments are used and to predict the need for maintenance and limit potential damages. Telcos have been able to gain better visibility on the congestion of their networks and take proper action to mitigate possible issues.

The problem is that you cannot do such analysis on the cloud. Why?

Imagine yourself as the CIO of a manufacturing company. The CEO has asked you to find a way to speed up the product quality checks on the production assembly line that at the moment are carried out manually. Your team has developed an ML-based image recognition solution to compare items in the assembly line with perfect products to quickly identify defects. The PoC that you decided to conduct to demonstrate the power of the solution has been a success—it identifies 98% of defects in an automatic fashion, and now you are ready to put it in production. How could you do this? What is the best way to proceed? The PoC process has been pretty straightforward:

- Collecting pictures that represent perfect items
- Collecting pictures that represent items with damages/imperfections
- Assigning a specific label for each picture (good item, item with defect)
- Developing and training an image recognition model to identify the two clusters of objects
- Deploying the model and making it available via an API
- Executing the following steps, for every item in the assembly line:
  — Take a picture of the item with a camera.
  — Upload the picture to the cloud environment as an input payload of the API invoking the developed model.
  — Based on the model output, decide to proceed (*item good*) or stop the process (*item with defect*).

This approach is good for testing purposes, but there are some caveats that make it impracticable to deploy it in a production scenario:

Bandwidth
> The system needs to take high-resolution pictures to be effective; every picture that needs to be uploaded into the cloud is of considerable size. Considering the number of items that have to be checked every day for every single assembly line, there is a huge amount of data that needs to be transferred, which requires a lot of bandwidth.

Latency
> To be effective and scalable, you need to get an outcome (item good versus item with defect) within a few milliseconds after taking the picture. Even with a high-speed connection, it would be difficult to make it fast enough to keep up with the assembly line.

Offline
> Factories are often in out-of-the-way places where it is difficult to maintain a stable network connection. So it is crucial these solutions are available even offline.

All these caveats are tied to a single point of failure: the need for a connection with the cloud environment. But what if you could bring more intelligence close to the physical devices/sensors and give them the ability to operate and make smart decisions with imperceptible latency or even offline? The goal of edge computing is aimed to do exactly this: bring a portion of storage and compute resources out of the cloud and closer to the subject that is generating/using data itself.

Use Cases

There are several situations where a centralized cloud environment won't work and an edge deployment can be beneficial. This is not an exhaustive list, but it should give you an idea of the possibilities:

Automated optical inspection
Use cases that leverage image analysis via deep learning models to identify something that is not aligned with the desired state—for example, automated checks to verify the quality of an item on an assembly line or a solution to speed up inspection checks on vehicle components to discover their wear level.

Improved security
Use cases where cameras and other sensors are leveraged to monitor people's safety in a specific location like a factory, workplace, or dangerous site. This may include thermal cameras to recognize people in dangerous places or close to dangerous machineries, or sensors to check if someone has fallen and needs help.

Agriculture
Using sensors to monitor the health, growth, and level of nutrients absorbed by plants. Collected data can be analyzed in real time to verify if there is something missing or exceeding.

Healthcare
Analyzing real-time patient data to extract more insight—for example, magnetic resonance images, echographies, glucose monitors, health tools, and other sensors.

Content Delivery Network (CDN)
To improve the browsing experience, content providers who deliver their data over the internet (e.g., music, video stream, web pages, etc.) usually cache information at the edge to reduce the latency when recovering it. Choosing what to cache can be greatly improved by real-time algorithms.

Immersive interactions
Real-time, speedy feedback is important to improve the realism of the immersive experience offered by VR headsets (e.g., augmented reality, gaming, etc.).

Smart cities
Applications aimed to make cities more intelligent and to avoid waste of energy and resources—for example, the automated lighting systems implemented by sensors that monitor and control a single light or group of lights to maximize efficiency and maintain security at the same time.

Traffic management system

Leveraging cameras and sensors, it is possible to adjust traffic signals in real time or manage the opening and closing of traffic lanes to avoid congestion. The importance of this case will increase even more when self-driving cars become more common.

You are now familiar with possible use cases where the pattern can be adopted; let's focus now on the benefits you may get.

Benefits

The role of edge computing is to extend centralized infrastructure and bring more computing power closer to the boundaries of the architecture. This enables connected (or disconnected) devices to execute tasks (e.g., ML inference) that require very low latency and power compute in place. This pattern addresses some infrastructure challenges like bandwidth limitations and network congestion. Other benefits include the following:

Reliability

The majority of IoT architectures include elements that are not in a fully connected environment like your office or home. There are pretty common situations where it is practically impossible to maintain a constant reliable connection with the world with a defined and constant low latency. Think about rural industrial sites where telcos are not investing in high-speed wired connections, or wind turbines in the middle of the sea leveraging old-style connectivity (2G/3G), or self-driving cars requiring microseconds of latency in making decisions (you would not want to wait for the response coming from the cloud if your car has to brake to avoid an accident). All these use cases, to be effective, require devices that can store and process data locally and that can handle temporary connectivity disruption without that having an impact on their functioning.

Legal/compliance

In some industries (e.g., financial services and insurance) in specific countries there are strict rules for storing, processing, and exposing the data (think about GDPR regulation). The ability to transform and use the data locally and potentially send back to the cloud a modified version of it (e.g., deidentification, encryption, etc.) would increase the ability of an organization to adopt a modern architecture while remaining compliant with regulations.

Security

Data exfiltration, distributed denial-of-service (DDoS) attack prevention, and data protection are some of the scenarios where edge computing can drastically reduce risk because devices can work fully offline and can even be forced to connect with the external world via a hardened gateway that can implement an extra layer of data protection, like ad hoc encryption.

Let's now shift our attention to the challenges you may face when dealing with an edge computing paradigm.

Challenges

Along with the benefits that this new paradigm can bring to the organization, there are some drawbacks that you may have to tackle, such as:

Limitations in computing and storage capabilities
> Devices deployed at the edge typically come with limited hardware that executes a defined operation very well (e.g., sensors collecting data of temperature, etc.). Because of this, devices tend to be super-specialized and not great for general-purpose tasks. Even if the device is capable of some general task such as locally running an ML model, the configured version of the device as installed may not have the necessary capabilities.

Device management/remote control
> As we outlined before, the connection between the cloud and these devices can be tricky due to the connectivity or because of strict access policies. You may need to physically access each device to check the status and, eventually, apply updates/patches that might be required. This may not be straightforward if some locations are inhospitable or devices are deployed in inaccessible positions.

Backup and restore
> Because these devices could be offline the majority of the time, you might need to implement extra local physical infrastructure (e.g., smart gateway plus network area storage) to backup and restore, which would raise the overall cost.

If any of these challenges apply to your use case, you'll need to evaluate whether they represent a blocker or whether there are valid workarounds to mitigate the issues.

Edge Computing Architectural Patterns

As with cloud, it is important to have a clear strategy in mind when defining an edge computing architecture: there could be situations where all devices are governed centrally (maybe by a cloud application), while there could be other situations where nodes are fully disconnected or partially connected just with the local network (to communicate with one another or with a local gateway).

There are, broadly, two types of edge computing architectures: one where the devices are smart and the other where a smart gateway is added at the edge. Regardless of whether you have a smart device or a smart gateway, ML activation works similarly. Let's look at both of these patterns.

Smart Devices

Smart devices are a straightforward (albeit expensive) way to implement an edge computing architecture. In our example scenario, the machines used to produce items that have to pass a quality check will all need to have hardware capable of executing the ML algorithm that is able to recognize defects in pictures. The devices that have to perform the logic can be called, for simplicity, "nodes," and their hardware can vary a lot depending on the use case they have to solve: they can come with general-purpose CPU or dedicated hardware to execute specific tasks.

Smart devices with nontrivial hardware that can directly execute complex logic (e.g., Raspberry Pi, Coral sensors, etc.), as shown in Figure 9-9, give a great level of flexibility but require a huge management effort (e.g., software updates, security patches, etc.) and an increased hardware cost.

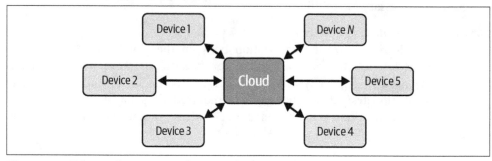

Figure 9-9. Edge architecture with smart devices

Smart Gateways

"Dumb" devices/sensors connected, via wire or wireless, to smart gateways that can execute the logic on their behalf, as shown in Figure 9-10, is the preferred approach for dealing with a huge number of sensors in the same place (e.g., within a factory) because it can reduce the management (one single smart device instead of n) and related cost. However, this introduces some security challenges in the architecture because it can become a single point of failure (SPOF).

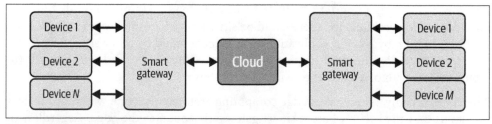

Figure 9-10. Edge architecture with smart gateways

ML Activation

We have discussed before a PoC scenario where machines, fully connected with a cloud environment, were continuously sending back and forth data to make a decision on how to handle items in the assembly line (*accept or reject*). You have seen, then, that the only way to make this architecture deployable in production was to extend it, making devices able to directly execute that logic at the edge.

The code executed by devices at the edge can vary case by case, but it can be generalized as an ML model that crunches some inputs (*the pictures* in this case) to get the desired output (*the final decision on items* in our example). In the previous chapters, when discussing modern data cloud architectures, you have seen that one of the main benefits of the cloud is its ability to collect and process data at scale, allowing developers to implement state-of-the-art ML algorithms easily.

Let's have a look at the different steps of the process (represented in Figure 9-11) of developing an ML algorithm and, for doing that, let's leverage the previous example:

1. Data collection

Everything starts with data that will be used as input to the process. In our scenario, we need to develop a model that can recognize information and features of items starting from pictures, so it is important to have access to a vast number of pictures of good items and items with defects. (Please note that you can create as many states as you want, but for the sake of simplicity we will consider only two states: good item and item with generic defect.)

2. Data analysis

The data collected at the previous step needs to be refined (e.g., cleaned, transformed, enriched) to be leveraged. In this specific example, we need to verify the quality of all shots (e.g., focus, alignment, noise, etc.), and then, for each image, we need to apply a label indicating what has been reported in the picture to produce two separated sets: good item and item with a defect.

3. ML model development, training, and test

It is time to develop the algorithm; there are plenty of tools and techniques you can use (e.g., scikit-learn, TensorFlow, PyTorch) and even automated solutions that make life easier (e.g., support in feature engineering, model selection, and parameters hypertuning). In our example, we can use transfer learning techniques to develop a deep learning model to recognize images.

4. ML model deployment

The model is ready to be used for predictions. It can be deployed as an API service in the cloud or directly in the edge nodes.

5. Feedback data collection

To improve the quality of the model, it is possible to collect data coming from the edge and then restart the process from the beginning in an interactive process aimed at making the prediction even better. In our case, the edge nodes will send back (leveraging, for example, a batch process) results of predictions together with the analyzed images.

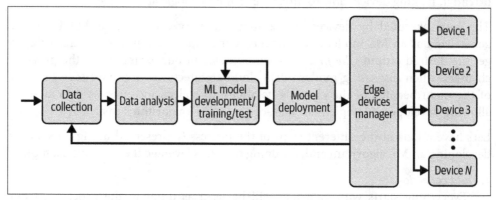

Figure 9-11. ML development/deployment on edge at scale

It is clear that these ML modeling steps impose certain requirements on the edge architecture:

1. Data collection requires the ability to store collected images for a long enough period of time that disks can be swapped out and moved to a location with better connectivity, and the data uploaded to the cloud.

2. Data analysis can be carried out in the cloud.

3. ML model development can also be carried out in the cloud. Testing, however, requires the ability to simulate the edge environment on the cloud.

4. Deployment requires that the characteristics of the edge hardware be kept in mind when developing the ML model. Deployment of the ML model to the edge may require an upgrade of hardware components to include ML inference chips such as a Google Coral Edge TPU or NVIDIA Jetson Nano.

5. Feedback of data collection requires the implementation of an application to keep track of situations where a human operator overrides the decision suggested by the ML algorithm.

Now that you are more familiar with the theory of the edge computing paradigm, let's have a look at how you can adopt it.

Adopting Edge Computing

Let's have a look at how the adoption of this paradigm may give greater visibility and more efficiency to a model organization.

The Initial Context

MagiCan is a (fictitious) manufacturing company specializing in the production of cans for beverages serving the most iconic brands in the world. The company has several production plants all around the world, and in each factory there are multiple machines working 24/7/365. The strategy of the company has always been to build plants in areas outside cities, and in some locations, local telcos provided the company with internet connections built on top of old wireless technology (e.g., 3G carriers).

One of the core values of the company is "high-quality product is a must, whatever it takes," and the organization has always invested a lot of money to ensure the quality of the end-to-end production cycle (for example, maintenance of the machineries and quality checks on produced items).

MagiCan discovered that there were several issues it needed to handle: too many faults on machines that caused multiple pauses in production at several sites, defects in produced items that resulted in fines, and difficulties in having a cohesive view of the status of its production plants. Because of this, the board decided to start a new project to improve the way it was collecting and elaborating data on its plants with the aim of addressing all these issues.

The Project

The organization was already leveraging cloud computing solutions for several workloads (e.g., DWH, website, SAP, etc.) and decided to expand its current architecture to invest in devices that would be directly connected to its machineries: the goal was not only to collect data directly from the plants for real-time visibility into how machines were working but also to allow users to operate on some parameters/components (e.g., actuators, assembly lines, etc.) to fix issues or correct inaccuracies and improve the overall quality of the production process.

The organization, with the help of a third-party partner specializing in IoT projects, defined a three-step journey:

1. *Improve overall system observability* by developing the architecture needed to collect data from the plants and build a near-real-time monitoring system.

2. *Develop automations* to tune actuators' functioning.

3. *Optimize the maintenance* of the machineries via the development of a predictive model.

Let's deep dive into the three steps of the journey.

Improve overall system observability

Considering the fact that MagiCan has plants in several locations globally distributed and the majority of them do not offer a reliable connection with the cloud world, it was impossible to develop a real-time architecture based on a streaming pattern. The company decided to split the problem in two different parts:

- *Local architecture* (at plant level), where all machines were connected in real time and all the information was immediately visible by a central but local application

- *Centralized architecture* leveraging the cloud system, where information coming from the plants was collected multiple times a day in a batch mode

The goal was to develop a standard way to monitor machines at every single plant and keep the data available even when the plants were offline. The central cloud brain had to collect all the data coming from the different plants and then give data scientists the ability to study that data so they could extract more insights and leverage the power of the cloud, as shown in Figure 9-12.

In each plant, devices with sensors were deployed to the various machineries to collect data coming from the different actuators (e.g., speed, rotation, temperature, etc.). These devices were locally connected to a smart gateway that was able to collect all the data in real time and via a custom-developed visualization tool, which provided users with a sort of continuous snapshot of the status of the plant. Every *x* minutes, data was compressed and sent to the cloud for further analysis and then aggregated with data coming from other plants. If there was an issue with the network, the batch would be enqueued and data sent to leverage the following batch.

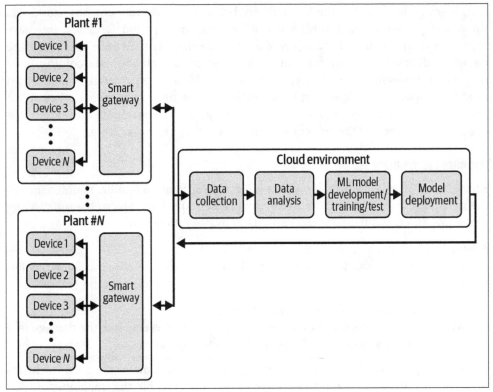

Figure 9-12. High-level IoT platform architecture

Develop automations

Once the data coming from all the plants was available in the cloud, it was time to start having some fun! The amount of information available allowed the team to gain visibility on several things, such as:

- How workers were interacting with the machineries
- Correlation between configuration of the actuators and defects on cans
- Average inactivity time due to a mechanical problem
- Ideal machine configurations when using specific raw materials

Considering the fact that the connectivity between the devices and the cloud, via the smart gateways, was bidirectional, it was possible to send feedback and have machines receive that updated information to tune the way they were operating. The company developed a near-real-time process to crunch all the data coming from the plants, understand the discrepancy with the ideal target operation mode, and send back updated configuration to immediately tune the actuators' behaviors. With this process, centrally governed, it was possible to provide machines with a tailored configuration based on the current scenario where they were operating.

Optimize the maintenance

The last step was to tackle an issue that was pretty difficult to handle: maintenance of the machines. Before having the ability to get a cohesive overview of the functioning of the machines, maintenance was carried out in two different ways:

Planned maintenance via scheduled intervention
> Machines were checked on a regular basis with a well-defined calendarization based on the machine model, its history, and the way it was operating.

Unplanned maintenance via ad hoc intervention
> Machines were checked on purpose because of some events like the damage of a component or a failure caused by an error of the operator.

Considering the fact that a maintenance operation could pause a machine for hours or even days, it was important to reduce as much as possible the unplanned downtime. Leveraging the data coming from the plants (the analysis has been possible after some months from the initial go live, since an adequate amount of historical data was needed), a predictive ML model algorithm was developed to calculate the probability of a failure in a machine: when the percentage was superior to a certain threshold, an alert was sent to the plant manager, who had to decide how to handle that (i.e., schedule an unplanned maintenance operation or wait for the next scheduled one).

The Final Outcomes and Next Steps

The entire end-to-end project took more than one year to complete, but the first release of the most important part (that is, the development of a unified view of all the machines in the various plants) was implemented relatively quickly (in less than six months). Thanks to this distributed architecture, the company was able to increase its observability both at plant level and at company level, leveraging a common, standardized, and unified process. At the same time, it was able to improve the efficiency of the entire production chain. MagiCan is now focusing on a brand-new project aimed at reducing the cost of the quality check, automating as much as possible in the process. Similar to what was presented at the beginning of this section, the organization wants to extend the architecture already in place to implement a process to automatically identify defects directly on the assembly line: to achieve that, it will leverage new camera devices with the ability to execute logics on frames based on ML models. The goal is to reallocate the majority of the workforce currently performing quality checks to other activities.

Summary

This chapter has provided you with a high-level understanding of how to handle hybrid and multicloud architectures when a single cloud provider is insufficient to meet all of the business's analytical requirements. It has presented you with the various factors to consider when dealing with such architectures as well as some common implementation patterns. Finally, it has given you some understanding of edge computing and how to use it. The key takeaways are as follows:

- Consolidating your entire software architecture on a single cloud provider is very appealing for the simplicity of the overall architecture, ease of learning/adoption, and overall costs.

- Small and medium-sized businesses should choose a single cloud provider and design their architecture using fully managed services available on that hyperscaler.

- Multicloud architectures may become inevitable because of acquisitions or the desire to use a service that is available on one of the clouds.

- Multicloud strategy has to be considered when the organization has fear of lock-in, needs to implement an exit strategy, has some stringent regulatory requirements, or wants to increase the level of workload portability, innovation, knowledge, and sustainability.

- The adoption of a multicloud strategy is a journey that requires a clear definition of the strategy to be followed and an extension of the skills of the team.

- There are various architectural patterns that you may leverage when dealing with multicloud architectures, like the development of a single pane of glass, bursting Hadoop on-premises workload, using Hadoop pass-through to enable data processing in the cloud, and change streaming to enable data integration.

- Edge computing is a paradigm that aims to bring a portion of storage and compute resources out of the cloud and closer to the subject that is generating/using data itself.

- Bandwidth limitations, network congestion, reliability, legal compliance, and security are just some of the benefits that the edge computing paradigm can bring.

- The main challenges of edge computing are limitations in computing and storage capabilities, management/remote control, and backup and restore.

- The main use cases that leverage such an edge computing paradigm are automated optical inspection, improved security, farming, healthcare, CDNs, immersive interactions, smart cities, and traffic management systems.

- When choosing an edge architecture, smart devices are simpler but more expensive than using a smart gateway. In either case, ML activation involves adding capabilities such as on-device storage and ML inference chips.

In the next chapter you will learn the high-level decisions you should make on architecture and frameworks in AI and ML.

CHAPTER 10

AI Application Architecture

In this chapter, you will learn the high-level decisions you should make on architecture and frameworks when building an AI and ML application. We start by considering what kinds of problems AI/ML is good at addressing and how to develop and deploy AI responsibly. Once you have decided that ML is a good fit for a problem, you will have to move on to deciding the enterprise approach you take: do you buy, adapt, or build? We look at examples of each of these scenarios and the considerations if you choose to adopt each of these approaches. If you are building, there are several choices of architectures, and the choice depends on the type of problem being solved.

This chapter covers AI architecture considerations and decision criteria at the application level. The platform on which data scientists and ML engineers will develop and deploy these applications is covered in Chapter 11. Do not skip this chapter and dive straight into the technical details in the next chapter—as a cloud architect, you will need to advise every application team on making the right decision regarding buy, adapt, or build and the choice of AI architecture for each application that they build on your platform.

 The purpose of this chapter and the next is to show you how to architect an ML platform using cloud technologies. Just as we did not cover SQL in the chapter on data warehousing, we do not cover TensorFlow in these chapters. If you wish to learn how to do ML, we heartily recommend the book *Hands-on Machine Learning with Scikit-Learn, Keras, and TensorFlow: Concepts, Tools, and Techniques to Build Intelligent Systems* by Aurélien Géron (O'Reilly).

Is This an AI/ML Problem?

To learn what kinds of problems you can solve with ML, let's start with a few fundamentals we briefly touched on in Chapter 1. We'll begin with some definitions, and we'll then consider the sorts of problems where ML as a solution is generally a good fit.

Subfields of AI

AI is the field of study that solves problems by getting computers to think and act like humans. Historically, there have been several approaches tried in AI. One approach is to write code that explicitly tells the computer what to do in each potential situation. This is how many robot devices such as manufacturing robots and home vacuums work even today. The problem is that writing such rules is hard. Another approach is to interview or observe an expert and use their behavior to code up the rules. AI models to approve whether patients are accepted into trials of experimental medicines work this way. But even experts can't tell you why they do what they do. There is a lot of intuition underlying human decision making, and the more someone is an expert, the more intermediate steps they jump. The difficulty of these approaches led to what is referred to as an "AI winter," a period of time (loosely 1985–2014) when AI was stuck.

ML is a subfield of AI (see Figure 10-1) that solves AI problems using data instead of custom logic. This makes it particularly useful when you can't articulate the logic or if the logic will be too difficult to code up as a computer program. Instead of capturing all the differences between nails and screws, for example, an ML system is shown hundreds of nails and told they are nails, and hundreds of screws and told they are screws. The ML model then figures out how to tell them apart by tuning an internal, very general mathematical function. ML is many decades old, but until about 2014 it worked only on structured data of the sort that you can store in a database.

Deep learning is a subfield of ML that shot into prominence in the late 2010s. It uses highly complex functions (which add "depth" to a pictorial representation of the function, hence its name). Deep learning has been successfully used to understand unstructured data like speech, images, video, and natural language. Deep learning is why you have been seeing smart speakers (Google Assistant, Alexa, Siri, etc.), image search (Google Photos), automatic translation, and instant video highlights (in sports shows) take off in the past few years. Deep learning is powerful, but it requires a lot of data to create the ML model in the first place.

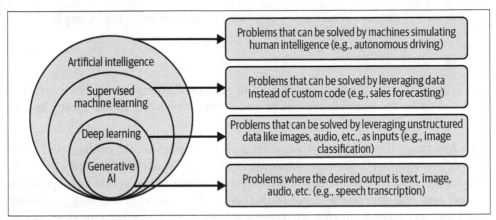

Figure 10-1. Relationship between AI, ML, deep learning, and generative AI

Generative AI

Traditionally, ML has involved solving classification and regression problems. There is a third form of AI that is becoming increasingly capable: *generative AI*. Generative AI is a type of deep learning that shot into prominence in the early 2020s. Here, the output of the model is text, image, music, video, etc. For example, an LLM like ChatGPT is trained by showing the model large amounts of natural language text so that it can predict the most likely next words given the preceding text. The LLM is used by having it generate an initial set of words given a prompt and then complete the sequence in a likely manner given this initial sequence and the prompt. Similarly, image generation models are trained to predict pixel values and speech models can generate audio frequency and amplitude values. The initial uses of generative AI were in sentence completion (e.g., Smart Compose in Gmail) and code completion (e.g., Tabnine, GitHub Copilot), but increasingly sophisticated products now use generative AI to generate initial drafts of emails and articles in sales, marketing, etc.

How it works

ChatGPT, Bard, LLaMa, etc., are LLMs that have been trained to generate text in a variety of styles and for different purposes while maintaining a high level of accuracy and detail. At the most basic level, these kinds of ML models have been trained to be able to complete sentences. Imagine you start writing something like the following:

We were floating

The model will propose some ways to proceed with the sentence. For example:

... on the river [80%]
... in space [15%]

The language model has been shown a lot of published examples—speeches, articles, books, reviews, etc.—which allow it to understand which words are most likely to follow others.

But what about if you pass to the model a previous phrase that contains the word "rocket" or "summer"? The relative probabilities of the words that are likely to follow will change. Based on the extensive training dataset, the model seems to adapt to the context and will generate a response that seems accurate, detailed, and consistent. The LLM has learned, during its training phases, which words or phrases to pay attention to. In addition, human feedback is employed in the training process for an LLM so that it prefers word continuations that are most pleasing to humans.

Foundational LLMs like GPT-4 (behind ChatGPT) and PaLM (behind Bard) are trained for general tasks that involve common language problems such as text classification, question answering, document summarization, and text generation across industries. These models provide an interactive way to summarize large amounts of knowledge and information. This can be multimodal—that is, in different unstructured formats such as text, images, or even videos. These models can achieve satisfactory results even with a small amount of domain-specific training data.

Fine-tuned LLMs go beyond global knowledge and focus on specific tasks and domains. For example, an LLM focused on healthcare such as Med-PaLM is trained on specific labeled datasets to adapt the model to perform specific tasks within the healthcare domain. These labeled datasets are crucial for training the model to accurately recognize medical entities, write medical care instructions, and perform other healthcare-related tasks.

Strengths and limitations

This technology is still in its infancy, and it comes with a lot of promise but also several limitations that need to be considered, especially for enterprise adoption at scale. Let's take a look at the most important factors to consider.

Do LLMs memorize or generalize?

Although LLMs may appear to be able to handle any type of context because they have been trained on a massive dataset with billions of parameters, they are not actually able to store all of the digital information available on the planet. Because they can't remember all possible word sequences in context, they instead interpolate between probable words and contexts. Then they select similar continuations in comparable contexts.

Does that mean that an LLM is able to generalize beyond the text it was trained on? Debatable. The model may generate text that is consistent with the given context, but this does not necessarily mean that it has truly understood the real world. More research is needed to determine whether models like this can truly generalize beyond the text they are trained on.

This area is fast-changing, however. At the time of writing, it is possible to get an LLM to make use of external datasets and services to "ground" the LLM or tell it to reason. Doubtless, the capability of LLMs will continue to get better.

LLMs hallucinate

One of the most significant constraints of current LLMs is that they can "hallucinate," which means that they may produce text that is syntactically correct but illogical or untrue. In this case, we say that the model has clearly hallucinated.

This is a significant constraint that must be carefully addressed. Given that most readers skim over some parts of the text they're reading, it is possible that not all people would be able to identify that there was a hallucination in the text. At the time of writing, the amount of human work needed to check for accuracy is something to be considered when planning for production adoption of this technology.

Human feedback is needed

To reduce the amount of nonsense generated, an extra step is usually added when training a consumer-facing LLM. This is called *reinforcement learning through human feedback* (RLHF) and involves training the model to choose between generated text documents based on human ratings.

In addition, humans help to train the model to create documents in specific formats (e.g., emails, blog posts, bullet points, etc.) and guide the model away from toxic text.

Weaknesses

Now that you understand how LLMs are trained, it is clear that they will have certain limitations:

- If any of the input sources is wrong, that wrong continuation is part of the probable set of continuations. So the LLM could reproduce misinformation and/or outdated concepts.
- The model is better in domains where there is a lot of text that is published in digital formats. Therefore, the LLM will be better in domains such as coding and politics, but worse in domains such as anthropology.

- It is hard to tokenize unusual numbers and names (LLMs use subword tokens). Therefore, you should always double-check factual information such as numbers, authors of articles, etc., that comes out of an LLM.

- Like all ML models, LLMs should not be used in situations where deterministic outcomes are expected.

It is important to keep these limitations in mind when building applications that rely on generative AI.

Use cases

These limitations do not mean LLMs are not useful. Already, we see various good uses of them:

Domain-specific assistants
The LLM is trained on your organization's data to answer specific questions that would require your employees to read through a large number of documents. For example, an LLM can answer questions about internal regulations. This can save your employees time and improve efficiency.

Code snippets
Generative models can write code snippets or review existing code (like an automatic peer programmer) to speed up development or documentation writing. However, the code may not do what you want it to do, so you should test and edit the generated code in small pieces.

Document summarization
The LLM could help with summarizing long documents that would take ages to read to extract relevant information (e.g., financial data on balance sheets). This can also be part of making workflows more efficient.

Content generation
Content generation at scale—for example, for personalized marketing or sales—is unlocked by generative AI.

Some production use cases of LLMs include Gmail's Smart Compose, Jasper AI's ability to create marketing copy, Salesforce's ability to craft personalized sales emails, and GitHub Copilot's ability to generate code. We are seeing many organizations leveraging generative AI to provide their employees better access to their private knowledge bases through a natural language question-answering bot. Another widespread and successful use case involves using image generation algorithms to improve the level of differentiation of marketing ads. However, do not discount the difficulty of creating such products where generated text or images solve a human pain point, are accurate, and meet human standards.

Problems Fit for ML

What kind of problems can you solve with ML? The most compelling use cases of ML happen when you have many of these conditions in operation:

Repeated decision
> You have a simple "brain" task that has to be done so many times that it becomes very expensive or impossible for humans to do it. If you are a medical insurance firm and you get thousands of requests per day for reimbursement, it is very expensive to have a human look at the reimbursement request and determine if the procedure was needed or not. If you can get a computer to identify suspicious-looking claims, that will save you a lot of money. Conversely, there is not much of a business benefit to automating rare decisions. Yet it is surprising how often data scientists get carried away trying to apply ML to a problem that needs to be solved only a few times a year.

Labeled data
> ML works when you can teach the ML system by showing it examples of correct decisions. Anomaly detection where you cluster the data and look for outliers is an exception to this. However, the vast majority of ML problems require you to have examples that have the correct answer attached.

Fault-tolerant use case
> Because no ML algorithm is perfect, you should not use ML in cases where errors are fatal to life or property. You will have to consider the implications of the ML system being wrong and be willing to live with the consequences. In situations where errors have significant impact, having a human in the decision loop or having stop-loss provisions is common.

Logic that is hard to articulate
> The more complex some logic is to articulate, the better ML is at it. Note that it is quite easy to write up the logic of how to calculate the area of a polygon. That is not the sort of problem that ML is good for. When it is easy to capture the logic, you should use traditional programming methods. Save ML for situations where human logic is hard to come by (e.g., calculate the area of a room from a photograph).

Unstructured data
> Traditional rules tend to work quite well for processing structured data, but ML is needed for unstructured data. If you receive an HTTP response consisting of what buttons on a website a user clicked on, and you wish to see if they bought an item, it is quite simple to see if the Buy button was one of the buttons they clicked. On the other hand, if they entered some review text into a form and you want to know if the review mentions a shipping issue, you will need to process unstructured data (the text of the review).

Now that you have a better grasp of what ML is and when to use it, let's examine the best way to adopt it.

Buy, Adapt, or Build?

Once you decide that you need some AI capability, the question shifts to whether this is something you can buy off the shelf or it is something you have to custom build. An AI cloud architect increasingly has to choose the areas where buying an off-the-shelf capability is the better approach and the areas where it is possible to build a better, more differentiated capability. This decision may also be driven by the need to prioritize scarce data scientist resources.

Let's look at the decision process and some scenarios and capabilities where one or the other approach is better.

Data Considerations

In general, the quality of an ML model improves with the size and quality of the data used to train it. Dramatic ML performance and accuracy are driven by improvements in data size. Also, ML systems need to be retrained for new situations. For example, if you have a recommendation system for expense categories and you want to provide recommendations for hotel accommodations, you can't use the same recommendations model. You have to train it in the second instance on hotels that were picked by other employees at the travel destination. So even though the model code may be the same, you have to retrain the model with new data for new situations.

Taking these two concepts together (you get a better ML model when you have more data, and an ML model typically needs to be retrained for a new situation), you get a strategy that can tell you whether to buy or build:

- Determine if the buyable model is solving the *same problem* that you want to solve. Has it been trained on the same input and on similar labels? Let's say you're trying to do a product search, and the model has been trained on catalog images as inputs. But you want to do a product search based on users' mobile phone photographs of the products. The model that was trained on catalog images won't work on your mobile phone photographs, and you'd have to build a new model. But let's say you're considering a vendor's translation model that's been trained on speeches in the European Parliament. If you want to translate similar speeches, the model works well as it uses the same kind of data.

- Does the vendor have *more data* than you do? If the vendor has trained their model on speeches in the European Parliament but you have access to more speech data than they have, you should build. If they have more data, then buy their model.

In a nutshell, if the vendor has a solution that solves the problem you want to solve, and they have more/better data, then you should buy it. If not, build your own. Increasingly, there is a third choice: to adapt a prebuilt model. Let's look at architectural and other considerations in each of these three cases.

When to Buy

When a credible service provider offers a turnkey service or API that works for your problem, you should seriously evaluate purchasing that service. It will almost always be less expensive and better maintained than something you can build—remember that a popular service will be able to amortize its development budget among hundreds of users, whereas you will have to pay for all improvements yourself.

Moreover, the fact that there is a marketplace of applications means that the capability is not core to your business. Plus, your team can be doing something more distinctive and differentiated than implementing something that can be purchased.

When alternatives are offered by other clouds or credible third parties, it is possible to run a bakeoff on your own workload and choose the one that fits best. Buying ML capabilities is one of the places where you don't have to worry about what cloud you use primarily—in many cases, these are simply APIs, and you can invoke them regardless of which cloud your application is running on. For example, you can run your website on AWS, but it might invoke Google's Translate API on the text of reviews.

There are three levels of abstraction at which you can buy AI capabilities:

SaaS
> Some AI capabilities are made available through turnkey APIs. For example, Retail Search from Google Cloud is a turnkey service that can be used by any business to provide ML-powered search within its ecommerce site. Amazon Connect is a turnkey service that provides contact center capabilities. Azure's Computer Vision API can be invoked by sending it an image and getting back information of what's in the image. All of these are examples of services that are invoked through APIs directly used to integrate with your applications. These models are trained on diverse datasets and are likely more accurate and more resilient than anything you can put together.

Building blocks
> Sometimes the capability that can be bought off the shelf is not something that constitutes a complete business use case. Nevertheless, you might want to use that AI capability as a building block in your applications. For example, you might be able to use the entity extraction or form parser capabilities of Google's DocAI in your NLP pipeline. Azure Computer Vision could be

used to prescan images for adult content before you ingest those images into your system. Amazon Rekognition can be used to identify people in an onboarding system.

Enterprise applications

Sometimes, the capability is too bespoke to buy as SaaS and too complex to be available as a building block. In such cases, you might be able to nevertheless purchase the capability as a combination of products and services. The supplier has experience implementing the capability in your industry and can reuse quite a bit of its earlier work to build the capability for you. The relative mix of reusable code to on-site code varies between providers and from use case to use case. For example, C3 AI will build an anti-money laundering solution off your first-party data but leverage its experience building similar answers for other financial firms.

The source of such capabilities is not limited to the major cloud providers. The marketplace on Google Cloud, AWS, and Azure all have a wide selection of SaaS capabilities from a wide variety of vendors. Systems integrators (like Accenture and Wipro) and AI application providers (like C3 AI [*https://oreil.ly/SHnU8*], SpringML, and Brightloom) offer AI solutions to improve customer engagement, pricing, digital marketing, revenue intelligence, yield optimization, and so on.

What Can You Buy?

A cloud architect in a company that is adopting AI has to become familiar with vendor choice and vendor management. Knowledge of ML frameworks like TensorFlow and MLOps platforms like SageMaker and Vertex AI is not sufficient.

With the explosive growth in AI-based startups and the addition of AI practices at global and regional systems integrators, the number of capabilities you can buy rather than build continues to dramatically expand. Whatever we write in this section will be obsolete in months, so we will paint with a broad brush and encourage you to do research, ask for demos, and make a well-informed decision. You could save months of effort and dramatically lower the risk of failure by choosing the right vendor.

Here are some capabilities that existed in early 2023:

Better customer service

There are a number of AI solutions that improve every step of the customer service chain, from automatic handling of calls, creating chat transcripts, and improving call center agent efficiency to obtaining product insights. The solutions are usually omnichannel and can support voice, chat, and email. Generative AI solutions exist that can search through your document archives and provide answers to user queries.

Workflow assistance

Coding assistants can improve software engineering productivity. Workflow copilots can streamline many corporate functions such as reviewing legal contracts and processing invoices.

Improving marketing spend

Digital user activity provides a lot of signals, and the impact of digital marketing is measurable. This leads to a number of AI solutions around privacy-safe marketing analytics, brand measurement, lookalike audiences, and improving campaign performance.

Writing sales and marketing content

Generative AI solutions to craft campaigns and help write copy also exist. They can also use alternative datasets and first-party data to craft responses to RFPs, personalized invoices, sales emails, etc.

Recommendations

Product and next-best-action recommendations are so widespread that these capabilities are available as industry-specific, easy-to-deploy solutions.

Publicly available or gatherable data

Capabilities that are based on publicly available or gatherable data such as social media posts, weather, internet images, stock market trades, etc., are often available for purchase.

Retail

All sorts of capabilities, from shelf management to omnichannel marketing attribution, demand forecasting, and price optimization, are available for purchase.

Manufacturing

While equipment may vary, capabilities like preventive/predictive maintenance, yield optimization, and quality control are available and can be customized.

Supply chain management

Many capabilities, from reading customs forms to inventory management and managing drivers' routes, are available for purchase.

Healthcare

Many stages of pharmaceutical research, detection of many diseases and medical conditions, and optimal use of facilities at healthcare providers have corresponding capabilities.

Media and entertainment

Many capabilities such as tracking of a puck in hockey, estimating the likelihood of a high-scoring football game, creating thumbnails of images and highlights of videos, etc., are already available.

Back-office operations

Many back-office operations can be improved by automating the work. There are robot process automation (RPA) solutions in everything from insurance application processing to classifying invoices. Generative AI solutions exist that can use first-party data to automatically fill forms and invoke backend agents through APIs.

Financial services

Several capabilities like personalization of customer interactions, embedded finance solutions, value-at-risk and "what-if" analysis, and real-time fraud analysis are available.

We are avoiding naming example providers of the preceding capabilities because there will doubtless be many more options by the time you are reading this. In any case, before you commit to building, find out how good the off-the-shelf solutions are at addressing your problem. You might be pleasantly surprised.

How Adapting Works

Training a state-of-the-art (SOTA) image classification model requires more than 10 million images. Chances are that you don't have that kind of a large dataset for the use case that you are interested in.

The solution is to take a SOTA model trained on an appropriately large dataset that is similar to yours (often, this is called a *pretrained model* or *foundational model*) and then adapt that SOTA model to fit your data. Your data can be as few as 10 images consisting of both positive and negative examples, although the more (high-quality) data you have, the better the model will perform.

Adapting is an in-between choice, between buying and building. You get the benefits of the vendor's large dataset and the customization afforded by your own data.

There are two ways to do this adaptation:

Transfer learning

This keeps 99%+ of the original model and tunes the remaining weights on your data. Specifically, it keeps the 99% of the model that has learned how to extract information from data and then trains the remaining 1% of the model that operates on the extracted information to come up with the result.

Fine-tuning

This keeps the entire original model and tunes the entire model on your data but keeps the magnitude of the weight updates small enough that the original information that was learned is not completely lost. Instead of modifying the weights directly, some "low-rank" generative AI fine-tuning methods train an ancillary model that adapts the weights of the foundational model.

You can find pretrained models that are ready for adaptation on sites such as Tensor-Flow Hub (*https://oreil.ly/GRfl5*), PyTorch Hub (*https://oreil.ly/wAxQj*), and Hugging Face (*https://oreil.ly/zJbVe*). These tend to be open source models for building block capabilities such as image classification, optical character recognition, and speech to text. Fine-tune or transfer learn these models with your own data.

Pretrained core LLMs such as OpenAI GPT and PaLM are trained for general purposes to solve common language problems across industries. It is possible to fine-tune these models for specific tasks, such as creating a checklist for medical procedures. However, it is important to recognize the limitations of fine-tuning in the case of generative AI. To teach the model new information, it is necessary to retrain (not just adapt) the models on that industry's data. Labeled industry-specific datasets are crucial for training the model to accurately recognize medical entities or classify medical texts.

Hyperscaler ML platforms provide a fully managed experience for adapting pre-trained models. For example, AutoML Translate provides a way to adapt Google's Translate API with your own phrase pairs—for example, of industry-specific language. The resulting model can do all the translation that Google's Translate API does but also knows about the industry-specific terms that you have added. Similar options exist on other hyperscalers.

So the full decision criterion becomes: buy the vendor's solution if it's trained on the same problem and has access to more data than you do. Then, consider if you can adapt (transfer learn from or fine-tune) the vendor's solution if you have unique data of your own to train it to do custom tasks. As with any situation where you incorporate externally created artifacts into your software, you will have to make sure that the vendors are in compliance with your legal requirements.

Examples of things that you can buy, adapt, or build from cloud providers and partners are summarized in Table 10-1. This is an incomplete list even at the time of writing and doubtless will have grown by the time you read this. The inclusion of a technology (e.g., Azure ML Computer Vision or AWS Lex) in Table 10-1 does not imply any endorsement over similar services available in other clouds (AWS Rekognition, GCP Vision API, Azure ML NLP, GCP DocAI, etc.).

Table 10-1. Example cloud capabilities that you can buy, adapt, or build

Strategy	Example ML capabilities	Why
Buy SaaS	• Amazon Forecast • Amazon Connect • Azure ML Computer Vision • GCP Retail Search • GCP Translate API • Google Enterprise Search	Turnkey service or API that can be easily integrated. These models are trained on diverse datasets and are likely better than anything you can put together.

Strategy	Example ML capabilities	Why
Buy building blocks	• AWS Lex • Amazon Polly • Hugging Face on AWS • Azure OpenAI GPT • GCP DocAI form parser • GCP NLP entity extraction	Use as building blocks in your ML applications. Why reinvent the wheel for functionality that is not core to your business? Plus, it is rare that you will have enough data to train a better model.
Buy enterprise application	• AWS Preventive Maintenance • Azure Price Optimization • GCP Contact Center AI • GCP Recommendations AI • GCP Med-PaLM • C3 AI Yield Optimization • Symphony Retail	Combination of products and services to deploy and configure the application to meet your organization's needs.
Adapt	• AWS Jumpstart • Azure OpenAI Studio • GCP AutoML Vision • GCP AutoML Video Intelligence • Vertex AI Fine-tune PaLM	Fine-tune AI models on your own tasks. Until you get to incredibly large datasets, these are likely to outperform custom models built solely on your data.
Build	• AWS SageMaker • Azure Machine Learning • GCP Vertex AI • GCP Dialogflow	Managed frameworks to build end-to-end ML models. This is covered in Chapter 11.

The strategies in Table 10-1 are tailored to different sets of technical skills. While the first three approaches require system-integration capabilities, data scientists are required for the last two.

Next, let's look at the considerations once you have determined that the AI capability you need has to be built by your team.

AI Architectures

Broadly speaking, there are seven types of AI applications that are currently successful:

Understanding unstructured data

For example, you may have a photograph of a piece of equipment and you would like the ML model to identify the model number. Understanding the content of images, videos, speech, and natural language text fall into this category of applications.

Generating unstructured data

You may receive a set of documents as "discovery" during a lawsuit and may need to summarize the information received. Or you may want to create a personalized ad based on the last five purchases of the customer, weaving them into a story. It is now possible to generate text, images, music, and videos using AI.

Predicting outcomes

For example, you have information about the basket of items in a shopping cart and the purchase history of the shopper, and you'd like to determine whether the shopping cart is likely to be abandoned without a purchase happening. Predicting the likelihood or magnitude of an event falls into this category of applications.

Forecasting values

For example, you would like to predict the number of items in a particular category that will be sold at a particular store over the next week. Predicting time-varying quantities like inventory levels at a future point in time falls into this category. The difference between predicting an outcome and forecasting a value is not always clear. In predicting an outcome, the other attributes are the primary determinant of whether the event will happen. In forecasting, the pattern of change over time is the most important factor. There are some problems that you might have to try out both ways.

Anomaly detection

In many cases, the goal is to identify unusual events or behavior. For example, in a gaming scenario, anomaly detection might be employed to identify cases where cheating might be happening.

Personalization

You might want to recommend products or craft experiences based on what the user and other users like this user have liked in the past.

Automation

This is where you take a process that is carried out inefficiently today and attempt to replace part or all of it using ML.

In this section, we will look at canonical architectures and technology choices for each of these. All these architectures will be built on top of the platform discussed in the next chapter.

Understanding Unstructured Data

The capability of deep learning to understand the content of images, videos, speech, and natural language text has kept on getting better over time.

Just a few years ago, the capability of speech recognition models lagged far behind that of humans. Now, while not perfect, speech-to-text models are routinely used to caption uploaded videos and live speeches. The same sort of improvement has been seen in all the other types of unstructured data.

Deep learning does not require the feature engineering step that is usually necessary for traditional ML methods. Because of this, you can build deep learning systems in a very generic way. The ML model architecture required to differentiate screws from nails will also work if you need to distinguish fractured bones from intact ones. Note that we said the same *architecture*, but not the same *model*. This is because the model in the first instance will be trained on images of screws and nails whereas the model in the second instance will be trained on images of broken versus unbroken bones. While the architecture is the same, the weights will be different.

The research community has developed and published model architectures for standard problems in image, video, speech, and text analysis. Unlike the prebuilt models discussed in the section on buying AI, these models have not been trained on very large datasets, or if they have, the characteristics of the datasets they have been trained on are very different from your data—you will have to train the models from scratch using your own data.

Therefore, when it comes to problems that involve unstructured data, it is usually not necessary to design your own model architecture. Just pick a model that is SOTA or close to it and train it on your data. All the major cloud providers provide easy mechanisms to do this. They usually start with unstructured data held in AWS S3, Google Cloud Storage, or Azure Blob Storage. Then use a no-code or low-code service such Vertex AI AutoML to train and deploy the model (see Figure 10-2).

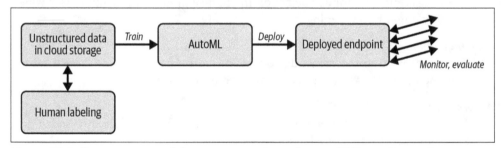

Figure 10-2. For unstructured data, use no-code, end-to-end ML services such as AutoML in Google Cloud Vertex AI or AWS SageMaker

The hardest thing might be to supply the AutoML model with *labels* for the training data—the label is the correct answer. It might involve human labeling. You can use crowd compute services like Amazon Mechanical Turk or SageMaker Ground Truth or third-party providers of equivalent services to avoid the drudgery of doing the labeling yourself.

Generating Unstructured Data

Generative AI is a type of AI that can create new content, such as text, images, music, and video. It does this by learning the structure of existing data (such as what English words tend to follow other English words) and then using that statistical knowledge to generate new content that is realistic. The architectures that work in generative AI are rapidly evolving at the time this book is going to press (in October 2023). Doubtless, by the time you are reading this, the choices will be broader and/or more streamlined.

At the time of writing, most use cases of generative AI involve invoking a pretrained model offered by an LLM vendor through an API that takes a text prompt as input. This is called *zero-shot learning*. For example, images can be created by supplying a text prompt to an image generation API such as DALL-E on Azure OpenAI, Imagen on GCP, Stable Diffusion on AWS SageMaker Jumpstart, or Midjourney. Similarly, you can ask PaLM on Vertex AI, GPT-4 on Azure OpenAI, Cohere on AWS Bedrock, etc., to generate an outline for a new article by sending it a natural language request. Code completion and code generation in response to natural language descriptions of the code to be generated are supported by the different hyperscalers (GitHub Copilot on Azure, Codey on Google Cloud, CodeWhisperer on AWS) and by independents such as Tabnine and Replit. Crafting the language of the prompt is important, leading to *prompt engineering* as an experimentation and development framework. In hybrid architectures, use managed LLMs offered by startups such as Perplexity AI and Ryax. Use a microservices architecture to build products that employ zero-shot learning, with the LLM being one of the microservices. While prompt engineering is good for prototyping, version changes in the models can cause existing prompts to break. Most practitioners guard against this by fine-tuning a model under their control for production use cases (*https://oreil.ly/sJtXI*).

It is possible to fine-tune LLMs on the public clouds using their platforms. Commonly, this is done for instruction tuning (teaching the LLM new tasks) so that the LLM can respond to prompts that it doesn't currently know how to handle or that it handles somewhat poorly, or to guard against breaking changes. Fine-tuning is done by training the LLM for a few epochs using supervised parameter-efficient methods (PEFT or SFT) such as Quantized Low-Rank Adaptation (QLoRA). You can fine-tune proprietary models such as OpenAI GPT-4 and Google Cloud PaLM through services that they provide and somewhat open LLMs such as Falcon, Dolly, and Llama 2 on PaaS ML platforms such as SageMaker, Databricks, and Vertex AI.[1] Open source

---

1 Researchers (*https://oreil.ly/m178J*) make the point that these LLMs are not truly open source (*https://oreil.ly/4BrtJ*). They do, however, allow you to fine-tune and deploy them in commercial applications without many restrictions.

model hubs (such as Hugging Face) are increasingly popular as a way to abstract out the necessary code. Deploy fine-tuned LLMs as APIs on ML platforms such as SageMaker, as you would any other ML model.

Instruction tuning can teach the model new tasks but not new knowledge (at the time of writing, that requires retraining the model from scratch on new data). To teach LLMs new knowledge cheaply, it is common to use patterns that take advantage of an LLM's ability to solve new tasks from a few examples (*few-shot learning*), to use information *stuffed* into the prompt (*retrieval-augmented generation*), or to generate structured data that can be passed into an external API (*agents*). For example, to answer questions, the embedding of a question or its hypothetical answer is searched against a vector database of document chunks to find relevant documents, and the LLM is asked to summarize these document chunks to answer the question posed (see Figure 10-3). Open source abstraction layers (such as LangChain) are becoming popular ways to implement these patterns. Architect production use cases in such a way that each step of the chain is a container in an ML pipeline. Containerized ML pipelines are covered in the next chapter.

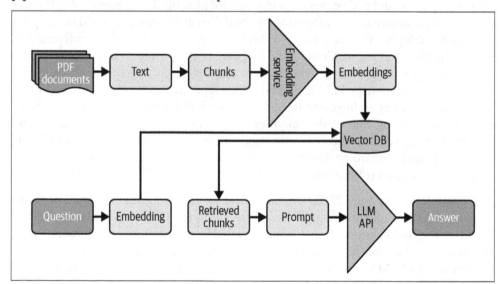

Figure 10-3. Architecture for retrieval-augmented generation, a pattern for question-answering using LLMs

Predicting Outcomes

The historical data that will serve as training data for predicting outcomes usually exists in logs data and transactional databases. For example, if you are interested in predicting whether a shopping cart will be abandoned, you have to get the history of all website activity—this will be present in logs data. You might choose to include information such as the price of the item, discounts in effect, and whether the customer actually paid for the item. While some or all of this data might also be retrieved from website logs, it might be easier to query them from a database. Thus, the historical data also contains the labels in this situation (see Figure 10-4).

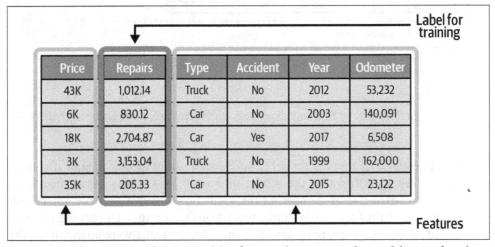

Figure 10-4. Outcome prediction models often involve training the model to predict the values of one column in the DWH based on other column values

Therefore, the architecture (see Figure 10-5) involves using replication mechanisms and connectors to land all the necessary data into a DWH. It is then possible to train regression or classification ML models on the DWH directly—both Amazon Redshift and Google BigQuery support the ability to train models directly from SQL and defer more complex models underneath the covers to SageMaker and Vertex AI, respectively. The model, once trained, can be exported and deployed into the managed prediction service on both clouds. Typically, all the predictions or at least a sample of them are stored back in the DWH to support continuous evaluation and drift detection.

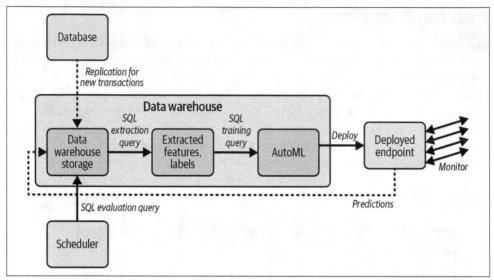

Figure 10-5. Architecture of training, deploying, and monitoring an outcome prediction model

Training is relaunched anytime there is a sufficient amount of new data or if continuous evaluation identifies that the model or one of its features has drifted. This evaluation is carried out by comparing the predictions against the true values that are obtained after the fact. For example, predictions of whether a shopping cart will be abandoned can be compared a day later with the carts that were abandoned. The evaluation query is carried periodically by means of a scheduler.

Forecasting Values

Most ML models do inference—they "predict" the value of an unobserved value based on other factors. For example, an ML model might predict whether a transaction is fraudulent based on factors such as the transaction amount and the location from which the credit card is being used. Key is that the input factors do not include past values of the thing (fraud) to be predicted (see Figure 10-6).

In contrast, in a forecasting problem, one of the inputs to the ML model is a previous value of the thing to be predicted. For example, if you are trying to predict the number of sandwiches that will be sold 3 days from now, one of the inputs might be the number of sandwiches that were sold in each of the past 28 days.

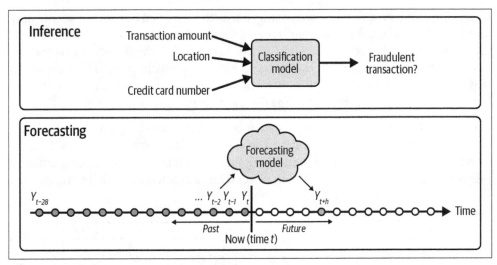

Figure 10-6. Inference versus time series forecasting

Notice that, in essence, forecasting problems require you to feedback the ground truth of past predictions. This real-time feedback loop makes the data engineering architecture considerably more complex. One approach is shown in Figure 10-7. Here, training is done on historical data in the DWH, with the data collected using windows in SQL. These are queries that partition the data into segments that consist of the current row and a certain number of preceding rows:

```
WINDOW fourweek_window AS
    (PARTITION BY store_id, sandwich_id
    ORDER BY purchase_date ASC ROWS 27 PRECEDING)
```

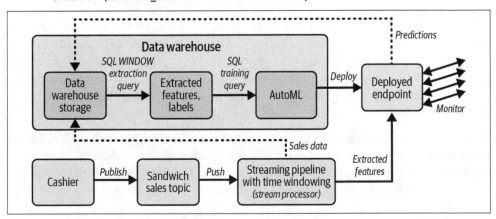

Figure 10-7. Architecture for time-series analytics with separate batch and streaming pipelines

In real time, however, the time windowing needs to be carried out within a streaming pipeline. The streaming pipeline pulls the 28 days of data and sends it to the forecasting model for prediction. It also takes care of keeping the DWH updated so that the next training run happens on up-to-date data. The problem with this approach is that you need to maintain two data pipelines: a batch pipeline for training based on historical data and a streaming pipeline for forecasting based on real-time data.

A much better approach is to use a data pipeline framework such as Apache Beam that provides the way to execute the same code on both batch and stream datasets. This limits the exposure to training-serving skew, which is caused by having different preprocessing steps happen in training versus during prediction. Such an architecture is shown in Figure 10-8.

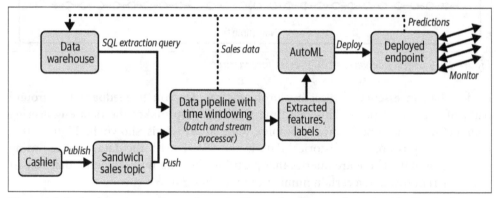

Figure 10-8. Architecture using a data pipeline technology such as Apache Beam that supports both batch and stream

Anomaly Detection

In anomaly detection on time-varying data, there are two time windows. Data over the longer time window (say, one month) is clustered. Then, data over the shorter time window is compared with the clusters. If data in the shorter window is unlike the larger data (i.e., if the distance between the new data and the clusters is high), an anomaly is flagged.

The architecture here is similar to the forecasting case depicted in Figure 10-8, except there are two time windows that need to be maintained. Make sure that the streaming pipeline infrastructure you choose (such as Cloud Dataflow, AWS Kinesis, Apache Flink, or Confluent Kafka) is capable of maintaining the length of time window that you require.

In anomaly detection on individual events, the principle is the same except that the second (shorter time) window consists of a single event or user session. So events over the past month are aggregated to learn what usual events look like. Outliers from the distribution are treated as anomalies. For example, if the goal is to identify bots in a multiplayer game, the typical behavior of players (time between moves, likelihood of repeated moves, likelihood of subsequent moves involving different hands, etc.) is collected and aggregated. Any player who deviates significantly from the overall distribution is flagged.

Personalization

One of the most common uses of ML is to tailor an experience (such as a game), product (such as a music playlist), service (such as a spam filter), or communication (such as a sales outbound) on an individual basis. Doing so in the context of respecting users' privacy concerns requires some fundamental guarantees about data confidentiality and security, including whether information leaks from one user to another.

Such tailoring requires knowledge of the preferences not only of the specific individual but also of individuals like the user for which the personalization is happening (e.g., next best action for a marketing funnel). The tailoring will also try to highlight items similar to items that this individual has liked or positively reacted to in the past. Therefore both the demographics of the individual (expressed as customer segments, such as "single, age in the 20s, urban, nonsubscriber") and the characteristics of the item (e.g., price, release date, etc.) are key features to a personalization ML model (see Figure 10-9). Given a person-item pair, the personalization model computes a score for how interested the individual would be in the item. Starting from a list of candidate items (such as all the items meeting the user's search query or all the ongoing sales promotions), the personalization model is thus able to rank the items in a way that captures that user's preferences.

A good personalization model will also need to handle the *cold-start* problem—if you have a new user, you still need to provide a reasonable experience to them, and if you have a new item, you still need the model to recommend the item to some customers. The cold-start problem is typically handled as a preprocessing step that looks for users or items with insufficient history and provides a reasonable experience to them (for example, that you recommend the most popular items over less popular ones).

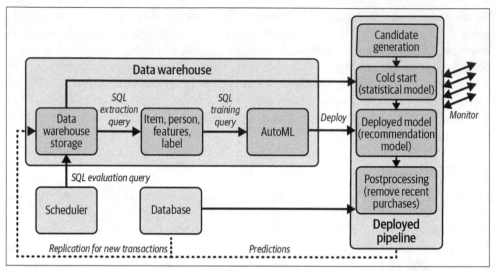

Figure 10-9. Architecture for personalization that involves only a small number of potential choices; the deployed model is part of a pipeline that also includes handling of cold starts and pruning of recent purchases

A personalization model will usually need to do some postprocessing on the recommendations. For example, if the user has just seen *The Shawshank Redemption* in your video-streaming service, you probably do not want to recommend the same movie again. Postprocessing consists of rules such as these to prune the automatically generated list of recommendations.

The architecture shown in Figure 10-9 is the same as that of outcome prediction (depicted in Figure 10-5) except that there are additional preprocessing and postprocessing filters required. Therefore, the model is deployed as a pipeline. The preprocessing step requires that a statistical model (e.g., the most popular item) be used to create a model that can be used in cold-start situations. The postprocessing step requires filtering out recent purchases and requires a connection to the real-time transactional database.

The architecture in Figure 10-9 breaks down if the number of candidate items is too large. For example, when you visit the YouTube homepage, you are presented with a set of recommended videos. The candidate space for that list is the entirety of the YouTube catalog. Ranking the entire catalog for you at the moment you visit the webpage is not feasible. Therefore, when the list of candidates is large, the architecture consists of a batch pipeline that precomputes a smaller list of candidate recommendations for each user. The frequency at which this batch pipeline runs might vary depending on how active the user is, and these precomputed candidates can be supplemented with trending topics for an experience that is not stale. This is shown in Figure 10-10.

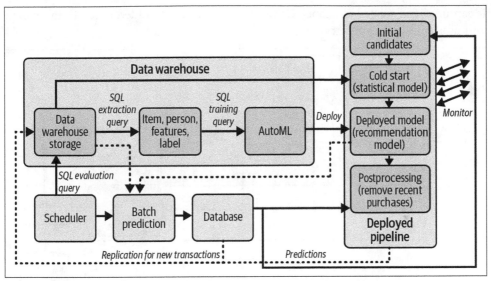

Figure 10-10. When the overall space of candidates is large, a smaller list of candidates is precomputed using a scheduled batch pipeline

Let's have a look now at the last type of AI application: automation.

Automation

Like personalization, automation of back-office processes requires multiple models and pre- and postprocessing filters. Each of the models has to be trained on its own data, and the deployed pipeline consists of the ML models invoked as a directed acyclic graph (DAG).

The ML models themselves may not all be trained from scratch. Building block models (such as a form parser, translation tool, etc.) are common components of these automation model pipelines.

Typically, in automation pipelines, the model decision on high-confidence predictions is automatically carried out, but some provision is made for human oversight, as shown in Figure 10-11. For example, a small sample of high-confidence predictions is sent to a human expert for ongoing validation. This is termed *human-over-the-loop*. In addition, decisions that are costly, low-confidence, or difficult to reverse are also subject to human approval. This is termed *human-in-the-loop*. Both are important.

Only high-value predictions from any model are fed to the next step of the ML pipeline. Low-confidence predictions from any of the models mean that the input is sent to a queue for human processing. A key component of automation pipelines is labeling—it is essential that the human decision on these low-confidence predictions is captured and treated as a label. Once labeled, this data is added to the training data and used in subsequent retraining.

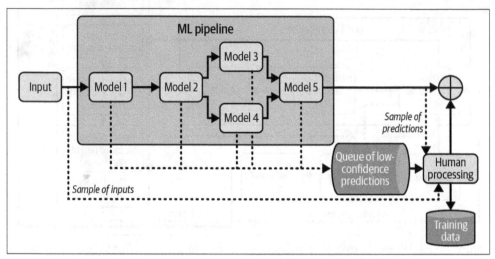

Figure 10-11. An automation pipeline consists of many ML models chained together

The ML models are trained and deployed depending on their type (e.g., AutoML, prebuilt APIs, or custom models). The set of models is tied into a pipeline and orchestrated in a system such as Kubeflow Pipelines for which managed services exist in the public cloud. The queue could be any distributed tasks queue: AWS Simple Queue Service, Google Cloud Pub/Sub, etc. The training data will be on cloud object storage or in a DWH, depending on whether it is unstructured or structured.

Responsible AI

Because ML is such a powerful tool, you have to be careful to not misuse it. Be aware of your organization and government policies and regulations. Consider this use case, for example: you wish to reduce the time people spend waiting on an elevator. So you want to automatically identify the people walking into the lobby of the building and use your knowledge of which floor their office is on. That way, you can optimally direct the individuals into elevators to minimize the number of stops. This use case would violate privacy regulations in many jurisdictions, as photographing and tracking people may be forbidden.

Because ML models are never perfect, you have to be careful about using ML in situations where decisions are made automatically without any human intervention. Zillow, famously, had to shut down its automated home-buying models (*https://oreil.ly/atiBv*) after it ended up building excess inventory—people whose houses were undervalued would not sell to Zillow, but people whose houses were overvalued would rush to sell.

For a more detailed coverage of these concepts, we recommend *Responsible Machine Learning* by Patrick Hall, Navdeep Gill, and Benjamin Cox (O'Reilly).

AI Principles

Your organization will probably have set up principles for when and where AI can be used and not used. As an example, these are Microsoft's AI principles (*https://oreil.ly/XuW7E*):

Fairness
> AI systems should treat all people fairly.

Reliability and safety
> AI systems should perform reliably and safely.

Privacy and security
> AI systems should be secure and respect privacy.

Inclusiveness
> AI systems should empower everyone and engage people.

Transparency
> AI systems should be understandable.

Accountability
> People should be accountable for AI systems.

Microsoft's Responsible AI Toolbox is a collection of integrated tools and functionalities to support the responsible use of AI by developers. The company also helped create a dataset named ToxiGen (*https://oreil.ly/MedGc*) to enable ML practitioners to detect toxicity against several minority groups.

As another example, here are Google's AI principles (*https://oreil.ly/6moeJ*) and how they propel or constrain Google's use of AI in their own products:

Be socially beneficial.
> For example, Google Maps uses AI to suggest the most eco-friendly route (*https://oreil.ly/-2R2z*). Google estimates that eco-friendly routing has the potential to prevent more than one million tons of carbon emissions per year, an obvious societal benefit.

Avoid creating or reinforcing bias.
> In February 2021, Google Cloud's Vision API stopped attaching gendered labels (*https://oreil.ly/RSNwL*) like "man" or "woman." The problem was that automatically identifying gender leads to use cases that create or perpetuate bias.

Be built and tested for safety.

Waymo, Google's self-driving car project, shared its safety framework (*https://oreil.ly/_qK3U*) when opening its fully autonomous ride-hailing service to the public.

Be accountable to people.

For example, even though the Google Nest Learning Thermostat can learn users' daily routines and automatically create a temperature schedule, users can turn Auto-Schedule off.

Incorporate privacy design principles.

In order for Google Assistant to reduce mistriggering when the device thinks it heard users say "Hey Google," the on-device model is fine-tuned to the user of that device. However, this uses federated learning, a privacy-enhancing technology that can work without sending users' raw data to Google servers.

Uphold high standards of scientific excellence.

Google publishes a lot of its work at reputed scientific conferences such as Neur-IPS (*https://nips.cc*). By making publishing at peer-reviewed venues a key part of the role for engineers working in ML, Google fosters high scientific standards.

Be made available for uses that accord with these principles.

Google makes AI technologies available both as open source (e.g., TensorFlow, BERT, etc.) and through Google Cloud (Vertex AI, Retail Search, etc.).

Do not design or deploy AI if the technology is likely to cause overall harm.

For example, do not design or deploy AI if its primary purpose is as a weapon that injures people, does surveillance, or contravenes human rights. In 2020, for example, the Google Cloud CEO said that the company had received confirmation from the US Customs and Border Patrol that its technology would not be used for immigration enforcement (*https://oreil.ly/s9wlB*) at the border.

While the Google or Microsoft principles may not fit your company's mission and goals (for example, if you work in the defense industry, the last principle will definitely not be applicable), verify with your AI governance board before embarking on a new AI project and double-check for any recent changes in regulations, as they are frequently updated.

ML Fairness

You also have to be careful about the use of historical data in training ML models that make irreversible decisions that affect people, because the ML model will pick up the biases inherent in the historical data. For example, consider whether it is responsible to use an ML model that is based on historical data of previous jail sentences to recommend the length of jail time for people convicted of a crime today. If prosecutors and judges in real life tend to be prejudiced against racial minorities, the ML model will pick up that bias (*https://oreil.ly/VxVdt*)—even if race is not an explicit input to the ML model, it can get picked up implicitly based on where the convicted person lives or the crime they are charged with. This is not an easy problem to resolve—pretty much any measure of fairness that you can think of (not using protected attributes, achieving classification parity, or calibrated outcomes independent of protected attributes) turns out to be problematic (*https://oreil.ly/TmD41*).

There are a number of tools that are part of cloud ML frameworks to help with diagnosing ML fairness issues. For example, it is possible to do sliced evaluations, carry out what-if tests, and continuously monitor model performance on protected criteria.

Explainability

Often, stakeholders (end users, regulators) will refuse to adopt an ML model unless they get some indication of why the model is making the recommendation that it is making. Few doctors will accept an automated X-ray model that simply says whether there is a fracture or not without any other explanation. Few regulators will take a bank's assurance that it is not being discriminatory in its loan approvals unless the bank can explain the rationale behind its loan decisions. Explainability can also be important for explaining to laypeople how the model works and the risks inherent to it, to build societal acceptance for technologies such as self-driving cars. This also plays out in organizational training, as everyone within the company, from marketing to sales to data teams, must understand how the model is making recommendations against the data available.

Cloud ML frameworks provide explainable AI (XAI) tools that can help you understand how your ML models make decisions. This isn't a complete step-by-step deconstruction of an AI model, which can be close to impossible if you're attempting to trace the millions of parameters used in deep learning algorithms. Instead, XAI aims to provide insights into how models work, so human experts are able to understand the logic that goes into making a decision.

When applied successfully, XAI offers three important benefits:

Increases trust in the ML model
> XAI tools can be used to provide clear and understandable explanations of the reasoning that led to the model's output. Say you are using a deep learning model to analyze medical images like X-rays; you can use XAI to produce saliency maps that highlight the pixels that were used to get the diagnosis.

Provides a way to troubleshoot ML

Explainability in AI can also enable you to debug a model and troubleshoot how well a model is working. The What-If Tool allows you to change one of the model inputs and see what the model would have done in that case.

Identifies fairness issues

For example, you might have a model to identify when cars are making illegal lefthand turns. The explanation might suggest that the model, instead of focusing on cars turning left illegally, is looking to see if there is a pothole. This influence could be caused by a skewed dataset that contained a large number of images taken on poorly maintained roads, or even real bias, where a ticket might be more likely to be given out in an underfunded area of a city.

Cloud ML frameworks provide XAI support during development as part of their notebook development experience. For example, What-If Tools are integrated into Vertex AI Workbench. They also provide XAI support for deployed models so that model predictions can have explanations attached to them. Saliency maps are integrated into Vertex AI Predictions. Because the What-If Tool from Google is open source, it can be used from notebooks on other clouds as well. Both Azure Machine Learning and AWS SageMaker, like Vertex AI Predictions, offer support for explaining predictions.

Summary

This chapter has provided you with an overview of the most relevant things you should consider to effectively include AI and ML applications in your data platform perimeter. The key takeaways are as follows:

- AI is the field of study that solves problems by getting computers to think and act like humans.

- ML is a subfield of AI that solves AI problems using data instead of custom logic.

- Deep learning is a subfield of ML that has been successfully used to understand unstructured data like speech, images, video, and natural language.

- Generative AI can be used to create unstructured data.

- Generative models can be used to generate text, images, music, and video. They are commonly invoked as APIs that take text prompts as inputs.

- It is possible to fine-tune large models to make them do tasks for which they were not trained. This is usually done in a parameter-efficient way using methods such as QLoRA.

- It is possible to use patterns such as retrieval-augmented generation and few-shot learning to get a generative model to learn new information.

- The most compelling use cases of ML happen when you have many of the following: repeated decisions, labeled data, a fault-tolerant use case, hard-to-articulate logic, and unstructured data.

- If the vendor has a solution that solves the problem you want to solve, and they have more data, then you should buy it. If not, build your own. The third option is to adapt a solution to your data.

- There are three levels of abstraction at which you can buy AI capabilities: SaaS, building blocks, and enterprise applications. Buy SaaS for turnkey services or APIs that can be easily integrated. Buy building blocks such as form parsers for use in your ML applications. Enterprise applications can be configured to meet your organization's needs.

- Adaptation of prebuilt ML models can be done through transfer learning or fine-tuning. Until you get to incredibly large datasets, these are likely to outperform custom models built solely on your data.

- Use AWS SageMaker, GCP Vertex AI, and Azure Machine Learning to build end-to-end ML models. This is covered in the next chapter.

- When it comes to problems that involve unstructured data, it is usually not necessary to design your own model architecture. Use a no-code or low-code service such Vertex AI AutoML to train and deploy the model.

- When predicting outcomes, train ML models within your DWH using SQL. Do batch predictions within the DWH itself. For online predictions, deploy the trained model to a managed ML service.

- The best approach to forecasting problems is to use a data pipeline framework such as Apache Beam that provides the way to execute the same code on both batch and stream datasets.

- The architecture for anomaly detection is similar to the forecasting case, except there are two time windows that need to be maintained.

- In personalization, the deployed model is part of a pipeline that also includes handling of cold starts and pruning of recent purchases. When the overall space of candidates is large, a smaller list of candidates is precomputed using a scheduled batch pipeline.

- An automation pipeline consists of many ML models chained together. It will typically include a human over the loop to verify a sample of predictions, a human in the loop to make decisions on low-confidence predictions, and a way to capture human decisions for subsequent retraining.

- Because ML is such a powerful tool, we have to be careful to not misuse it. Verify with your AI governance board or legal counsel before embarking on a new AI project.

- Sliced evaluations, what-if tests, and continuous monitoring of model performance on protected criteria are ways to track ML fairness.
- Cloud ML frameworks provide XAI tools that offer insights into how models work, so human experts are able to understand the logic that goes into making a decision.

In the next chapter you will learn how to support the development and deployment of custom ML models. We will cover the various development stages and the frameworks that can support such activity.

CHAPTER 11

Architecting an ML Platform

In the previous chapter, we discussed the overall architecture of ML applications and that in many cases you will use prebuilt ML models. In some cases, your team will have to develop the ML model that is at the core of the ML application.

In this chapter, you will delve into the development and deployment of such *custom* ML models. You will look at the stages in the development of ML models and the frameworks that support such development. After the model has been created, you will need to automate the training process by looking into tools and products that can help you make this transition. Finally, you will need to monitor the behavior of your trained models that have been deployed to endpoints to see if they are drifting when making inferences.

In earlier chapters, we discussed ML capabilities that are enabled by various parts of the data platform. Specifically, the data storage for your ML platform can be in the data lake (Chapter 5) or DWH (Chapter 6), the training would be carried out on compute that is efficient for that storage, and the inference can be invoked from a streaming pipeline (Chapter 8) or deployed to the edge (Chapter 9). In this chapter, we will pull all of these discussions together and consider what goes into these ML capabilities.

ML Activities

If you are building an ML platform to support custom ML model development, what activities do you need to support? Too often, we see architects jump straight to the ML framework ("We need to support XGBoost and PyTorch because that's what my data scientists use") without consideration of the many activities that data scientists and ML engineers need to be able to do on the platform.

Typically, the ML platform has to support the activities in Figure 11-1.

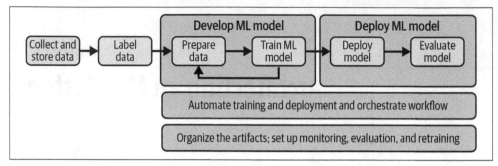

Figure 11-1. Activities that an ML platform needs to support

You need to clean and process the raw data to make it more suitable for ML and for the resulting trained models to be more accurate. Data preparation requires exploratory data analysis to examine the data, plot its distribution, and study its nuances. Then, an ML model is trained on a subset of the data and evaluated using another subset. Based on this, the data scientist will make changes to the data preparation or modeling steps. This process is iterative and usually involves a great deal of experimentation.

After model training is finished, you need to assess it against test data, check for compliance and performance, and then deploy it to an endpoint. Clients of the ML model may then send prediction requests to the endpoint.

A trained model does not remain fit for purpose indefinitely. The environment typically changes, and over time, the model starts to become less accurate. Therefore, you have to automate the steps for model training and deployment to ensure that your models are always up to date and accurate.

Also, you have to carefully and continuously monitor the model (to ensure it is handling the incoming prediction requests), evaluate it (to ensure predictions remain accurate and features have not drifted), and retrain it whenever there is new training data or new code or model drift is detected.

Let's look at how to design an ML platform to support all these activities.

Developing ML Models

Developing ML models involves iterative development that consists of:

- Preparing the data for ML
- Writing the ML model code
- Running the ML model code on the prepared data

To support these steps, your data scientists will need a development environment for ML.

Labeling Environment

To develop custom ML models, you need to have the data that will be used to *train* the model. Let's assume the data needed has been collected and stored, either in a DWH or in a data lake.

In the case of supervised learning, the training data will need to have labels, or correct answers. In some cases, these labels may be naturally present in the data, and in others, you will need to get the data labeled using human experts. Quite often, this tooling is outsourced and is not done by the data science team itself, but it is worth asking whether a labeling application needs to be supported by your ML platform.

Development Environment

Because the ML development process is so iterative, data scientists are most productive in an environment where they can write code, run it, view the results, change the code immediately, and rerun the code. Data scientists need to have the ability to execute their code in small snippets—it should not involve having to rerun the entire program. The code and its outputs live in a document that is called a notebook, as we anticipated in "Interactive Analytics with Notebooks" on page 138. The notebook will be rendered by a web browser, and this is how users will access the notebook. Code within the notebook is executed by software called a notebook server (see Figure 11-2). The notebook server software is installed on cloud VMs, and their lifecycle is managed through managed notebook services such as SageMaker, Databricks, Vertex AI Workbench, or Azure Machine Learning.

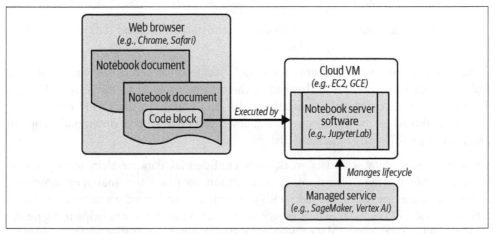

Figure 11-2. High-level architecture for notebooks

Jupyter Notebook, as you have already read in previous chapters, has become the de facto standard for data science development because it supports such interactive workflows. Managed services for running Jupyter Notebook servers exist on all the major cloud providers. These typically come with necessary statistical and ML software frameworks preinstalled and offer the ability to run on GPU-enabled machines for speeding up mathematical computations.

Notebook services are also provided as part of cloud-agnostic data frameworks like Databricks—this will work on all the major clouds in a nearly identical way. Google Colab provides free managed notebooks, but these have time and hardware restrictions. These limits are removed in a professional version of Colab that is also offered. Finally, there are domain-specific managed notebooks such as Terra.bio— these add, for example, biology-specific libraries and visualization capabilities to generic notebooks.

As coding assistant tools based on generative AI (such as Replit, GitHub Copilot, and Google Codey) are incorporated into notebook services like Colab and Jupyter, things may change significantly. At the time of writing, it is difficult to predict what the future holds, but AI assistants are likely to greatly streamline and simplify software development.

User Environment

The typical approach is for the notebooks to be user managed. In essence, you treat the VM on which Jupyter runs as the data scientists' workstation. No one else will be able to log in to that workstation. The data scientist will spend the majority of their workday in it. The notebook files are placed under version control, and the version control system (such as GitLab or GitHub) provides the collaborative, consistent team view of the project.

User-managed notebook instances let data scientists access cloud data and ML services in a simple way that is auditable.

When data scientists need to store the data, it has to be stored in such a way that all collaborators have access to it. Instead of the data being local to the Jupyter VM (as it would be in a traditional workstation), the data is held in the DWH or in object storage and read on the fly. In some instances, it can be helpful to download a copy of the data to a sufficiently large local disk.

In many cases, data scientists work with confidential data or data with privacy-sensitive information. Therefore, it is common to place the managed notebook service and the source of the data within a higher trust boundary such as a virtual private cloud (VPC), as shown in Figure 11-3. Such an architecture helps mitigate the risk of data exfiltration by data scientists, protects notebook instances from external network traffic, and limits access to the VM that hosts the notebook server.

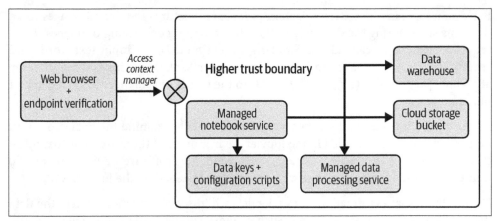

Figure 11-3. Use a higher trust boundary to encompass notebook servers, data keys, and training data

Make sure that you use fine-grained access controls such as column-/row-level security when providing access for data scientists. Data owners should ensure that data scientists have access to redacted or tokenized datasets to the maximum extent possible. Apply a crypto-boundary to all the datasets and manage these keys through a cloud key management service. This ensures that encryption keys are needed before any data can be read, and key management teams are kept separate from data owners.

Data scientists require VMs with GPUs when training deep learning models on unstructured data. If you provide each data scientist their own managed notebook instance, cost could become an issue. As a first step, make sure to set up features of the managed service to automatically pause or stop the VM if it hasn't been used for some number of hours.

For large teams (more than 50 data scientists), stopping idle instances may not be sufficient cost optimization. You would want multiple users to share the same hardware so as to amortize the computational power across those users. In such cases, the architecture involves running the notebook server on a Kubernetes cluster rather than on a VM (JupyterHub supports this) and then serving out notebooks to multiple users from the same cluster. Because this architecture is multitenant, it makes security considerations harder. Consider whether the cost savings are worth the increased security risks.

Preparing Data

The first step in many ML projects is to extract data from source systems (typically a DWH or a relational database), preprocess/clean it, and convert to a format (such as TensorFlow Records) optimized for ML training. The resulting ML data is stored in an object storage service for easy access from notebooks.

For example, many image classification model architectures require all images to be the same size. During the data preparation step, cropping or resizing of images to the requisite size can be carried out. Similarly, in text models, the input text words and sentences have to be converted into a numeric representation. This is often done by applying a large model (e.g., BERT, GPT-3) to the words or sentences to get a batch of numbers.

At this point, it is essential for data scientists to visually examine the data. Common plotting libraries are included in the Jupyter environment. If there are tools that make this easier for the data scientists (e.g., video rendering software or domain-specific frameworks and libraries), make sure to have them installed on the Jupyter VM.

During the visual examination, data scientists will discover situations where the data needs to be corrected or discarded. Such changes can be made to the dataset and a new dataset created. Or they can be added to the software that reads in the data. It's more common for this cleanup to be done in software because it provides a consistent way to treat such data if provided during prediction.

Then, it is common for the data to be split into subsets. One subset will be used for training and another subset to ensure that the model is not overfitting. Sometimes, a third subset is kept aside for final evaluation.

There are several ways that data scientists can read the data from source systems, filter out bad values, transform the data, and split it into subsets. Doing data preparation in SQL within the DWH is often a convenient choice for structured data. However, there are limitations to the types of statistical processing that can be carried out in SQL. Therefore, data processing will typically be carried out using pandas— while pandas will work for small datasets, you will need a framework such as Dask, Apache Spark, or Apache Beam to process large amounts of data. Therefore, a cloud managed service that will allow you to run Dask, Spark, or Beam at scale needs to be within the high trust boundary.

All such activities should be carried out in coordination with the business to have a clear understanding of the organization's objectives and to ensure that the correct information is retained during the preparation phase.

Training ML Models

Your data scientists will write model code within the Jupyter notebooks in frameworks such as scikit-learn, XGBoost, Keras/TensorFlow, or PyTorch. Then, they will execute the model code over the training dataset multiple times to determine the optimal weights of the model.

Writing ML code

The code will typically read training data in small batches and run through a training loop that consists of adjusting weights. The data pipeline that reads the data might carry out data augmentation to artificially increase the size of the dataset by, for example, flipping images. The model architecture will be closely tied to the inputs that are read and how they are transformed. The data scientist will typically experiment with many options for representing data, many types of models, and many methods of optimization.[1]

Model code is developed iteratively, and so a low-latency connection to the cloud and the ability to have quick turnaround time are essential. It is important to try out small changes to the code without having to run the entire training program again. Writing code is typically *not* the time to use managed training services—at this stage, data scientists use notebooks in their local environment.

Doing interactive development on a large dataset will impose unnecessary delays. To speed up development, it might be useful to provide a sample of the large dataset that can be downloaded to the notebook VM. In the case of situations involving privacy-sensitive data, the sample might have to consist of simulated/synthetic data.

Once the code has been developed, the data scientist will typically want to run the training job on the entire dataset. Whether they can do so from within the notebook depends on the size of the dataset and the capability of the VM on which the notebook server is running.

Small-scale jobs

For small datasets and simple models, where a training run can finish in under an hour, it can be helpful to provide the ability to run a training job in the notebook itself.

Managed notebook services offer the data scientist the ability to change the machine type on which their notebook runs, to make it more powerful—this can be accomplished by switching to a machine with GPUs or TPUs attached. This will provide the necessary horsepower to train the model on moderately sized datasets.

For even larger datasets and/or complex models or where a training run can take longer than an hour, it is preferable to use a managed training service. It is possible to submit a notebook to a managed training service like SageMaker or Vertex AI, have the notebook be executed in its entirety, and receive the updated notebook after a few hours.

---

1 The reference here is to regularization, learning rate schedules, optimizers, etc.

Distributed training

For extremely large datasets, simply scaling up to a more powerful machine is not sufficient. You will have to run the training job on a cluster of machines that communicate with one another in a special way. Essentially, every batch of training examples is distributed among the machines in the cluster, each of the machines does mathematical calculations on its subset of the batch, and the intermediate calculations are used to determine the actual result on the match. Frameworks such as TensorFlow and PyTorch support distributed training, but the cluster has to be set up in specific ways.

To get distributed training of the code in the notebook, it is necessary to run the notebook server on an appropriately configured cluster (e.g., JupyterHub on a Kubeflow cluster). Unless this is the user environment you have created, making this change is not a quick one.

A better option is to skip ahead to the automation step discussed in "Automation" on page 293 and use managed training frameworks.

No-code ML

Custom models do not always require coding in TensorFlow, PyTorch, etc. Low-code and no-code options exist. For example, it is possible to use the cloud console or create and deploy an AutoML model. Tools such as Dataiku and DataRobot provide completely point-and-click ways to train and deploy models.

The capabilities of no-code ML models continue to become better and better. For unstructured data (images, video, text), it is hard to do better than the AutoML options available. On images, you can use AutoML for classification, segmentation, and even generation from text prompts. On text, you can use it to parse forms, extract entities, detect sentiment, summarize documents, and answer questions.

In all these cases, you can treat the model that comes out of AutoML as a custom model that can then be deployed just like models that were coded up by a data science team.

Deploying ML Models

As discussed in Chapter 10, batch prediction is used to periodically score large amounts of data, whereas online prediction is used for near-real-time scoring of data.

If you will only be doing batch predictions, it is possible to directly use the trained model files from large-scale data processing frameworks such as Spark, Beam, and Flink. You will not need to deploy the model. Some DWHs (such as BigQuery) allow you to provide a trained TensorFlow model on Cloud Storage for batch predictions.

To use a model for online predictions, you need to deploy it as a microservice in a serving environment. The major cloud ML frameworks (Vertex AI, SageMaker, Azure Machine Learning) have similar concepts and support similar capabilities for online predictions.

Deploying to an Endpoint

Clients access an endpoint through the URL associated with it (see Figure 11-4). The clients send an HTTP POST request with a JSON payload that contains the input to the prediction method. The endpoint contains a number of model objects, among which it splits traffic. In Figure 11-4, 80% of traffic goes to Model 1, 10% to Model 2, and the remainder to Model 3. The model is an object that references ML models built in a wide variety of frameworks (TensorFlow, PyTorch, XGBoost, etc.). There are prebuilt container images for each framework. In the case of TensorFlow, the container image looks for SavedModel files, the format that Keras/TensorFlow 2.0 models are exported into by default.

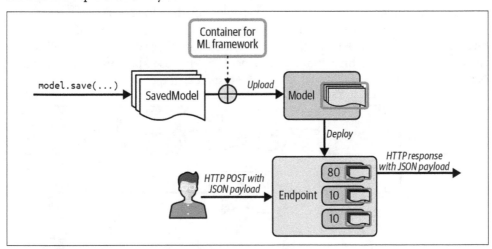

Figure 11-4. Deploying a trained model to an endpoint

The endpoint is backed by an autoscaling service that can handle variability in the traffic. However, it is still up to the ML engineer to choose a machine large enough to support a few simultaneous requests by carrying out measurements. The computation can be sped up by running the endpoint on machines that have accelerators (such as GPUs or field-programmable gate arrays [FPGAs]) attached. If working with large models such as text models, it may be necessary to ensure that the machine has sufficient memory. Autoscaling might also introduce unacceptable latencies since it can take a bit of time for a new machine to come online. Therefore, it can be helpful to ensure that there is a warm pool with some minimum number of machines available.

Evaluate Model

The reason to deploy multiple models to an endpoint is so that ML engineers can control the traffic split to them. This is because the ML platform will need to allow for A/B testing of models so that ML engineers can decide whether to replace the current production model with a newly developed one.

The ML managed services provide the ability to monitor resource usage and ensure that the deployed model can keep up with the input requests. A sample of the inputs and corresponding predictions can be sent to a DWH and used to compare the performance of different model versions.

Hybrid and Multicloud

Because moving data around is costly and adds governance and security considerations, you will usually choose to train ML models on the cloud where the majority of your historical data lives. On the other hand, to minimize network latency, you will need to deploy the models to an endpoint on the cloud (or edge) where the consuming applications run. In Figure 11-5, you can see an example of training on one cloud (where your data lives) and deploying to another (where your applications run). To do such a hybrid training and deployment, use standard model formats (such as TensorFlow SavedModel, ONNX, or *.bst* files) and containers.

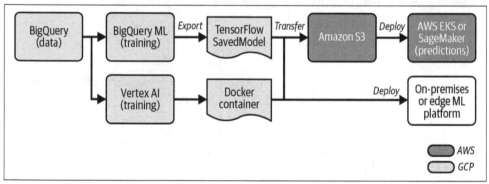

Figure 11-5. It's possible to train ML models on one cloud and deploy them to another

This flexibility, to run inference disconnected from the cloud, is an important consideration when building an ML platform. Choose frameworks that are not tied to proprietary implementations.

Training-Serving Skew

One of the major challenges in ML is *training-serving skew*. When an ML model is trained on preprocessed data, it is necessary to carry out the identical steps on incoming prediction requests. This is because you need to provide the model data with the same characteristics as the data it was trained on. If you don't do that, you will get a skew between training and serving, and the model predictions will not be as good.

There are three ways to ensure that preprocessing done during training is repeated as-is during prediction: putting the preprocessing code within the model, using a transform function, or using a feature store. Let's discuss them one by one.

Within the model

The simplest option, as shown in Figure 11-6, is to incorporate the preprocessing steps within the model function itself. For example, preprocessing might be carried out within a Lambda layer in Keras. This way, when the model is saved, the preprocessing steps will automatically be part of the model.

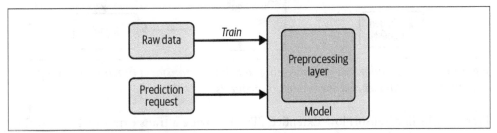

Figure 11-6. Incorporating the preprocessing code into the model function

The advantage of this method is the simplicity. No extra infrastructure is required. Preprocessing code is carried along with the model. So if you need to deploy the model on the edge or in another cloud, there is nothing special you have to do. The SavedModel format contains all the necessary information.

The drawback to this approach is that the preprocessing steps will be wastefully repeated on each iteration through the training dataset. The more expensive the computation, the more this adds up.

Another drawback is that data scientists have to implement the preprocessing code in the same framework as the ML model. Thus, for example, if the model is written using PyTorch, the preprocessing also has to be done using PyTorch. If the preprocessing code uses custom libraries, this can become difficult.

Transform function

As you have understood, the main drawback with placing the preprocessing code within the model function is that the code needs to be used to transform the raw data during each iteration of the model-training process, and this needs to be in the same language as the training code.

This can be optimized if you capture the preprocessing steps in a function and apply that function to the raw data. Then, the model training can be carried out on the preprocessed data, so it is more efficient. Of course, you have to make sure to invoke that function from both training and prediction code (see Figure 11-7). Alternatively, you have to capture the preprocessing steps in a container and interpose the container between the input and the model. While this adds efficiency, it also adds complexity—you have to make sure to save the transform function as an artifact associated with the model and know which transform function to invoke.

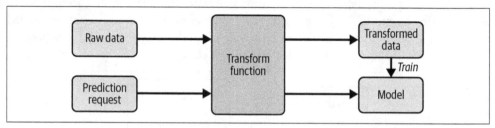

Figure 11-7. Encapsulate the preprocessing code into a transform function that is applied to both the raw dataset and the prediction requests

Frameworks like TensorFlow Extended (TFX) provide a transform capability to simplify the bookkeeping involved. Some SQL-based ML frameworks like BigQuery ML also support a TRANSFORM clause. Vertex AI supports a Feature Transformation Engine.

You should prefer to use a transform function over putting the transformation code into the model if the extra infrastructural and bookkeeping overhead is worth it. This will be the case if the feature is computationally expensive.

Feature store

Placing the preprocessing code within the model function or encapsulating it in a transform function (or SQL clause or container) will suffice for the vast majority of features.

As you will learn soon, there are two situations where these won't suffice and you will need a *feature store* (see Figure 11-8), a repository for storing and serving ML features. The feature store is essentially a key-value store where the key consists of an entity (e.g., hotel_id) and a timestamp and the value consists of the properties of that entity (e.g., price, number of bookings, number of website visitors to hotel listing over the past hour, etc.) as of that timestamp. All the major ML frameworks (AWS SageMaker, Vertex AI, Databricks, etc.) come with a feature store.

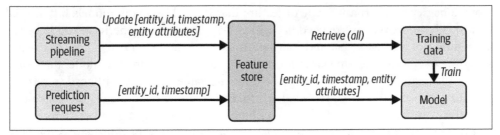

Figure 11-8. A feature store is a central repository that provides entity values as of a certain time

The first situation where you will need a feature store is if the feature values will not be known by clients requesting predictions but have to instead be computed on the server. If the clients requesting predictions will not know the feature values, then you need a mechanism to inject the feature values into incoming prediction requests. The feature store plays that role. For example, one of the features of a dynamic pricing model may be the number of website visitors to the item listing over the past hour. The client (think of a mobile app) requesting the price of a hotel will not know this feature. This information has to be computed on the server using a streaming pipeline on clickstream data and inserted into the feature store.

The second situation is to prevent unnecessary copies of the data. For example, consider that you have a feature that is computationally expensive and is used in multiple ML models. Rather than using a transform function and storing the transformed feature in multiple ML training datasets, it is much more efficient and maintainable to store it in a centralized repository.

Don't go overboard in either scenario. For example, if all the features of the model that will need to be computed server-side are computed in the same way (for example, they are retrieved from a relational database or computed by a streaming pipeline), it's perfectly acceptable to have the retrieval code in a transform function or container. Similarly, it is perfectly acceptable to repeat some feature processing a handful of times rather than to complicate your ML platform with a feature store.

The canonical use of a feature store

The most important use case of a feature store is when situations #1 and #2 both apply. For example, consider that you need a "point-in-time lookup" for fetching training data to train a model. Features such as the number of website visitors over the past hour or the number of trips made by a driver in the past hour, etc., are used in multiple models. But they are pretty straightforward in that they are computed by a streaming pipeline and so their real-time value can be part of the DWH. Those are relatively easy and don't always need a feature store.

Now consider an alternative type of feature that is used by many models but also is continually improved, as sketched in Figure 11-9—for example, perhaps you have an embedding of a song, artist, and user in a music-streaming service. There is a team updating user and song embeddings on a daily basis. Every time the model that consumes this feature is retrained—high commercial value use cases will need to retrain periodically—the training code will need to fetch the values of this feature that align with the training labels and the latest version of the embedding algorithm. This has to be done efficiently and easily across all labels. And this has to be done across the tens or hundreds of features used by the model. The feature store makes periodic model retraining on hard-to-compute, frequently improved features exceptionally useful.

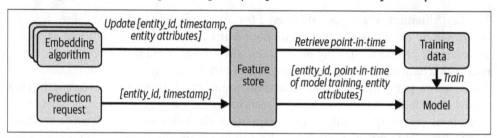

Figure 11-9. A feature store is particularly useful for hard-to-compute features that are frequently updated, since models will have to be trained on "point-in-time" embeddings

Decision chart

The considerations discussed here are summarized in Figure 11-10. This is not a decision tree to decide whether your organization needs a feature store—there are probably a handful of features for which you do. This is a decision tree to decide whether to use a feature store for the particular feature/model you are building or operationalizing.

All three major cloud ML frameworks (AWS SageMaker, Vertex AI, Azure Machine Learning) come with a feature store. Databricks and Tecton.ai provide feature stores that are cloud agnostic.

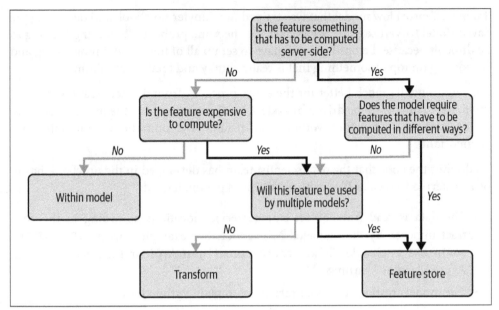

Figure 11-10. Choosing between different options for capturing preprocessing

Automation

As you have understood so far, it is possible to use the cloud consoles to deploy a custom model. It is possible to develop and deploy a TensorFlow or PyTorch model to AWS/GCP/Azure using just a notebook. Neither of these approaches scale to hundreds of models and large teams.

Automate Training and Deployment

When you create an AutoML model using the web console, for example, you get back an endpoint that can be monitored and on which you can set up continuous evaluation. If you find that the model is drifting, retraining it on new data automatically is difficult—you don't want to wake up at 2 a.m. to use the user interface to train the model. It would be much better if you could train and deploy the model using just code. Code is much easier for your team to automate.

Taking a TensorFlow model that was trained in a Jupyter notebook and deploying the SavedModel to Vertex AI or SageMaker has the same problem. Retraining is going to be difficult because the ops team will have to set up all of the ops and monitoring and scheduling on top of something that is really clunky and totally nonminimal.

For retraining, it's much better for the entire process—from dataset creation to training to deployment—to be driven by code. Clearly separating out the model code from the ops code and expressing everything in "regular" Python rather than in notebooks is important.

To do this, the code that the data scientist team has developed in the notebook has to be transferred to regular files, with a few things parameterized:

- The data is read from object storage service locations according to the contract imposed by the managed ML service. For example, this is `AIP_TRAINING _DATA_URI` in Google Cloud, `InputDataConfig` in AWS, and the `Run` context in Azure Machine Learning.
- The model creation code is extracted out to plain Python files.
- The model output (in SavedModel, ONNX, *.bst*, etc.) is saved into an object storage service location provided as part of the contract imposed by the managed ML service.

Let's focus now on how to orchestrate all the steps needed to train your model.

Orchestration with Pipelines

Simply converting the Jupyter Notebook steps that your data scientists prepared to an executable script is not sufficient. It is necessary to *orchestrate* the steps on the appropriate infrastructure:

- Prepare the dataset using Spark, Beam, SQL, etc.
- Submit a training job to the managed ML service.
- If the model does better than previously trained models, deploy the trained model to the endpoint.
- Monitor the model performance and do A/B testing to evaluate the model on real data.

There are, broadly, four options for orchestration: managed pipelines, Airflow, Kubeflow, and TFX.

Managed pipelines

If you are using a single cloud for your complete development and deployment workflow, use the provided ML workflow orchestration mechanism. Every task that is carried out using the managed services on that cloud will have a corresponding operator, and these jobs will understand dependency tracking. For example, Vertex AI provides Vertex AI Pipelines, a fully managed service that allows you to retrain your models as often as necessary. Azure Machine Learning has a native designer that serves the same purpose.

All the managed-pipeline offerings make available programming SDKs that provide handy automation capabilities. In the case of Databricks, this pipeline SDK is provided by MLflow, an open source framework that runs on Spark but provides integration to TensorFlow, PyTorch, and other ML libraries and frameworks.

Airflow

If you are already using Airflow for scheduling and orchestration of data pipelines, extending its use for ML will allow you to have a simple, consistent system. The drawback is that Airflow does not have custom ML operators, so you will find yourself using generic Python or bash operators that, in turn, call out to the cloud SDK. Airflow is open source, and you can use managed services to run Airflow—Google Cloud Composer, Amazon Managed Workflows for Airflow, and Astronomer.io, which is cloud agnostic.

Kubeflow Pipelines

Each of the steps can be containerized and the containers orchestrated on Kubernetes. Kubeflow operators already exist for popular ML frameworks, ML metrics, etc. Kubeflow is also open source, and you can use the managed Kubernetes services (Google Kubernetes Engine, Amazon Elastic Kubernetes Service, or Azure Kubernetes Service) on the public clouds to run Kubeflow. There are also cloud-agnostic managed Kubeflow providers like Iguazio.

TensorFlow Extended

If you are using the TensorFlow ecosystem, TFX provides convenient Python functions for common operations such as model validation, evaluation, etc. This provides a prescriptive, easy-to-use approach for orchestration that avoids the need to build and maintain operators or containers. TFX is an open source package that can be run on managed pipelines, Airflow, and Kubeflow.

TFX is an integrated ML platform for developing and deploying production ML systems. It is designed for scalable, high-performance ML tasks. The key libraries of TFX for which prebuilt Python libraries exist are as follows:

TensorFlow Data Validation (TFDV)
Used for detecting anomalies in the data

TensorFlow Transform (TFT)
Used for data preprocessing and feature engineering

Keras
Used for building and training ML models

TensorFlow Model Analysis (TFMA)
Used for ML model evaluation and analysis

TensorFlow Serving (TFServing)
Used for serving ML models at endpoints

These libraries implement their tasks using open source Apache Beam and Tensor-Flow. The tasks can run locally on the Kubeflow or Airflow cluster on which TFX is being run, or they can submit the jobs to managed services such as Dataflow and Vertex AI.

Continuous Evaluation and Training

Each step in the ML workflow results in output artifacts that you need to organize in a systematic way.

Artifacts

User notebooks, pipeline source code, data processing functions, and model source code need to be stored in the source code repository.

Every experiment that the data scientists carry out needs to be kept track of: the parameters, the metrics, which datasets were used, and what models were created. This is a capability that all the ML orchestration frameworks provide.

Model training jobs, the subsequent trained model files, and deployed models are tracked in the managed ML service (such as Azure Machine Learning, Vertex AI, or SageMaker).

The environment used for development, training, and deployment is containerized and kept track of in a container registry. This is essential for reproducibility.

Dependency tracking

Steps in the ML pipeline should do dependency tracking and not launch the task unless one of the dependencies has changed. For example, unless the raw data has changed, an invocation of the pipeline should not cause the training data to be re-created. This is something that the prebuilt operators and managed ML pipelines provide but that custom-built operators and pipelines may not.

Once you have automated the training and prediction code into an ML pipeline and captured the artifacts systematically, it is possible to set up a continuous integration/continuous deployment (CI/CD) pipeline. This involves, in the ML context, continuous evaluation and continuous retraining.

Continuous evaluation

To set up continuous evaluation, you will need to configure the prediction endpoint to store a sample of inputs and corresponding predictions to a DWH. If necessary, a labeling job can be periodically run to submit tickets for humans to validate the predictions that have been made. A scheduled evaluation query will compare the human labels against predictions that have been made to monitor for drift in the performance of the model over time. This is automatically handled in TFX by the Model Analysis component.

The scheduled evaluation query will also need to examine the distribution of model features and monitor them for drift. This is automatically handled in TFX by the Data Validation component. Skew and drift detection are also provided out of the box for all model types by the managed predictions service in Vertex AI.

Continuous retraining

Whenever the evaluation query identifies skew or drift, an alert should be raised for human overview into what sorts of changes are needed. Other types of changes can trigger an immediate retraining.

Whenever code changes are checked in, the model training pipeline might need to be kicked off. This can be handled by GitHub/GitLab Actions.

Finally, whenever a sufficiently large amount of new data is received, the model training pipeline will need to be kicked off. This can be handled by triggering a Lambda or Cloud Function off new files in the cloud object storage and having the function invoke the pipeline endpoint.

Choosing the ML Framework

In Chapter 10, you looked primarily at prebuilt ML models and how to build ML applications on top of such foundational capabilities. You also looked at low-code and no-code ways of creating ML models. In this chapter, you looked at custom ML models.

As a cloud architect, you should choose the tools available in the ML platform based on the skill set of the people who will be building the ML application. If ML models will be built by data scientists, you need to enable them to use a code-first ML framework such as Keras/TensorFlow or PyTorch and operationalize it using SageMaker, Vertex AI, Databricks, etc. If the models will be developed by domain experts, provide them a low-code ML framework such as BigQuery ML or AI Builder. While a data scientist may be unhappy with prebuilt models (and the corresponding lack of flexibility), the ease of use and data wrangling capabilities that BigQuery ML provides will be perfect for domain experts. Practitioners in the field will need a no-code ML framework such as DataRobot or Dataiku to create ML models.

Team Skills

The answer for the same ML problem will vary from organization to organization. For example, consider using ML for pricing optimization. Teams will tend to choose the approach based on their skill set:

- A team of data scientists will choose to build dynamic pricing models. They will probably start with controlled variance pricing methods and proceed to incorporate factors such as demand shocks. The point is that this is a sophisticated, specialized team, using sophisticated methods. They'll need to do it with code.

- A team of domain experts might choose to build tiered pricing models. For example, a product manager might use historical data to craft the pricing for different tiers and adapt the pricing to new market segments based on the characteristics of that market segment. This involves analytics or a regression model and is very doable in SQL.

- A team of nontechnical practitioners determines the optimum price. For example, you could have store managers set the price of products in their store based on historical data and factors they find important. This requires a no-code framework (e.g., DataRobot to price insurance (*https://oreil.ly/kML83*)).

The correct answer depends on your business and the ROI that your leadership expects to get from each of the above approaches.

Task Considerations

Model training needs a data science skill set (stats, Python, notebooks), and deployment needs an ML engineer skill set (software engineering, cloud infra, ops), while invoking the model can be done by any developer. However, it's important to recognize that the ML workflow is more than just model training and deployment. The end-to-end ML workflow consists of: (1) training, (2) deployment, (3) evaluation, (4) invocation, (5) monitoring, (6) experimentation, (7) explanation, (8) troubleshooting, and (9) auditing. As a cloud architect, you need to identify who at your company will be doing the task for each ML problem. Very rarely will these other steps be carried out by an engineer (indeed, it's a red flag if only engineers can do these things).

For example, a model that is created by a data scientist may have to be invoked as part of reports that are run within Salesforce by a practitioner (a salesperson, in this case) and audited by a sales manager. If data scientists build such models in Spark, productionize them as notebooks, and deploy them as APIs, how will the sales manager do their audit? You now need a software engineering team that builds custom applications (maybe leveraging a Streamlit framework or similar) to enable this part of the ML workflow. This is a serious waste of time, money, and effort. This is a problem that the cloud architect could have avoided by deploying the model into a DWH that readily supports dashboards.

User-Centric

It may sound obvious, but we see so many organizations making this mistake that it is worth calling out: organizations that try to standardize on an ML framework disregarding the skill set of the people who need to carry out a task will fail. Because skill sets vary within your organization, you will have different ML frameworks and tools in your organization.

Make sure to choose open, interoperable tools so that you don't end up with silos. It is also helpful to go with solutions that address different levels of sophistication—this way, the vendor takes care of interoperability.

Summary

In this chapter, we covered how to architect an ML platform for the development and deployment of custom ML models. The key takeaways are as follows:

- An ML platform needs to support model development, deployment, orchestration, and continuous evaluation and retraining.

- When writing code and doing exploratory data analysis, data scientists are most productive in notebook environments.

- All the major cloud providers provide managed notebook servers for Jupyter Notebook.

- When working with confidential or private data, place the notebook server, input data, and encrypted keys within a higher trust boundary that will reduce the risk of data exfiltration.

- Data preparation on small datasets can be done using pandas. On larger datasets, scale out data preparation using Dask, Spark, or Beam.

- Writing of the model code is typically done with a small sample of the dataset. In the case of private or confidential data, provide a sample that can be downloaded to the notebook VM.

- Model code in a notebook can be executed on small datasets by changing the machine type to one with a GPU. On larger datasets, use a notebook executor service to execute the notebook within the managed training service. The latter option also works for distributed training on enormous datasets.

- Deploy models to an endpoint that is backed by an autoscaling service capable of running on GPUs.

- Evaluate models by doing A/B testing of the models deployed to an endpoint.

- Hybrid and multicloud scenarios are supported through the use of standard model formats and frameworks or by the use of containers.

- To prevent training-serving skew, encapsulate preprocessing code within the model or in a transform function. Alternatively, use a feature store.

- For retraining, it's much better for the entire process—from dataset creation to training to deployment—to be driven by code.

- There are four options for orchestration: managed pipelines, Airflow, Kubeflow, and TFX. Use managed pipelines if you are using a single cloud, Airflow to have consistency with data pipelines, Kubeflow if all your steps are containerized, and TFX if you are within the TensorFlow ecosystem and want an easy-to-use, prescriptive system.

- Artifacts such as notebooks, pipeline source code, etc., should be backed up so that they can be used to reproduce errors.

- Continuous evaluation is achieved by configuring the prediction endpoint to store a sample of inputs and corresponding predictions to a DWH.

- Continuous retraining is triggered by new code, new data, or detected drift.

- Make sure to choose the ML framework based primarily on the skill set of the users who will be building ML applications.

- Consider each of these tasks separately: (1) training, (2) deployment, (3) evaluation, (4) invocation, (5) monitoring, (6) experimentation, (7) explanation, (8) troubleshooting, and (9) auditing. Then, ask who at your company will be doing the task for each ML problem.

In the next chapter, you will learn how to apply the principles you have learned so far via the description of a model case. You will understand what it means to transform an old-fashioned data platform into something that is modern and cloud native.

CHAPTER 12

Data Platform Modernization: A Model Case

In the previous chapters we explored ways to leverage the cloud to build a modern data platform that can handle data at scale, help your organization remove silos, enable more employees to access data, make obtaining insights from data easier, and speed up AI/ML adoption. Together, these capabilities facilitate the extraction of value from data. In this final chapter we will apply the principles to a model case to explain what it means to transform an old-fashioned data platform into something that is modern and cloud native. Please note that the model case is purely fictitious to help ground the discussion.

New Technology for a New Era

YouNetwork is an important video broadcaster that serves 15+ million customers throughout Europe. Over the 30+ years that it has operated, YouNetwork has navigated several technology transformative cycles, from a pioneering adoption of satellite broadcasting in the early 1990s to a recent implementation of the Internet Protocol television (IPTV) protocol. The adoption of IPTV enabled YouNetwork to launch a service that delivers real-time shows and video on demand (VOD), leveraging tailored set-top boxes (STBs) connected to the internet.

Over this time, the organization has been able to adapt its offering to customer needs by enlarging its video catalog (e.g., TV shows, movies, sports events, etc.) every year. Impressively, it has also successfully diversified its portfolio, adding new services (e.g., online gaming, internet connections, etc.) to enable and boost the adoption of its brand-new IPTV service.

In other words, YouNetwork is a successful business that both innovates in its core business (content) and successfully integrates newly available technologies to expand its market. The recent explosion of data generated by new services and the inability to be agile based on the real-time data have caused the company to reflect on the future of its technology stack. The main drivers have been (1) the scalability of services with increasing data volumes, (2) the necessity to quickly implement and put into production new analytics-based solutions, and (3) the need to offer more tailored content streams to customers who increasingly expect such personalization.

The Need for Change

At the beginning of the last fiscal year, the board of directors scheduled a meeting to discuss the business strategy, and one of the main topics of discussion was the need for a change in the technology stack. Traditionally when YouNetwork invested in technology, this has involved building the capability in its own data centers. However, the scalability issues were making this harder and harder to do. The biggest concern of the board was that every single development that aimed to put in place innovative solutions like collections of tailored customer information, predictions of what users would love to see next, and real-time fraud detection systems became a challenge and ended up being impossible to implement in a timely manner.

The board discussion highlighted the need for a radical change. From a technological perspective, especially on the data side, YouNetwork has gone through two main digital transformations in its history:

COTS era
> Where the company invested a huge amount of money in purchasing hardware and software coming from a single vendor and working all together in carrying out all the activities (e.g., DWH/data marts/cubes analysis)

OSS era
> Where the company tried to differentiate between hardware and software, adopting a more open source (mainly Hadoop) approach, being able to cope with new use cases like unstructured data management and time-series analysis

The board recognized the fact that the company now needed a new transformation, a third big evolutionary step—the board made the decision to adopt a new journey, leveraging one of the most disruptive technologies of recent times: the public cloud.

Since nobody in the company had sufficient experience to drive such a transformation, the first decision was to establish a technical "SWAT" team (consisting of internal leaders and contractors coming from top-tier consulting companies) with the aim to scout all possible solutions available in the market and prepare a solid business plan to modernize YouNetwork's current data platform.

It Is Not Only a Matter of Technology

The SWAT team organized a series of one-on-one meetings with the major cloud vendors to gain a better understanding of how to transform the data platform architecture into a modern stack. Even after the first interaction, it became clear that the journey to the cloud was more than just a technological journey. It also required an organization-wide transformation in the way that YouNetworkers used data.

The SWAT team found that it was necessary to align the cloud strategy with the overall organizational strategy to consider how the business would evolve in response to the technological update. For example, the deep investment in internet-based technologies and protocols required a corresponding investment in a scalable data platform to cope with the real-time terabyte-scale data that the new system would generate. Such a scalable data platform would support the extraction of actionable information and enable YouNetwork to improve the quality of service (QoS) and gain a better understanding of the users. The QoS, in turn, would change the mix of programs that could be offered, and a better understanding of users permitted personalization that would change the shows being produced. This meant that the content acquisition team was now a stakeholder in the data-platform transformation.

Another key outcome was the need for sponsorship from the top, but since in this case the program was initially generated by the board of directors, the KPIs and the backing from C-suite were already a thing. However, there was a need for a flow of this sponsorship down through the chain of the company, a sort of advocacy within the organization, and the best way to achieve that was via the establishment of a dedicated group of people named the Cloud Center of Excellence (CCoE) that had to become a point of reference for such a transition. Considering the initial legacy footprint of the organization, it was not an easy task to clearly identify people who were able to drive such a transformation. YouNetwork adopted a hybrid approach, starting from the SWAT team, where both internal and external individuals partnered in building the CCoE:

Internal resources

> Three people respectively from the product, architecture, and engineering areas who brought internal knowledge and expertise about what was working and what was not. They were selected for their openness to cloud and a bias toward bringing change to the company—YouNetwork picked people who were already running some "unofficial" research and experimentations leveraging cloud services.

External resources

> Third-party senior-level consultants who brought expertise and experience helping with the definition of the overall strategy, its adoption, and related governance. They acted as leadership and advisors where their main goal was to

bring order, methodology, and support with vertical knowledge when needed, especially during the initial phase. At the beginning, there were multiple people in this group because of the lack of solid cloud knowledge within the internal team.[1] The number of people reduced over time as the internal team became more and more capable.

The initial achievement was mainly strategic and focused on finding a solid response to the question: "How do we guide the company into a new chapter?" As you will see throughout this chapter, the pivotal task was to carefully analyze, compare, and judge the proposals made by cloud vendors to select the best one that fit the organization's needs.

The CCoE, as shown in Figure 12-1, identified the strategy and clarified the process to be followed in four stages:

Governance
Identify and implement standards to guide the use of the newly created data platform, measure its success, manage related spending, and strive for efficiency

Migration management
Push and control the migration of workloads in the cloud

Operationalization of the running environment
Control the cloud team's operations for workloads that have been migrated to the cloud

Training and support
Serve as an SME for the engineering, product, and operations teams to foster further adoption of the cloud for new projects while empowering the business to understand and leverage the organization's newly created cloud capabilities, especially via massive training sessions (i.e., change management)

By the completion of the development of the new data platform, internal people fully drove the CCoE. The CCoE had also expanded—it had added brand-new roles like security, site reliability engineers (SREs), data engineers, data scientists, cloud operations, technical support engineers, etc.—developing new teams within the company's business units to execute on each stream. Today, the CCoE at YouNetwork consists of 10 individuals.

---

1 The actual number is hard to pin down because several consultants rotated into and off the project and each was part-time, splitting their time among multiple clients. Initially, the number of external consultants ranged from 5 to 10, and toward the end, it became 2 to 3.

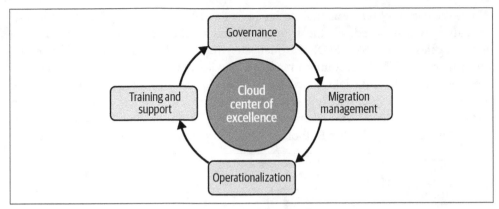

Figure 12-1. The role of the CCoE

It is important to note that one of the CCoE's responsibilities is to consider potential organizational changes that the company may face in the future (see "Step 3: Break Down Silos" on page 50). To help with the transition into the new world, follow the team's recommendations.

The Beginning of the Journey

As highlighted before, after understanding the challenges and effort needed to adopt a complex transformation and modernization journey, YouNetwork had to first identify a possible target architecture and then define how to make it real considering its on-premises/legacy heritage. The CCoE, based on the preliminary discussions with the cloud vendors, prepared some documents describing a high-level picture of the current environment and an envisioned target architecture.

The Current Environment

The technological footprint of the data platform needed, as already mentioned, an evolution, and the company decided to issue an RFP (that is in practice a tender, an offer for supply products and services) to the various cloud vendors to get an offer for a possible target architecture and related program to get there.

When the legacy system was first designed as described in Figure 12-2, some standardization was imposed: all the source systems of the legacy architecture had to generate files (e.g., CSV, JSON, Parquet, etc.) to be uploaded into an FTP server. From there, a COTS ETL solution read and transformed the data to be ingested into the DWH and the data lake based on Hadoop/Spark technology. Communication between the Hadoop cluster and the DWH was achieved via an ad hoc connector. Data analysts and decision makers were carrying on all their activities and analysis mainly using Excel and other BI tools that were based on commercial solutions.

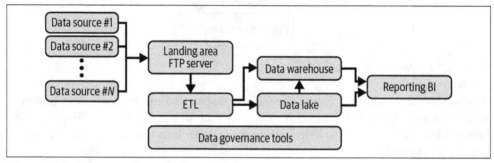

Figure 12-2. On-prem data platform architecture

Configuration information of each of the current workloads was added as an annex of the RFP to help cloud vendors size the final solution both from a technology and an economical perspective:

- Number of environments (usually three: dev, test, and prod)
- Number of nodes
- Number of cores per node
- CPU average utilization (e.g., 92%)
- CPU utilization peak (e.g., 100%)
- Memory size per node
- Memory average utilization (e.g., 92%)
- Memory utilization peak (e.g., 100%)
- Storage size per node, storage for backup, and total storage
- HDFS replication factor (e.g., 3)
- Operating system type and version (e.g., Windows Server 2008/Linux CentOS 7)
- Nodes uptime (e.g., 24/7/365 or 160 hours/month)
- Generated data per day (e.g., ~350 GB)
- Data retention policy (730 days on average)

A legacy solution like that, with hardware close to the end of life and software that surpassed the end of support, was hard to maintain, and the cost for the licenses, especially on the DWH side, was exploding. Furthermore, the architecture was very limited because streaming patterns could not be adopted. The Hadoop cluster needed to be updated in terms of both hardware (the system was close to collapse, and new jobs could remain in queue days before being executed) and software (Hadoop distribution was out of date).

The system resided in two physically separated data centers: the main site and a failover site. They had been configured in active/active, which means that in both facilities there was adequate infrastructure to run the business and reduce system degradation in case of disaster (i.e., failure of an entire data center), improving reliability. DWH data was synchronized in real time, achieving a recovery point objective (RPO) close to zero. The data lake data was aligned multiple times a day using the tool DistCp with a targeted RPO of six hours. In case of disaster, it was possible to route the traffic from one data center to the other one with a minimum downtime, achieving a recovery time objective (RTO) close to zero.

The Target Environment

In the RFP document, the CCoE team outlined the desired end state of YouNetwork's new cloud environment. From a general point of view, the goal was to have one single system (i.e., a data lakehouse) as a single point of truth for the entire company. All users should be able to get access to the data, based on their access rights, and perform self-reporting. The idea was to limit the number of tools to be used for such activities, with the goal of getting rid of offline spreadsheets as much as possible and transitioning toward OSS. The ETL part had to be modernized wherever possible with an ELT approach. The goal of adopting OSS was to terminate as many of the COTS licenses as possible. The team chose a SQL-first data lakehouse (see Chapter 7) approach because even though Hadoop was an important pillar of the legacy architecture, the number of people who were familiar with SQL was higher than the number of users able to play with Spark. The intention was to simultaneously (1) value the work already done by the organization in landing all source data into a data lake and (2) help reduce the constraints, promoting a more democratic data access approach.

Since the current architecture was showing limits in elasticity and cost optimization, what the organization wanted to achieve was a cloud solution that provided unlimited scalability and the ability to rely on modern techniques like ephemeral clustering to optimize resource usage and costs. The size of the Hadoop cluster, where unstructured data sits, had to be reduced as well since the majority of the activities should be carried on directly by the DWH.

Another key element was the ability to handle data processing in real time: in the past, a batch approach was enough for the requested analysis, but the need to provide customers with immediate and tailored feedback pushed the company toward streaming use cases. Furthermore, considering the high number of tasks to be managed and controlled, there was a clear need for a workflow management platform layer that helped orchestrate all the data tasks with a "configuration as a code" approach. Every single component of the architecture had to be secured with fine-grained control policies and governed with a solution that allowed users to have complete visibility and understanding of what was happening.

Finally, the platform had to be the home for innovation by enabling and expanding the adoption of ML to improve the customer experience, reduce costs, increase revenue, and gain a competitive advantage by providing more valuable services to the customers. This led to the intended target architecture shown in Figure 12-3.

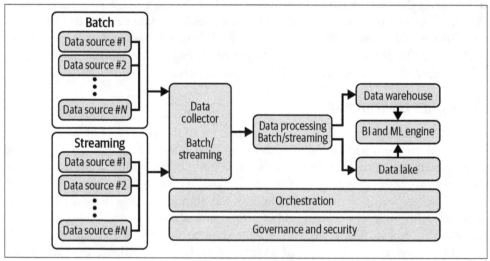

Figure 12-3. Envisioned high-level cloud data platform architecture

In our experience, the difference between a successful vendor choice and a poor one is alignment between your business goals and the vendor's products. YouNetwork took particular care in making sure it got this right. YouNetwork explained to the vendors why it wanted to invest effort in the move to cloud. As highlighted at the beginning, there were three main motivations behind the renovation of YouNetwork's technological stack:

- The organization wanted to *grow its market share*, increasing the number of users accessing the services with a direct impact on the scalability of the platform: more users, more access, and more resources needed to serve the system following (probably) unpredictable patterns.

- The company wanted to *offer more attractive services*, and this implied a *fail fast* approach with a lot of experimentation and A/B testing.

- YouNetwork wanted to *develop fidelity*, giving to the users not only even more tailored content but also an even more robust service via a granular control of the QoS of their hardware devices.

YouNetwork clearly laid out the expectation to see its goals reflected in the RFP response, and in fact, the company asked for the development of a PoC to demonstrate the value of a modern data platform.

The PoC Use Case

YouNetwork decided to pose to the cloud vendors a specific scenario that was generating a lot of pain in the on-premises world, especially for two of the main motivations: space needed to accomplish the task and time requested to get to the final results. The company was collecting data coming from its customer STBs every 15 minutes to analyze the QoS and generate a heat map of the status of its devices network. Each STB generated a file containing a snapshot of its status, and then it connected to the FTP server to upload the content. From there, an ETL batch job processed all the data present in the FTP server, aggregating all the files and extracting relevant information to be uploaded into the DWH. From there, a SQL job processed the data and materialized the result into a table that was the base for a dashboard that visualized the status of the STBs, as shown in Figure 12-4.

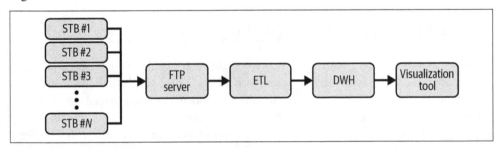

Figure 12-4. PoC on-prem use case architecture

The major drawbacks of such an architecture were as follows:

Inability to scale
There were 15+ million devices that could potentially send information every 15 minutes, but the backend was not able to handle such a big number of multiple connections, so in reality, data was not sent every 15 minutes for each device but just for some devices selected in a round-robin fashion.

Size of the requested space
Each individual file was not so big by itself (more or less 1 MB), but considering the frequency of generation, the size of the data stored in the DWH was

unmanageable, and this meant that YouNetwork could maintain online a very short amount of history (just seven days generating 100+ TB of data with 100+ million rows).

Time to access the data

Because the DWH was already under stress handling several use cases, the time needed to execute the query to materialize the table used by the visualization tool was around 55 minutes.

 The choice of a use case to do a PoC on is important. Note that YouNetwork chose a use case that, if successful, would provide a justification for building a cloud native data platform. You too should choose a use case that is harder than typical, has significant business impact, and can shed light on the relative benefits of a move to cloud over the status quo. What you should not do is select a use case that is one-off or mostly operational in nature. This can be particularly difficult when most of the people doing the evaluation sit in the IT department. The PoC should not be about ingesting a random file and doing a query on it (one-off use case, no business impact) or about being able to fulfill a "right-to-be-forgotten" request (operational in nature). So get out and talk to business users when selecting a PoC use case!

The RFP Responses Proposed by Cloud Vendors

To have a better understanding of how to achieve its goals, YouNetwork decided to prepare a detailed tender to be shared with all the cloud vendors that had submitted ad hoc proposals. Even though the value propositions were based on different differentiators, the proposed high-level architectures were very similar. The following sections will discuss the key components of cloud vendors' responses that outline their proposals for the modernization journey. This is a typical procedure when working on such a project with an organization of this size. However, please keep in mind that other organizations may use different approaches, which may be more or less formal. Please concentrate on the material in the various sections rather than the structure of the overall process.

The Target Environment

Each of the cloud vendors' proposals followed the architecture sketched in Figure 12-5 (the one that you saw in Chapter 7) and leveraged the highlighted PoC use case to explain it.

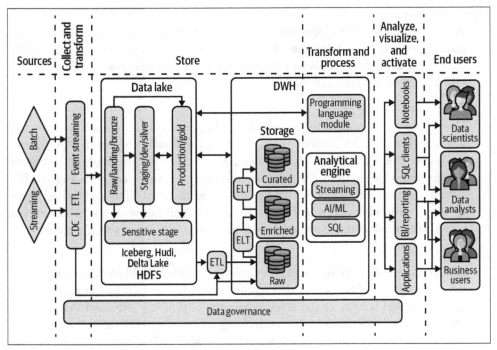

Figure 12-5. Proposed cloud data platform architecture

The main components of the architecture included the following:

Data sources
> STBs send the data to the backend. They can do that both in real time and/or batch:

> *Real time*
>> The devices send information about their status every x seconds, usually in JSON format.

> *Batch*
>> The devices send multiple messages at the same time or a single message containing multiple messages, maybe after a reboot or an update operation.

Ingestion
> This is the component that reads messages coming from the STBs and that is responsible for the collection and storage of the data. For the real-time messages, it makes use of a publisher/subscriber serverless solution that is able to handle millions of messages per second. From there, the data is pushed into the raw landing zone (bronze) of the data lake that is based on an object storage solution that is infinitely scalable by nature. This will become the home both for real-time and batch messages that will be processed by subsequent pipelines.

Transformation

At this stage, the system processes the JSON data to extract relevant information (and to enrich it with internal data for governance purposes) like bandwidth, latency, jitter, or packet loss and stores it both in the production zone of the data lake and in ad hoc tables in the DWH.

Analytics

Now it is time to analyze the collected data to figure out if there is any issue or if the situation is under control. Users can read information via pure SQL queries to double-check the status of their devices or to analyze the evolution of some parameters over the time. But they can also carry out more complex analysis like the effectiveness of plan policy change for a specific set of STBs and related users, or they can double-check if there is any correlation between a specific level of video compression and the number of hours spent in front of specific content.

BI and AI/ML

Analysts can now develop some real-time visualization dashboards to easily identify the usage of STBs—via heat maps, for example—or monitor in real time the level of packet latency or the level of compression of the streamed videos. They can do that at scale because the underlying infrastructure is capable of carrying out several analyses on multiple datasets in parallel without degrading the overall performance. With the huge amount of new and historical data available, data scientists can work on the implementation of ML algorithms to predict when STBs will have a failure, suggesting to the customer the need for a new device or, better, automatically triggering a procedure to ship them a new one.

Data consumers

They could be users or other systems. Consumers can leverage the data as it is (i.e., raw) or curated from an extrapolation from the analytics or BI and AI/ML systems. In this specific scenario, the majority of data consumers are automatic solutions that, based on the result of some elaboration (e.g., analysis of the level of jitter), can automatically trigger some procedures to improve the quality of service like, for example, bandwidth shaping or traffic policing.

Transverse to the preceding sections, there were horizontal services:

Orchestration

Solutions to coordinate all the data processing tasks generally described via a DAG that defines all the dependencies of various jobs handling failures, retries, and backfill

Catalog and privacy

Solutions for data cataloging operations (e.g., metadata management, data lineage, etc.) and for preventing data exfiltration/leaking, protecting the content of sensitive information (e.g., credit card numbers)

IAM/operations/logging and monitoring

Solutions to control "who is accessing what" and to log every single step (e.g., number of loading events, dimension of the ingested data, user who performs a specific query, etc.) of the data journey with the ability to monitor and control the health of the entire data platform

Continuous integration and continuous delivery

Solutions for version control of source code, scripts, configuration, and infrastructure as code; automatic building, testing, and deployment; and environment setup, isolation, and separation from production

In terms of development, cloud vendors decided to opt for a high level of the flexibility that the company wanted to have:

IaaS

The best level of control with the burden of management; compliant both with COTS and OSS. The organization had to fully manage the entire infrastructure and take care of activities like patching, updates rollout, maintenance, etc. Here we are talking about configurations based on VMs where YouNetwork has to deploy selected solutions.

PaaS

The solution that lets the organization focus on the development of the proper solutions instead of having them working on managing the underlying infrastructure that scales automatically based on the application needs. Examples are AWS Lambda, Azure Functions, Google Cloud Functions, AWS Redshift, Azure Synapse, or Google BigQuery.

SaaS

Solutions that can be directly leveraged by users. They can be deployed anywhere (in cloud or even on premises), but this is totally transparent for users who will access the services online. Examples are Salesforce, Looker, and Palantir.

It has to be noted that from the RFP it was not super clear what the preferred strategy of YouNetwork was: its past expertise was in handling VMs and servers, so an IaaS approach was the easiest one to tackle, but to really achieve the level of envisioned transformation, cloud providers pushed for a more PaaS and SaaS approach, freeing the organization from infrastructure maintenance completely and focusing all the users on creating value for the company. To avoid having the organization perform a double somersault, one of the vendors proposed a hybrid approach where the pivotal components were based on PaaS technology (e.g., DWH, data lake) but others (e.g., scheduler) were deployed on IaaS to streamline the adoption process.

It is important to note that RFPs are not always 100% clear on the requirements that the organization wants to achieve or the KPIs that will be used to evaluate them. It is standard practice to have a dedicated section where vendors can ask detailed questions to relevant stakeholders before submitting their official response. Sometimes these questions are made public to all participants, and sometimes they are not, depending on the rules established by the organization.

The Approach on Migration

Another key part of the RFP was aimed at getting a response to a simple question: "How do we get there?" Migrating from an on-premises environment to a modern one that is outside the boundaries of the proper data center is something that appears daunting at the beginning. This is why you need to have a clear understanding of the approach and the different phases required to complete such a transformation. Besides a suggested initial discovery and planning phase that was recalling what was described in Chapter 4, all the vendor proposals converged on a multistep approach based on four different phases with related focus and purpose:

Foundations development
> Where the basis of the architecture has to be built both for IaaS and PaaS/SaaS solutions

Quick wins migration
> Migrate specific workloads that can easily find a fit in the new world, thereby enabling downstream applications (e.g., data collector for JSON data coming from STBs)

Migration fulfillment
> Complete the migration of all the data behind the workloads (e.g., historical STB data)

Modernization
> Introduce new functionalities (e.g., streaming and AI/ML capabilities) and redesign/reimplement old-fashioned workload to leverage cloud native functionalities (e.g., the data lake and the DWH adopting a more SQL-first data lakehouse approach)

Let's have a deep dive into all the steps proposed by the cloud vendors.

Foundations development

This is the step where YouNetwork has to develop the basis for all future workloads in the cloud. It refers to the baseline and structural configuration of a cloud environment. You can consider it as the minimum configuration you have to put in place to enable the migration of legacy workloads and the implementation of new ones, and it generally includes all the horizontal services that make the platform the perfect place for your workload.

The vendor proposals aimed to target the following elements that have been identified as critical factors for the YouNetwork adoption:

Identity management

You have to handle authentication of users and services in a secure and reliable way:

- *Cloud Identity Services* with an initial integration with the current on-premises solutions (i.e., Microsoft Active Directory in this case) followed by a complete adoption of the fully managed solution in the cloud environment and a natural dismission of the legacy solution
- *Authentication options* (e.g., user/password or single sign-on) and related security (e.g., two-factor authentication) to allow YouNetwork users to get rid of a VPN approach and adopt a modern zero trust security approach to enable secure, fast, and easy remote working
- *Auditing* activities to keep track of and monitor all the activities (e.g., user login) made by each single identity within the platform for compliance and control purposes

Access management

You have to ensure that only authorized identities can get access to selected resources with the correct set of rights:

- IAM solutions to handle at scale permissions to all identities
- Organization policies to define all the rules that should be applied at the organizational level (e.g., audit team can access all cloud resources in read mode)

Security

You have to define the policies and actions to secure the new environment that take into account the shared responsibility that comes with cloud technology (i.e., security of the cloud environment handled by the cloud vendor and security in the cloud environment that has to be managed by the final user).

Networking

You define the way all the new components in the cloud environment will communicate and how they can eventually interact with external and on-premises resources.

Visibility

You describe how to get access to real-time information related to the running workloads (e.g., logging, monitoring, error reporting, billing consumption and budgets, etc.).

The foundations proposal from all the vendors foresaw an N months period where YouNetwork, the cloud vendor professional services organization (PSO) team, and a third-party system integrator would work together on multiple deep dives into the topics mentioned earlier to prepare for the first workload deployment (i.e., the data collector of JSON data coming from the STBs).

Now is the time to reflect on the role of the CCoE and how to plan for its expansion. At the beginning, the CCoE was only a small group of people working in specific business units within the company (i.e., product, engineering, and architecture). However, the goal is to expand its reach to multiple other areas (e.g., security, operations, training, etc.) and to permeate the organization with cloud knowledge. The proposal for YouNetwork was in fact to have the PSO and system integrator collaborating with the CCoE in defining best practices, blueprints, and monitoring activities during the setup of the foundation. This allowed the organization to have firsthand experience on the approaches to be leveraged in a cloud environment and to understand how to harden and extend the CCoE team.

Please do not forget that your ultimate goal is to make the CCoE so successful that it can be disbanded when the project is completed, as all relevant functions within the organization will have the knowledge and tools to leverage and expand the cloud environment on their own.

Quick wins migration

This is the phase where YouNetwork can start the initial migration of specific legacy workloads (refer to the quick wins solutions mentioned in Chapter 4) that have been identified during the assessment and planning phase. The use case that was identified, as you have read before, was of course the data collector from STBs that enabled technical users to have a better understanding of the status of the footprint of the devices. Data was collected in batch mode, having STBs uploading data in an FTP server that was then ingested via an ETL pipeline into the DWH. The goal was to leverage this quick win to showcase a first modernization step: enable the system to collect metrics from multiple STBs, leveraging a full serverless pipeline. To do so, the file collection using an FTP server would be completely abandoned in favor of a publisher/subscriber message approach that was a first step toward a future full streaming application. The data, once ingested in the data lake, could be directly queried by the analytical engine and visualize results via dashboards. The entire data journey related to this use case could run in parallel on both systems (i.e., on-premises and cloud),[2] and after a period of parallelism the workload could be

---

2 It is important to note that, to achieve that, it was necessary to send a dedicated update to the firmware of all STBs.

fully decommissioned from the legacy system. You have to understand that this initial transition required a nontrivial set of manual activities not only because it was the first real migration activity but also because it was a good moment to start developing all the artifacts (such as infrastructure as code templates, general query transpiler, data validation pipelines, etc.) needed to implement automations that would have been leveraged in the following migration phases.

Migration fulfillment

Completing a successful migration for the first quick wins is an incredibly important milestone to set a trajectory for the success of the overall project, and you should put a lot of focus on it. Leveraging a fully migrated solution into the new cloud environment, you can showcase to the business immediate benefits like scalability, elasticity, improved observability, and reduced time to data access. Such a showcase is important to build confidence in your next step, which is the full migration of the legacy platform. Considering that YouNetwork wanted to quickly dismiss its on-premises data centers, this phase is focused on *speed of migration* (especially on the data migration), and thus the suggested approach was to adopt a main rehost strategy with a replatform nuance when possible. This allows the organization to:

Define a standard for the various migration activities
> Definition of migration blueprints for every kind of workload that is part of the migration perimeter (e.g., custom applications, databases, etc.)

Automate migration activities
> Data extraction, compression, deduplication, transfer, ingestion and transformation, task orchestrations, monitoring, and validation

The proposal, except for the DWH that was already part of the quick wins strategy, was to generally maintain the original technological stack, introducing some native cloud features to improve the usability of the solutions. All transformative steps were deferred to the last step:

- FTP server (not used anymore for the data coming from the STBs but for other kinds of data like video content, imagery, etc.)
  - Scheduled VMs up and running only at specific periods of the day when data is expected to come in the form of a file
  - Integration with cloud native network-attached storage (NAS) system solution to store the temporary data
  - Integration with a cloud native blob storage solution to store a copy of the raw data for backup purposes

- ETL
  - Migration of the COTS solution as it is
- Hadoop environment
  - Migration of the Hadoop distro as it is
  - Integration with cloud native blob storage solution to reduce the size of the HDFS file system

You have to note that, when migrated, workloads will automatically benefit from all the horizontal solutions that have been put in place in the cloud foundations phase (i.e., networking, security, visibility, etc.). During the migration, there is of course an important topic you have to consider, which is the *data migration* that can be handled by various techniques; in this case, the data migration requires a two-leg approach:

Hot data
  Migration directly performed that leverages a high-speed connection between on-premises data centers and the cloud environment

Cold data
  Migration performed in a second moment that leverages physical transfer appliances:

  - Connect the physical appliance to the on-prem environment.
  - Download the cold data.
  - Transfer the physical appliance to a location connected to the target cloud data center with a super-high-speed connection.
  - Upload the data into the cloud environment, validating the content (e.g., CRC32C checksum).
  - Destroy the contents of the physical appliance.

Let's have a look now at how the architecture can be modernized.

Modernization

In this phase, you should think about how to enhance the migrated workload, extend the current capabilities, and implement new features. Streaming capabilities, real-time analysis, and ML to automatically extract value from the data are just a few of the activities that need to be carried out. The goal of the previous step was to migrate workloads as fast as possible with a more IaaS-oriented approach; the goal now is to change your mindset and start leveraging fully managed solutions—to remove the burden of infrastructure management and to let users focus on their business solutions, which are what really matter. The first thing to do is an extension of the preliminary workload analysis to discover:

- The best way to add new functionalities that weren't feasible in the on-prem environment

- The best way to redesign old-fashioned workloads to leverage PaaS and a server-less solution

One of the elements that you should not underestimate in the modernization journey is the fact that every single component of the platform has to be accessible via APIs: it is the core element of the transformation because it enables integrations between internal and external resources, future reorganization of the architecture, and real-time interoperability between components. When you look at the migrated elements, you can identify the main transformation for each layer:

Ingestion

This is the first component you should redesign, not only because it is essential to get rid of the FTP server approach (*slow, not scalable, and insecure*), but also because the batch paradigm is not enough for a company like YouNetwork, which is basing its business on streaming technology. It has to put in place a layer that is capable of handling data collection at scale (i.e., in parallel from multiple sources) and in real time, leveraging a message queuing/event paradigm (e.g., a Kafka-like solution). Integration between these solutions and data sources is generally carried out by third-party partners, in-house custom developments, or leveraging cloud-vendor native solutions (e.g., AWS Glue, Azure Data Factory, or Google Data Fusion). Data has to be stored, possibly in the original format, in a blob storage that is unlimited in scalability: here the data can be temporarily stored before proceeding with its transformation, or it can remain untouched for months or years—for example, in fully protected and certified storage areas for audit purposes.

Transformation

The approach you should follow here is to expand the usual technique based on ETL where all the logic resides within the transformation tool, adopting an ELT approach that can leverage the engine of the analytical layer. The original COTS solution has been migrated as-is in the previous step, but it is now time to change the approach and start implementing an open source solution that reduces vendor lock-in and offers a unified approach for both batch and streaming processing. This will avoid the need to learn and manage two separate models to handle the transformation (Apache Beam is an interesting example of that). The layer has to be capable of handling huge volumes, high levels of parallelism, and possibly processing real-time data coming from the production systems.

Analytics

Data lake and DWH are converging in a single environment where users leverage the engine they need (e.g., SQL, Spark) to analyze the data, as you have read in

Chapter 7. Here the concept of VMs is completely removed from the equation, having serverless and fully managed solutions (e.g., AWS Redshift and EMR, Azure Synapse, or Google BigQuery and Dataproc) leading the race to be able to cope with required scalability. The HDFS model can be surpassed in light of a better integration with other forms of storage (e.g., blob storage, DWH storage, etc.), bringing the capability to have better usage of the different resources (i.e., the system does not need to be up and running all the time as per the HDFS paradigm). It is obvious that even all the policies for retention and backup need to be revisited in accordance with users' needs.

BI and AI/ML

Besides the evolution of the migrated tools toward more modern BI solutions (e.g., Tableau, Power BI, Looker, etc.), the component you should leverage to achieve the highest level of modernization is of course the AI/ML. That kind of technology, not easy to scale using the on-premises YouNetwork architecture, is the core for the implementation of a series of features that will boost the adoption of the organization's services, such as:

Personalized recommendations
To increase engagement and satisfaction by analyzing the viewing history and preferences of customers

Content optimization
To identify clusters of interests to determine the areas of investment when producing or acquiring new content

Predictive maintenance
To monitor the health of the services, reducing downtime and improving the overall quality of service for customers

Audience analytics
To analyze viewing patterns and demographic information to get a better understanding of the customer and provide them with a better-tailored service and pricing strategies

Fraud detection
To detect fraudulent activity, such as sharing accounts among multiple users or using stolen credit cards to purchase services

Now that you have a better understanding of the responses made by cloud vendors, let's take a look at how YouNetwork evaluated them.

The RFP Evaluation Process

After a detailed analysis and evaluation of the different RFP responses, taking into account not only the technological vision and strategy but also the commercial figures (which are obviously outside the scope of this book but play a crucial role in the final decision), the YouNetwork team selected a restricted number of cloud vendors to proceed with the last step of the evaluation, which was to build the PoC. The aim was to understand the ease and the effectiveness of adopting the specific cloud solution.

The Scope of the PoC

The company decided to leverage the specific scenario described in the RFP to assess and validate the capabilities of the various cloud vendors. Cloud vendors had to implement a mockup to demonstrate their ability to handle the described use case at scale.

YouNetwork defined three specific KPIs to evaluate PoC results:

20M devices
Collection of data from an extended fleet of STBs

Two-week (nice to have one month) window
Extend the size of the historical data to be stored

Less than five minutes
Time to materialize the table

The time available to deliver the PoC was two weeks.

YouNetwork provided cloud vendors with:

- An example data file generated by STBs
- Guidelines to extract and transform needed data from the example file
- Model of the DWH tables
- Definition of the main information needed to be extracted and visualized into the report

Let's have a look now at how the PoC was executed.

The Execution of the PoC

The selected hyperscalers leveraged this opportunity to partner with their preferred system integrators to showcase, from the beginning, a pretty common model, where the cloud vendor working alongside a third-party company can bring deep architectural and product expertise coupled with the ability to scale: *a real scalable modernization team in action*. The approach of both participants to the tender was pretty similar, and it was based on following pillars:

- Design and configure a blob storage reachable via APIs where STBs can upload their files.
- Implement a custom application, in Java or similar, to mimic the behavior of multiple basic STBs with very basic goals:
  — Generate random data based on the example provided by YouNetwork.
  — Try to connect to the backend to send the data.
  — Send the data.
  — Destroy itself when it has received the acknowledgment that the data has been correctly delivered.
- Launch several VMs in parallel running multiple instances of the STBs emulator.
- Develop a batch ETL serverless pipeline to read and transform all the data at scale and ingest it into the DWH.
- Implement the dashboard to directly query the data from the DWH.

Let's have a look now at what the results were for each KPI after the implementation by one of the cloud vendors:

20M devices: ✔

How was it possible to achieve that? It is a huge number! Yes, it is, but this was a pretty common use case for the cloud: handle spikes! Let's imagine an initial state where you have your emulator running in a VM environment (e.g., AWS EC2, Azure Virtual Machines, Google Compute Engine): the emulator just has to mimic the behavior of an STB generating some random data, materialize that data in a file, and then upload it to a blob storage. Let's assume that the emulator can simulate multiple STBs in parallel; what you have to do to quickly reach your target number is to simply deploy other VMs with another running emulator for each instance. Following this approach you can easily reach (and even overcome) the target you have. Data can be uploaded in parallel to the blob storage, which is a serverless solution that can scale inherently (e.g., AWS S3, Azure Blob Storage, Google Cloud Storage): here you do not have a problem related to space because it can be considered unlimited.

Two-week window: ✔

> Again? Yes! As stated in the previous point, the storage available can be considered unlimited, and the same logic can be applied to the storage for the DWH, so no issue here. In terms of cost, cloud storage was inexpensive enough that the extension of the window would not have caused budgetary problems.

Less than five minutes to materialize the data: ✔

> What does it mean? It means that you can query the data directly from the ingestion table without needing to materialize it into a new table and still get a super-fast response. This can be achieved with serverless solutions (e.g., AWS Redshift, Azure Synapse, Google BigQuery) that (thanks to the separation of storage and compute) can easily boost their analytical engine to speed up query execution (fun fact: when the YouNetwork board saw with their eyes the time needed to render the dashboard from a query running in the DWH and crunching 100+ TB of data, the CDO said, "This is a Flash animation," and the consultant replied, "It would have taken longer").

Let's see now what the final decision of YouNetwork was.

The Final Decision

YouNetwork was impressed by the results achieved via the execution of the PoC because it was able to experience a portion of the value of the overall modernization. The final decision for the assignment of the modernization journey at the end was taken following these considerations:

Technical robustness of the solution

> Not only in terms of scalability and elasticity but also related to availability, disaster-recovery options, backup solution, etc.

Vision and roadmap

> Where we are now and where we are heading in the future, especially on the innovation side.

Team and organization

> Ability to deliver the migration project.

Partnerships

> Mainly but not limited to system integrators (even software vendors).

Training programs

> Mandatory to have a solid training plan for your staff.

Overall pricing

> Modernization is cool, but it has to be financially sustainable.

And now? Who was selected as the cloud provider (*only one?*), what was the system integrator (*only one?*), and how many months did it take to migrate the entire infrastructure? These are not the things that are important, because every company has a proper way to make decisions (and will weigh the above factors differently): what really matters is that YouNetwork now has a data architecture that enables it to build toward the future with more confidence. It has already implemented several new use cases for its IPTV and VOD system spanning across security (e.g., new fraud detection system in its online ecommerce website), user experience (e.g., real-time identifications of the actors in movies, real-time search for programs via voice interaction), and operations (e.g., real-time QoS analysis via anomaly detection). Many more innovative data products are, doubtless, still to come.

Peroration

We wrote this book as a guide to architects who wish to support data-driven decision making in their business by creating a data and ML platform using public cloud technologies. Our goal was to help you gain a better understanding of the main concepts, architectural patterns, and tools available to build modern cloud data platforms.

In this book, we have covered how cloud-based data platforms can reduce the technical barrier associated with getting access to data, running interactive queries, creating reports, making automated decisions, and personalizing the business's services. A well-designed data and ML platform makes it possible to access data from anywhere, carry out fast, large-scale queries even on edge devices, and take advantage of services that provide many analytics and AI capabilities.

When every stakeholder in your business has access to the data they need, they can make better decisions and solve problems more effectively. Making the use of data easy and widespread will give you a competitive advantage, help you make better decisions, improve your products and services, and grow your business. There are many challenges to democratizing data—beyond the technical aspects of building a data and ML platform, you also need to ensure that everyone has the skills and tools they need to access and use data, and you need to create policies that protect privacy and security. However, as this book showed, these challenges are not insurmountable.

The benefits of democratizing data far outweigh the challenges.

Summary

In this chapter, we have applied the principles you have learned in the previous chapters to a model case. You have seen what steps are needed to move from a legacy environment into a modern cloud native data platform. The key takeaways are as follows:

- When organizations recognize that their current data platform is not compatible with their current and future plans for business development, it is time to start working on a modernization journey.

- The very first step is to establish a dedicated SWAT team to work on the identification of a possible solution.

- The SWAT team, which can quickly become a first experimentation of CCoE, needs to have preliminary discussions with major cloud vendors to understand what a possible journey could be.

- It has to be clear to the organization's stakeholders that modernization projects are not just a matter of technology but also embrace the entire organization, including its people.

- When the organization decides to embrace the journey, everything starts with an analysis of the current footprint and with the identification of a possible target architecture. This is usually carried out by the CCoE team.

- Commonly, organizations issue an RFP to understand from a 360-degree perspective what it means to jump into the cloud.

- Top cloud vendors generally are invited, and they usually share a common vision based on four steps: *development of cloud foundations*, *migrations of quick wins*, *migration fulfillment*, and *modernization*.

- The company that issues the tender analyzes the different proposals and reduces the final list to two vendors.

- Once the organization's CCoE completes its initial analysis phase and identifies a problem in the on-premises environment, the top vendor candidates implement a PoC to demonstrate the power of the cloud in improving that specific use case.

- The organization at the end decides on a specific (single or multiple) cloud vendor(s) and implements the new platform, extending its current footprint with a series of use cases to improve the overall quality of its service and user experience.

Thank you for reading. We hope that what you have learned in this book proves beneficial as you build your enterprise's data platform on the public cloud or as you build data-enabled products on your enterprise's data platform.

Index

About the Authors

Marco Tranquillin is a seasoned consultant helping organizations undergo core technology transformations through cloud computing to discover and generate new value. He has over a decade of experience in cloud technology, having worked for firms such as Accenture, Microsoft, and Google. In his career, he has been involved in complex IT cloud projects for many global organizations.

Valliappa Lakshmanan works with management and data teams across a range of industries to help them employ data and AI-driven innovation to grow their businesses and increase value. Prior to this, Lak was the Director for Data Analytics and AI Solutions on Google Cloud and a research scientist at NOAA. He is a coauthor of *Data Science on the Google Cloud Platform*, *Google BigQuery: The Definitive Guide*, and *Machine Learning Design Patterns*, all published by O'Reilly.

Firat Tekiner, PhD in Reinforcement Learning, MBA, is currently a Senior Staff Product Manager in Data Analytics and AI at Google. Firat is a leader with over 20 years of experience in developing new products, designing and delivering bespoke information systems for some of the world's largest research, education, telecommunications, finance, and retail organizations. Following roles within National Supercomputing Services and National Centre for Text Mining, he worked as a Senior Consultant at Ab Initio Software prior to joining Google. He has written over 50 publications in the areas of parallel computing, big data, artificial intelligence, and computer communications.

Colophon

The bird on the cover of *Architecting Data and Machine Learning Platforms* is the blue-tailed bee-eater (*Merops philippinus*), a slender, multihued member of the Meropidae family of bee-eaters.

True to its common name, the blue-tailed bee-eater subsists primarily on a diet of bees, hornets, and wasps, hunting for these and other flying insects from perches throughout their coastal habitats. Like all near passerines, they are land birds, but they typically make their nests by burrowing into sandbanks and gently sloping hillsides, rather than in trees.

Blue-tailed bee-eaters are known to migrate seasonally throughout South and Southeast Asia, where they're widely distributed. Due to their distribution and stable population, the species has been classified by the IUCN as being of least concern.

The cover illustration is by Karen Montgomery, based on an antique line engraving from *British Birds*. The cover fonts are Gilroy Semibold and Guardian Sans. The text font is Adobe Minion Pro; the heading font is Adobe Myriad Condensed; and the code font is Dalton Maag's Ubuntu Mono.

Printed in the USA
CPSIA information can be obtained
at www.ICGtesting.com
JSHW051156041123
51447JS00006B/10